Hands On Google Cloud SQL and Cloud Spanner

Deployment, Administration and Use Cases with Python

Navin Sabharwal
Shakuntala Gupta Edward

Apress®

Hands On Google Cloud SQL and Cloud Spanner

Navin Sabharwal
New Delhi, India

Shakuntala Gupta Edward
Ghaziabad, India

ISBN-13 (pbk): 978-1-4842-5536-0
https://doi.org/10.1007/978-1-4842-5537-7

ISBN-13 (electronic): 978-1-4842-5537-7

Managing Director, Apress Media LLC: Welmoed Spahr
Acquisitions Editor: Celestin Suresh John
Development Editor: Siddhi Chavan
Coordinating Editor: Aditee Mirashi

Cover designed by eStudioCalamar

Cover image designed by Freepik (www.freepik.com)

Distributed to the book trade worldwide by Springer Science+Business Media New York, 233 Spring Street, 6th Floor, New York, NY 10013. Phone 1-800-SPRINGER, fax (201) 348-4505, e-mail orders-ny@springer-sbm.com, or visit www.springeronline.com. Apress Media, LLC is a California LLC and the sole member (owner) is Springer Science + Business Media Finance Inc (SSBM Finance Inc). SSBM Finance Inc is a **Delaware** corporation.

For information on translations, please e-mail rights@apress.com, or visit http://www.apress.com/rights-permissions.

Apress titles may be purchased in bulk for academic, corporate, or promotional use. eBook versions and licenses are also available for most titles. For more information, reference our Print and eBook Bulk Sales web page at http://www.apress.com/bulk-sales.

Any source code or other supplementary material referenced by the author in this book is available to readers on GitHub via the book's product page, located at www.apress.com/978-1-4842-5536-0. For more detailed information, please visit http://www.apress.com/source-code.

Printed on acid-free paper

Dedicated to the people I love and the God I trust.

—Navin Sabharwal

Dedicated to my family for being my rock and guiding light and to my God who shades every step of my life.

—Shakuntala Gupta Edward

Table of Contents

About the Authors

Navin Sabharwal has more than 20 years of industry experience and is an innovator, thought leader, patent holder, and author in the areas of cloud computing, artificial intelligence and machine learning, public cloud, DevOps, AIOPS, DevOps, infrastructure services, monitoring and managing platforms, Big Data analytics, and software product development. Navin is responsible for DevOps, artificial intelligence, cloud lifecycle management, service management, monitoring and management, IT ops analytics, AIOPs and machine learning, automation, operational efficiency of scaled delivery through Lean ops, and strategy and delivery for HCL Technologies. He is reachable at Navinsabharwal@gmail.com and https://www.linkedin.com/in/navinsabharwal.

Shakuntala Gupta Edward is an accomplished consultant in the areas of data and analytics with more than 16 years of experience. Shakuntala is a Big Data architect and is responsible for database design, database architecture, best practices for Big Data technologies, product development using databases, Big Data, NoSQL, analytics, and machine learning technologies. She has authored books on Big Data analytics, including *Practical MongoDB* from Apress. She is reachable at https://in.linkedin.com/in/shakuntala-edward-70343627/.

About the Technical Reviewer

Piyush Pandey works as a deputy general manager in the HCL DRYiCE practice, focusing on creating solutions catering to cloud adoption (including cloud landing zone, migration, and operations), automation, orchestration, and cloud lifecycle management.

Acknowledgments

To my family, Shweta and Soumil, for being always by my side and letting me sacrifice their time for my intellectual and spiritual pursuits. For taking care of everything while I am immersed in authoring. This and the other accomplishments of my life wouldn't have been possible without your love and support. To my mom and sister for their love and support as always; without your blessings, nothing is possible.

To my co-author, Shakutala. This is the third book we authored together and the journey over the last 10 years has been enriching. Thank you for your hard work and quick turnarounds.

To my team here at HCL who has been a source of inspiration with their hard work, ever engaging technical conversations, and their technical depth. Your everflowing ideas are a source of happiness and excitement every single day. Piyush Pandey, Sarvesh Pandey, Amit Agrawal, Vasand Kumar, Punith Krishnamurthy, Sandeep Sharma, Amit Dwivedi, Gauarv Bhardwaj, Nitin Narotra, Shoyeb, Divjot, Nitin Chand, and Vivek— thank you for being there and making technology fun.

To Celestine and Aditee and the entire team at Apress, for turning our ideas into a reality. It has been an amazing experience authoring with you over the years. The speed of the decision making and the editorial support have both been excellent.

To all my co-authors, colleagues, managers, mentors, and guides, it was and is an enriching experience to be associated with you and to learn from you.

Thank you goddess Saraswati, for guiding us to the path of knowledge and spirituality.

असतो मा साद गमय, तमसो मा ज्योतिरि गमय, मृत्योर मा अमृतम् गमय

(Asato Ma Sad Gamaya, Tamaso Ma Jyotir Gamaya, Mrityor Ma Amritam Gamaya)

Lead us from ignorance to truth, lead us from darkness to light, lead us from death to deathlessness.

—Navin Sabharwal

ACKNOWLEDGMENTS

First and foremost, my utmost thanks to my entire family. To my mom and dad (without you I am nothing), to Nitya (you are the very soul of my life, be you always), to Eddy (my husband, friend, and partner in crime), to Bindu, Eliz, and Vicky (for your love, being the energy in my life; you guys keep me grounded), to Amar, Jey, and Asper (for being there always), to my Savari mom and dad-in-law (for your support and blessings), and not to forget Ria, Asper, and Steve (my little angels). Without your unfaltering love and support, I would never be what I am today. Words cannot say enough.

I would like to thank my co-author Navin for believing in me and pushing me always to deliver my best.

Special mention to Ayush Aggarwal and Raja Bhattacharya, for helping me with the code in the book.

Finally, I would like to give a big thanks to Celestin, Aditee, and the whole team at Apress for believing.

—Shakuntala Gupta Edward

Introduction

Back in 2009, a new term was coined—"Big Data". Big Data is data that has a high volume, is generated at a high velocity, and has multiple varieties. This is data with the three Vs—Volume, Velocity, and Variety. Convergence of several technology trends fueled the progress further.

On the one side, Big Data poses challenges to organizations to store, transport, secure, process, mine, and serve that data. Cloud Computing on the other hand provides support to address these challenges by provisioning shared resources, such as compute, database storage, networking, security, and analytical offerings. In effect, the combination of both is spearheading new innovations in technology.

The Google Cloud Platform (GCP) is a suite of cloud computing services offered by Google. They run on the same infrastructure that Google uses internally for its own end-user products, such as Google search, Google Photos, YouTube, Gmail, etc. GCP services are well positioned for the modern application development user and have some unique offerings in the data storage, Big Data analytics, artificial intelligence, and containerization spaces. Google continues to innovate and strengthen its offerings.

This book takes a deep dive into the relational database service offering of Google— Cloud SQL and Cloud Spanner.

These database offerings from Google Cloud are increasingly being used by enterprises to develop their modern digital applications. The aim of this book is to provide guidance and best practices to architect applications using GCP database offerings.

We have tried to cover topics that will enable developers to make informed choices and also help cloud administrators administer these databases and manage them on a daily basis.

- Cloud SQL is Google's fully managed relational database service with two choices of database engine—MySQL and PostgreSQL.

- Cloud Spanner is Google's fully managed NewSQL database service, offering high availability with an industry leading 99.999% availability SLA.

Time is valuable, more so in today's world of ever-increasing data. We thank you for spending your valuable time and investing in reading this book.

We sincerely hope that you'll find the coverage useful and will be able to architect, develop, and manage GCP database offerings. We hope that you enjoy reading the book as much as we enjoyed writing it.

Wishing you the best on your cloud and Big Data journey.

CHAPTER 1

Getting Started with GCP

The cloud computing space is evolving. Every day new offerings from cloud vendors like Google, AWS, and Azure are launched. In the last few years, the offerings have become more mature and stable and are seeing rapid adoption in the enterprise world. Developers are moving from on-premises solutions to adopting the service offerings from cloud providers.

Many of you may be running workloads on the cloud and are aware of the benefits that you are deriving. Let's reiterate these benefits:

- *Pay per use:* This is efficient and cost effective. You pay for the exact amount of resources you consume.

- *Zero maintenance headaches:* Operating in the cloud also means no worries about physical hardware infrastructure provisioning, upgrades, or maintenance. The cloud provider takes the responsibility of upgrading and maintaining everything, allowing you to focus on application development.

- *Easy scalability:* Providers offer auto-scaling capabilities as your computing needs peek, freeing you from worries about workloads peaks and troughs.

- *Fully accessible:* Enables you to work from anywhere at any time and from any device.

- *Quick deployment:* Speeds up application development as provisioning with the cloud is just a matter of a few hours, whereas the traditional mode of setting up the infrastructure takes months.

Multiple cloud vendors are competing for the mindshare of the users, and these cloud providers each have their own strengths and capabilities.

© Navin Sabharwal, Shakuntala Gupta Edward 2020
N. Sabharwal and S. G. Edward, *Hands On Google Cloud SQL and Cloud Spanner*,
https://doi.org/10.1007/978-1-4842-5537-7_1

1

The Google Cloud Platform (GCP) is a portfolio of cloud computing services offered by Google. Their services are well positioned for the modern application development user. GCP has some unique offerings in the Big Data analytics, artificial intelligence, and containerization spaces.

Google's first foray into cloud computing was with Google App Engine, which was launched in April 2008 as a Platform as a Service (PaaS) offering. It enabled developers to build and host apps on Google's infrastructure. In September 2011, App Engine came out of preview, and in 2013 the Google Cloud Platform name was formally adopted. The company subsequently released a variety of tools, such as its data storage layer, Cloud SQL, BigQuery, Compute Engine, and the rest of the tools that make up today's Google Cloud Platform.

Figure 1-1 shows that, like any cloud provider, Google offers core IaaS (infrastructure as a Service) services for the compute, storage, networking, security, and databases spaces.

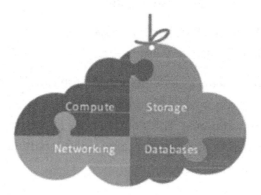

Figure 1-1. *Cloud providers' core services*

Apart from the core services, Google offers PaaS (Platform as a Service) services as well, such as Pub/Sub, DataFlow, AI Hub, and machine learning, to name a few. These PaaS services are built on top of the core stack of services. Google is constantly innovating to strengthen its base further and continues to add to these PaaS services.

This book focuses on the database service offerings in the relational space. Cloud databases are indisputably the future of enterprise databases. Database as a Service (DBaaS) solves the challenges inherent to the traditional on-premises model.

Google is one vendor that is leveraging its strengths in data processing and is establishing its dominance in the Big Data segment. Google's DBaaS services were born out of their internal database management models. It brings in differentiated products to this category. In addition, as compared to the other vendors, Google DBaaS users get to achieve high levels of customization, which are covered in the coming chapters.

Despite being a late entrant in the cloud domain, Google has quickly risen to deliver the best performance for the price in the DBaaS segment.

Before you start using any of the GCP services, you need to know how to get started with GCP. Let's begin exploring the platform. This chapter walks through the Google Cloud Platform.

Signing Up

It's time to get started with GCP. The first step is to sign up for GCP. The following steps are required for signing up and are more relevant to first time users.

The primary prerequisite for signing up is a Google account. GCP uses Google accounts for access management and authentication. As shown in Figure 1-2, you enter the `https://console.cloud.google.com` URL in your browser window and click the Try For Free button.

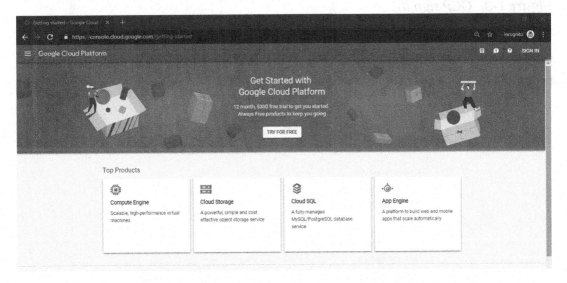

Figure 1-2. *Google Cloud Platform*

You will be redirected to the Sign In page, as shown in Figure 1-3.

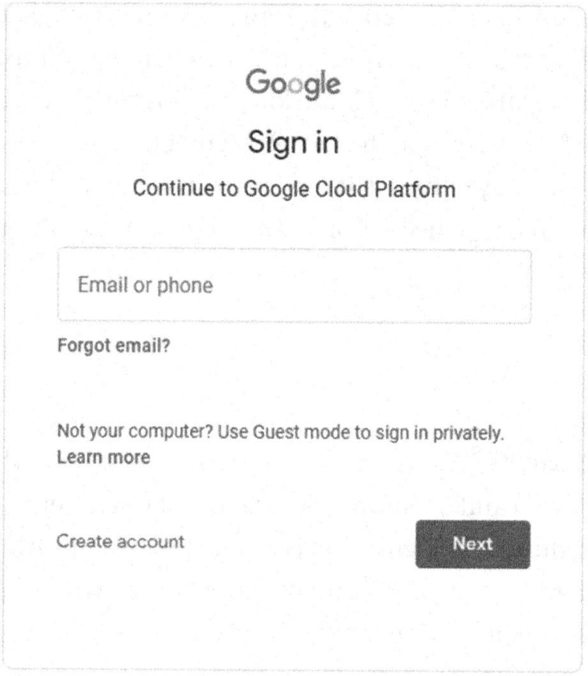

Figure 1-3. *GCP sign in*

This prompts you for a Google account. If you don't have a Google account, follow the Create Account process to create one. If you are eligible for the free tier, you will be prompted for the account details, as shown in Figure 1-4.

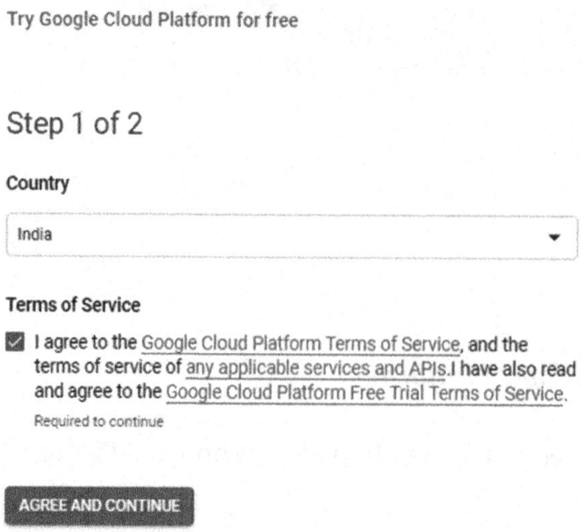

Figure 1-4. *GCP free tier registration, step 1*

Select your country, agree to the terms of service, and click the Agree and Continue button. This will take you to the second step, as shown in Figure 1-5, wherein you create and select your payment profile. Provide the required billing details; however, rest assured that the auto debit will not happen unless you manually choose that option.

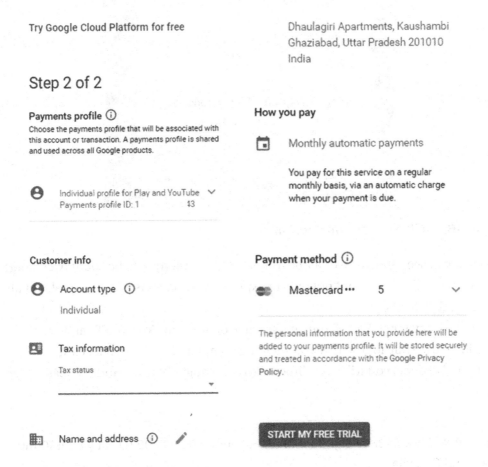

Figure 1-5. *GCP free tier registration, step 2*

While you create your payment profile and sign in, the right panel displays details, as shown in Figure 1-6.

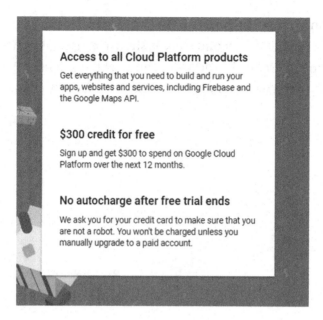

Figure 1-6. *GCP free tier information*

As you can see, Google gives a free trial of $300 to everyone to be spent over a period of 12 months. This is sufficient not only to explore all the exercises in this book but also to evaluate GCP further.

Once you have specified all the details, click on the Start My Free Trial button.

It will take a while for the registration to be completed. Once the necessary validations are done, you will be redirected to the Google Console and are ready to get started.

Note If you are already signed into an account, you will be directly sent to the GCP Cloud Console.

Accessing Google Cloud Platform

Now that you have signed up, you can next look at accessing the GCP services and resources using a web-based graphical user interface (a Cloud Console) and a command line (a Cloud Shell).

Cloud Console

Navigate to `https://console.cloud.google.com`. If you're not already signed in, it will prompt you to enter the Google account credentials. Once you're signed in, it will redirect you to the Cloud Console, as shown in Figure 1-7.

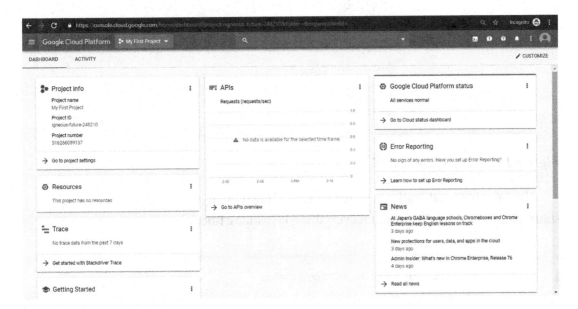

Figure 1-7. *GCP Cloud Console*

In the top-most panel, next to the GCP icon, a dropdown appears with My First Project selected. This is the project dropdown, and My First Project is a new project that's automatically created when you first sign in.

A project can be thought of as a container for your work, wherein all the resources are isolated from the resources created in other projects. You will learn about projects and how you create a project in a while.

The center of the console is a dashboard that gives you a bird's eye view of the selected project. The view is further divided into multiple cards wherein each card refers to specific information.

The Project Info card shown in Figure 1-8 gives details about the project, such as the names and IDs, along with a quick link at the bottom enabling easy modification of the project settings.

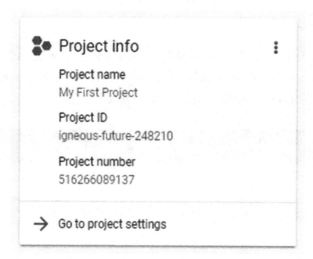

Figure 1-8. *Project Info card*

The Google Cloud Platform status card, as shown in Figure 1-9, gives you a quick status check. Green indicates that everything is working fine.

Figure 1-9. *GCP status card*

The billing card shows the billing details at a glance for the selected project, as shown in Figure 1-10.

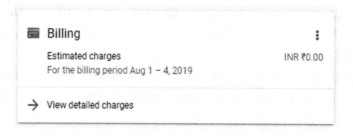

Figure 1-10. *Billing card*

There is also a card for Quick Starts, as shown in Figure 1-11, which you could use when exploring GCP services and offerings.

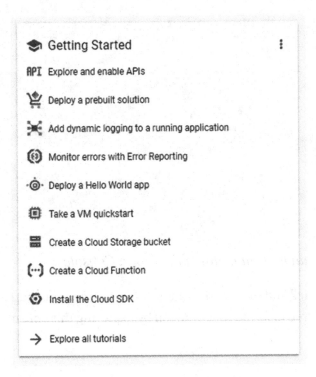

Figure 1-11. *Quick Start card*

On the left side of the top-most panel is the navigation button, as shown in Figure 1-12. Clicking this button opens the navigation menu where all the GCP offerings are categorized and listed.

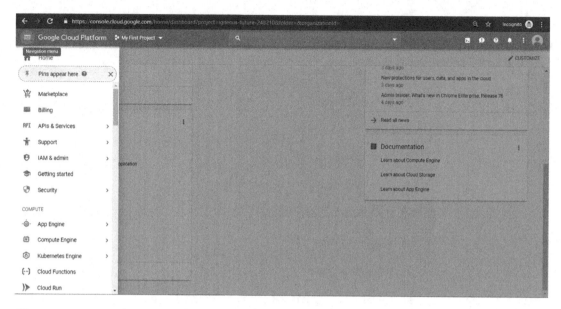

Figure 1-12. *Left navigation menu of the Cloud Console*

You will come back and explore the menu when subsequent chapters cover the relevant areas. Feel free to familiarize yourself by exploring this console.

Cloud Shell

Now that you have familiarized yourself with the web console, next you learn how to manage the resources using commands and scripts.

The GCP Cloud Shell option enables you to access and manage its resources directly from the command line. Click on the Activate Cloud Shell button in the top-right corner of the Cloud Console, as shown in Figure 1-13, to access the Cloud Shell.

Figure 1-13. *Activating the Cloud Shell*

This opens the pop up shown in Figure 1-14.

Google Cloud Shell

Free, pre-installed with the tools that you need for the Google Cloud Platform. Learn more

```
example-vm-1   asia-east1-a    f1-micro           10.240.160.142 104.155.216.228 RUNNI
example-vm-2   europe-west1-b f1-micro            10.240.119.112 104.155.36.122  RUNNI
example-vm-3   us-central1-f  f1-micro            10.240.57.1    104.154.76.241  RUNNI
writetoshakun8@cloudshell:~$
writetoshakun8@cloudshell:~$ git clone https://github.com/GoogleCloud/appengine-example.git
Cloning into 'appengine-example'...
remote: Counting objects: 476, done.
remote: Total 476 (delta 0), reused 0 (delta 0), pack-reused 476
Receiving objects: 100% (476/476), 432.65 KiB | 0 bytes/s, done.
Checking connectivity... done.
writetoshakun8@cloudshell:~$ cd appengine-e
```

Real Linux environment

- Linux Debian-based OS
- 5 GB persisted home directory
- Add, edit and save files

Configured for Google Cloud

- Google Cloud SDK
- Google App Engine SDK
- Docker
- Git
- Text editors
- Build tools
- View more [↗]

Popular language support

- Python
- Java
- Go
- Node.js

CANCEL   START CLOUD SHELL

Figure 1-14. *Google Cloud Shell*

Click on Start Cloud Shell to get started. The Cloud Shell session opens inside a new frame at the bottom of the console, as shown in Figure 1-15.

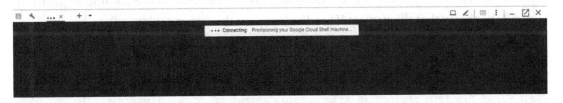

Figure 1-15. *Connecting a Cloud Shell session*

It takes a few seconds to initialize the Cloud Shell session as Google spins up an active instance for this. This instance runs on the Google Cloud and provides a complete environment to connect to the various resources in the cloud.

The Cloud Shell instances are provisioned on a per user and per session basis. The instances persist while the session is active and are terminated after an hour of inactivity.

After the initialization, a command prompt is displayed for you, as shown in Figure 1-16. You can start keying in your commands.

Figure 1-16. *Cloud Shell command prompt*

You can start multiple sessions to the same instance by clicking on the **+** icon, as shown in Figure 1-17.

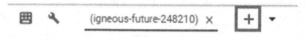

Figure 1-17. *Multiple Cloud Shell session*

This opens a new tab to the same instance, as shown in Figure 1-18.

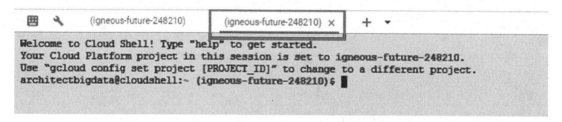

Figure 1-18. *Cloud Shell new session of the same instance*

The Cloud Shell automatically authenticates the logged-in account ID and picks the active/selected project as the current default. This can be seen on the command prompt. Figure 1-19 shows that the project ID is displayed on the command prompt.

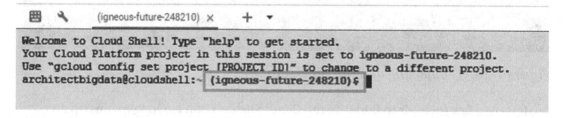

Figure 1-19. *Active project as default*

With Cloud Shell, the Cloud SDK gcloud command and other utilities are available. They enable you to work with the resources and perform a whole bunch of operations. There's no need to install or set up anything.

Let's start keying in a few commands using gcloud. You will start by validating the current default project set (see Listing 1-1). Enter the gcloud config list project command.

Listing 1-1. Validate Default Project Set

```
Welcome to Cloud Shell! Type "help" to get started.
Your Cloud Platform project in this session is set to igneous-
future-248210.
Use "gcloud config set project [PROJECT_ID]" to change to a different
project.
architectbigdata@cloudshell:~ (igneous-future-248210)$ gcloud config list
project
[core]
project = igneous-future-248210

Your active configuration is: [cloudshell-30918]
architectbigdata@cloudshell:~ (igneous-future-248210)$
```

This displays the selected project. Next, you validate which active account is authenticated to work with the selected project by using the gcloud auth list command (see Listing 1-2).

Listing 1-2. Validate the Active Account

```
architectbigdata@cloudshell:~ (igneous-future-248210)$ gcloud auth list
      Credentialed Accounts
ACTIVE   ACCOUNT
*        architectbigdata@gmail.com

To set the active account, run:
    $ gcloud config set account `ACCOUNT`

architectbigdata@cloudshell:~ (igneous-future-248210)$
```

You can see that the logged-in account is being set as the active account. The Cloud Shell is a full-fledged command line on the browser, so you can run Linux commands.

You can change the active account as well as the current default project set using gcloud commands. Type gcloud -h to get help on what commands are available with gcloud (see Listing 1-3).

Listing 1-3. Get Help on Commands

```
architectbigdata@cloudshell:~ (igneous-future-248210)$ gcloud -h
Usage: gcloud [optional flags] <group | command>
  group may be            access-context-manager | ai-platform | alpha | app |
                          asset | auth | beta | bigtable | builds | components |
                          composer | compute | config | container | dataflow |
                          dataproc | datastore | debug | deployment-manager |
                          dns | domains | endpoints | filestore | firebase |
                          functions | iam | iot | kms | logging | ml |
                          ml-engine | organizations | projects | pubsub | redis |
                          resource-manager | scheduler | services | source |
                          spanner | sql | tasks | topic
  command may be          docker | feedback | help | info | init | version
For detailed information on this command and its flags, run:
  gcloud --help
architectbigdata@cloudshell:~ (igneous-future-248210)$
```

You can see a list of all the commands. Using gcloud <<command>> --help or gcloud help <<command>>, you can check the usage of a specific command.

From the commands listed, determine what the config command is used for. Use the gcloud config help command (see Listing 1-4).

Listing 1-4. Help on Config Command

```
architectbigdata@cloudshell:~ (igneous-future-248210)$ gcloud help config
```

It displays complete information about the command, as shown in Listing 1-5.

Listing 1-5. Config Help Output

```
NAME
    gcloud config - view and edit Cloud SDK properties
```

SYNOPSIS
    gcloud config GROUP | COMMAND [GCLOUD_WIDE_FLAG ...]

DESCRIPTION
    The gcloud config command group lets you set, view and unset properties
    used by Cloud SDK.

    A configuration is a set of properties that govern the behavior of gcloud
    and other Cloud SDK tools. The initial default configuration is set when
    gcloud init is run. You can create additional named configurations using
    gcloud init or gcloud config configurations create.

    To display the path of the active configuration along with information
    about the current gcloud environment, run $ gcloud info.

    To switch between configurations, use gcloud config configurations
    activate.

    gcloud supports several flags that have the same effect as properties in a
    configuration (for example, gcloud supports both the --project flag and
    project property). Properties differ from flags in that flags affect
    command behavior on a per-invocation basis. Properties allow you to
    maintain the same settings across command executions.

    For more information on configurations, see gcloud topic configurations.

GCLOUD WIDE FLAGS
    These flags are available to all commands: --account, --billing-project,
    --configuration, --flags-file, --flatten, --format, --help,
    --impersonate-service-account, --log-http, --project, --quiet,
    --trace-token, --user-output-enabled, --verbosity. Run $ gcloud help for
    details.

GROUPS
    GROUP is one of the following:

     configurations

    :

> **Note**   Press Enter to navigate through the output. Once you're done, press q to
> return back to the shell.

Now that you know that the `config` command helps you manage properties, you can
use `gcloud config list` to view which properties are set in the configuration for this
instance. See Listing 1-6.

Listing 1-6. View Properties Set in the Configuration

```
architectbigdata@cloudshell:~ (igneous-future-248210)$ gcloud config list
[component_manager]
disable_update_check = True
[compute]
gce_metadata_read_timeout_sec = 5
[core]
account = architectbigdata@gmail.com
disable_usage_reporting = False
project = igneous-future-248210
[metrics]
environment = devshell

Your active configuration is: [cloudshell-30918]
architectbigdata@cloudshell:~ (igneous-future-248210)$
```

It displays only the properties that have changed and are different from the default
settings. For example, you can see the account is set to the Gmail ID and the project is set
to the selected project. You can use `gcloud config list -all` to view all the properties
that can be managed using this command.

It lists all the properties with a few marked as `unset`. These are the ones that are
either default or are not yet set. See Listing 1-7.

Listing 1-7. View All Properties of the Configuration

```
architectbigdata@cloudshell:~ (igneous-future-248210)$ gcloud config list
--all
enabled (unset)
[healthcare]
dataset (unset)
location (unset)
[interactive]
bottom_bindings_line (unset)
bottom_status_line (unset)
completion_menu_lines (unset)
context (unset)
fixed_prompt_position (unset)
help_lines (unset)
hidden (unset)
justify_bottom_lines (unset)
manpage_generator (unset)
multi_column_completion_menu (unset)
prompt (unset)
show_help (unset)
suggest (unset)
[metrics]
environment = devshell
[ml_engine]
local_python (unset)
polling_interval (unset)
[proxy]
address (unset)
password (unset)
port (unset)
rdns (unset)
type (unset)
username (unset)
[redis]
region (unset)
```

```
[scc]
organization (unset)
[spanner]
instance (unset)
[survey]
disable_prompts (unset)

Your active configuration is: [cloudshell-30918]
architectbigdata@cloudshell:~ (igneous-future-248210)$
```

You saw how easy it is to work with the Cloud Shell. It's an easy way to get up and running with the Google Cloud. The book uses the Console as it walks through the topics. Feel free to explore the other commands.

gcloud, the powerful and unified command-line tool for the Google Cloud Platform, is especially useful when you want to script operations that need to be performed on a regular, routine basis. Rather than running the steps manually, you can run the script and free up the manual resources from mundane tasks.

Cloud SDK

The Cloud Shell option is typically used when you can't download the software on your local machine. However, since the VM instances are spun up temporarily, it's not a very good option when you have to do development intensively using Google Cloud.

In that case, downloading and using Google Cloud SDK is the better option. Google provides command-line tools and APIs to interact with its services and resources via Google Cloud SDK.

The book will return to its usage when you start working with the services offered by GCP in the coming chapters. Before you go any further, it's important to briefly understand what a project is and how you create a new one.

Project

When you first signed up for GCP, you learned that GCP automatically creates a new project named My First Project, which is basically used to isolate the resources of the project from the resources of other projects.

A project is the base organizing entity; primarily a container for all the resources you create. It's a must to get started with GCP. For example, if you create a new instance, it will be owned by a project. Further, any charges incurred by the resources will be charged to its project.

Ownership: Projects and Billing

The project is the top-level billing instance, which implies that billing in GCP happens at the project level and not at the account level.

The billing account that you created at the start is by default associated with the project; however, different billing accounts can be specified for each project you create. That way, if you have a bunch of Google Cloud projects going on in the same organization, you can ask different departments or different teams within a department to pay for it.

So, you can have multiple projects associated with a single billing account or you can have multiple billing accounts, each associated with different projects. You use the billing menu to manage project-wise billing accounts. Figure 1-20 displays the default billing account overview and the projects linked to the account.

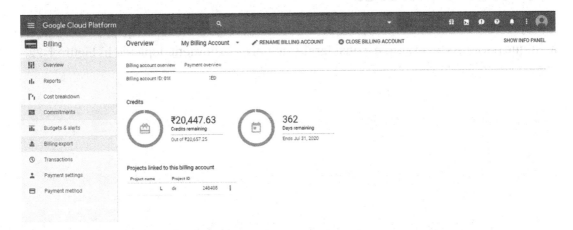

Figure 1-20. *Billing account overview*

Figure 1-21 shows the context menu associated with the accounts. Clicking on the context menu enables you to disable the billing account for the project or change the billing account. If no action is taken, the projects billing continues to happen through this account only.

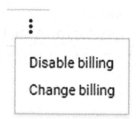

Figure 1-21. *Billing account context menu*

The billing of a project happens based on the services used within.

Projects and Isolations

Not only does the project own a resource, but it is also used to isolate the resources from one another. This means that if users have access to view a project, they will have access to all its resources but will not be able to view resources in other projects unless specified. This is very useful in controlling who views what.

Project as Namespace

A project also serves as a namespace, which means every resource in a project must have a unique name. As an example, consider the actual environment depicted in Figure 1-22.

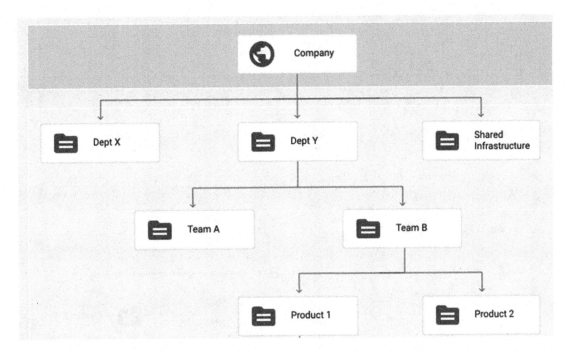

Figure 1-22. *Actual environment*

There are various departments and development teams. Teams work on various products. Each product has a Dev environment, a Test environment, and a Production environment.

In GCP, each environment should be represented as a project, which is an organizing unit of all resources required to achieve a precise objective. So in GCP, the environment from Figure 1-22 will look like Figure 1-23.

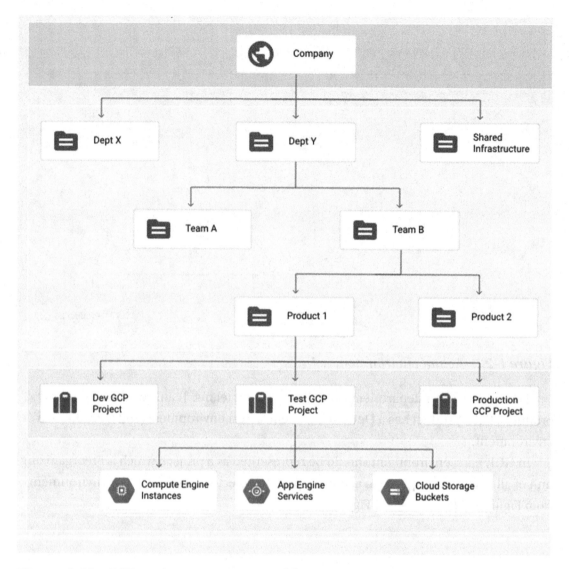

Figure 1-23. *GCP project organization of the actual environment*

You need to create multiple projects, each pertaining to a specific need or requirement.

In addition, say you have customer-specific implementations. You can then have customer specific projects, wherein resources and changes within a project are visible only to that customer's users and not to others.

Create a Project

Now that you're familiar with what a project is, it's time to create a project. Click on the Projects dropdown appearing in the top-most panel, as shown in Figure 1-24.

Figure 1-24. *Projects dropdown*

Figure 1-25 shows the pop up that will appear with all projects listed under Recent. In this case, the default created project is visible.

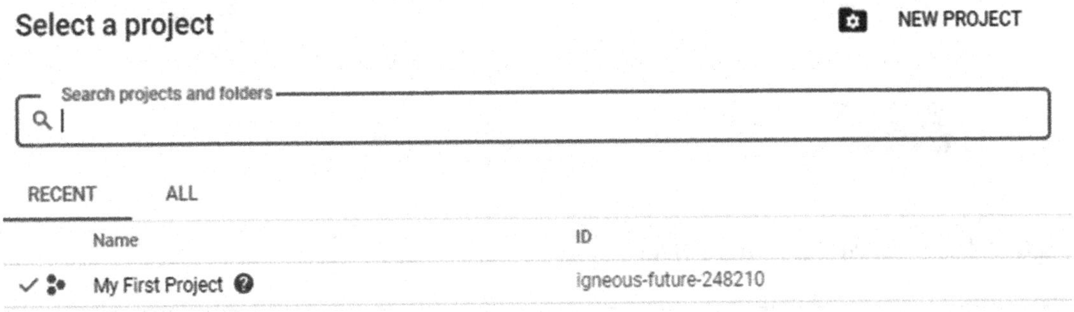

Select a project

NEW PROJECT

Search projects and folders

RECENT   ALL

Name	ID
✓ ⁑ My First Project ❓	igneous-future-248210

Figure 1-25. *Recent project list*

Click on New Project. A window will appear, as shown in Figure 1-26.

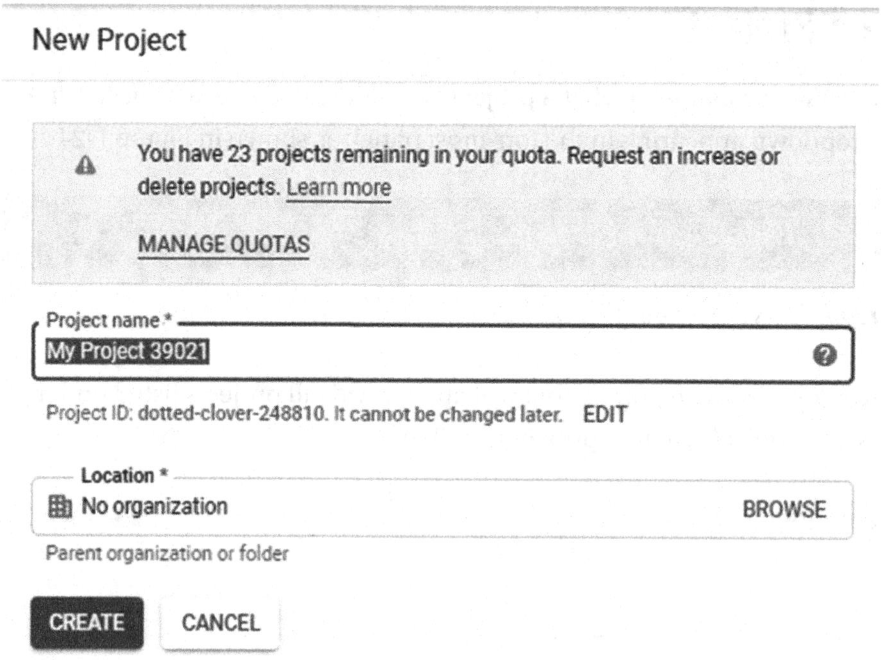

New Project

> ⚠ You have 23 projects remaining in your quota. Request an increase or delete projects. Learn more
>
> MANAGE QUOTAS

Project name *
My Project 39021   ❓

Project ID: dotted-clover-248810. It cannot be changed later.   EDIT

Location *
🏢 No organization   BROWSE

Parent organization or folder

[CREATE]   [CANCEL]

Figure 1-26. *Create a new project*

Note   If you are using the trial quota, you'll have a limit of 23 projects. This is sufficient for the examples in the book.

All projects consist of the following:

- *Project Name*: A display name that's mutable and is provided while creating.

- *Project ID*: This comes prepopulated but you can change it. The ID is unique across GCP. Once the project is created, it cannot be changed. The ID cannot be used again, even if you delete the project.

- *Project Number*: Provided by GCP. It is automatically assigned when the project is created and is read-only.

To follow along with the example here, try creating a project named ExampleGettingStarted. Figure 1-27 shows the pop up with the name specified.

Project name *

ExampleGettingStarted   ❓

Project ID: examplegettingstarted-248810. It cannot be changed later.   EDIT

Location *

🏢 No organization   BROWSE

Parent organization or folder

[CREATE]   [CANCEL]

Figure 1-27. *Project ExampleGettingStarted*

Click on Create to create the project. Once you have created the project, it will start appearing in the project dropdown, as shown in Figure 1-28. Click on the dropdown and select the project.

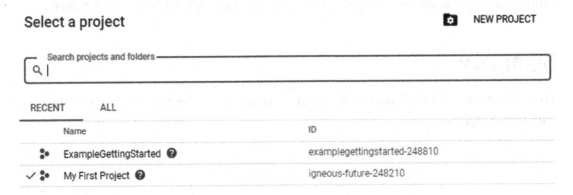

Select a project   ⚙ NEW PROJECT

Search projects and folders

🔍 |

RECENT   ALL

	Name	ID
⁑•	ExampleGettingStarted ❓	examplegettingstarted-248810
✓ ⁑•	My First Project ❓	igneous-future-248210

Figure 1-28. *Project created and displayed in the project list*

You will be redirected to the Cloud Console with the selected project set as active, as shown in Figure 1-29.

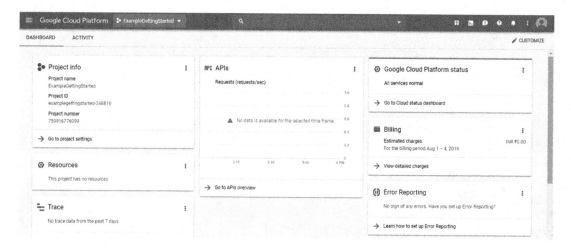

Figure 1-29. *Newly created project's Cloud Console*

In order to interact with most GCP resources, you must provide the identifying project information for every request. This is either a project ID or a project number.

Summary

This chapter covered the basics of getting started with GCP. The next chapter will start with Cloud SQL.

CHAPTER 2

Cloud SQL

Cloud SQL is Google's relational database. It's a cloud hosted MySQL or PostgreSQL database.

> *Cloud SQL is a fully managed database service that makes it easy to set up, manage, maintain, and administer relational databases on the Google Cloud Platform.*
>
> —Google

Cloud SQL enables you to run the same SQL queries you are used to but within Google's managed cloud. This offering is extremely helpful if you are migrating an existing application to a cloud database without much reengineering.

This chapter starts with Cloud SQL, and you will learn how to provision a Cloud SQL instance. However, prior to that, the chapter discuses what a relational database is.

Relational Databases

The following section introduces the relational database concepts and is more relevant to users who are new to RDBMS.

Relational databases have been a common choice of database for personal data, financial records, logistical information, manufacturing records, and other applications since the 1980s. This system complies with the relational model proposed by IBM's E. F. Codd in 1970.

Relational databases refer to databases that store data in a structured format in the form of tables using rows and columns. The values within each table are related to each other. See Table 2-1.

27

© Navin Sabharwal, Shakuntala Gupta Edward 2020
N. Sabharwal and S. G. Edward, *Hands On Google Cloud SQL and Cloud Spanner*,
https://doi.org/10.1007/978-1-4842-5537-7_2

Table 2-1. *Students*

23	Ram	IV	C	Vivekananda
25	Shyam	V	A	Thomas

As you can see in Table 2-1, each row refers to a student and the columns represent the attributes of that student.

In relational databases, tables and their schemas are defined before you start capturing the data. As an example, see Table 2-2, which specifies the attribute names, data type, and size.

Table 2-2. *Student Table Schema*

Roll Number	Number
Name	STRING [50]
Class	STRING [5]
Section	STRING [1]
Team	STRING [50]

Tables may also be related to each other. In order to understand relationships between tables, consider the following example.

In an organization there are various departments and each department has employees. Tables 2-3 and 2-4 show the schema definition for these tables.

Table 2-3. *Department Table Schema*

Department ID	STRING [5]	PRIMARY KEY
Department Name	STRING [50]	

Table 2-4. *Employee Table Schema*

Employee ID	STRING [10]	PRIMARY KEY
Employee Name	STRING [50]	
Department ID	STRING [5]	FOREIGN KEY

In addition to the data type and size, the attributes also include keys: the primary key and the foreign key.

Primary Key

Whenever an employee joins the organization, an ID is assigned to them, which uniquely identifies the employee. You cannot have two employees with the same ID and you can't have an employee without an ID. Similar to that in a relational table, there are columns whose values uniquely identify each row. These columns are called the primary keys. For example, the Employee ID in the Employee table and the Department ID in Department table.

Foreign Key

When an employee joins the organization, a department is also assigned to the employee. When storing that information in the form of the table, you store the department ID along with the employee. Since the Department ID is the primary key of the Department table, it becomes the foreign key in the Employee table.

A column in a table that serves as the primary key of another table is called the foreign key. The foreign key links the two tables.

In the previous example, the Department ID key is used to link the two tables— Employee and Department. If you look at the data in the individual tables, it will look like Table 2-5.

Table 2-5. *Department Table*

Department ID	Department Name
D01	IT
D02	Admin
D03	HR
D04	EHS
D05	Finance

Table 2-6. *Employee Table*

Employee ID	Employee Name	Department ID
E1	Mike	*D01*
E2	Michelle	*D01*
E3	Dave	*D02*
E4	Kate	*D03*
E5	Chintamani	*D04*
E6	Natalie	*D05*
E7	Steffi	*D02*

If you have to determine the name of the department that Employee E1 belongs to, you simply use Department Code D01 mapped to E1 to retrieve the department, which is IT. Tables in relational databases are linked or related using primary keys and foreign keys.

Constraints

In addition to the data type, size, and key specifications, relational databases also enable you to define constraints while defining the schema. For example, a Unique Key constraint ensures uniqueness within the data of the column and a NOT NULL constraint says that the column cannot have a NULL (empty) value. All these together maintain the referential integrity constraints.

If a department is to be deleted, the foreign-primary key will help ensure that all related employees are either deleted or moved to another department.

If you alter the employee schema and add a new column, called Nickname, with a UNIQUE constraint and then modify the Employee Name and Department ID to have a NOT NULL constraint, you'll get Table 2-7.

Table 2-7. *Modified Employee Schema*

Employee ID	STRING [10]	PRIMARY KEY
Employee Name	STRING [50]	NOT NULL
Nickname	STRING [10]	UNIQUE CONSTRAINT
Department ID	STRING [5]	FOREIGN KEY, NOT NULL

Note   Department ID is a foreign key and has the NOT NULL constraint associated with it.

If an employee is created, the UNIQUE constraint on Nickname will ensure that the same nickname is not used twice. The NOT NULL constraint will ensure that no employee is created without a Name or a Department. All these ensure that the table's data is consistent.

Operations

Now that you have understanding of the schema, this section looks at the type of operations that can be performed on the data. The operations are grouped into DDL, DML, and read requests.

DDL

DDL stands for data definition language and it includes operations dealing with schema creation or modifications such as CREATE TABLE, DROP TABLE, and ALTER TABLE, to name a few. See Tables 2-8 through 2-10.

Table 2-8. *CREATE TABLE: Employee Table*

Employee ID	STRING [10]
Employee Name	STRING [50]

Table 2-9. *ALTER TABLE: Employee Table Modified the Data Size for Column Name*

Employee ID	STRING [10]
Employee Name	STRING [100]

Table 2-10. *DROP TABLE: Employee Table Removed*

Employee ID	STRING [10]
Employee Name	STRING [100]

DML

DML stands for data manipulation language and this includes operations that are used for manipulating data such as inserts, deletes, and updates. See Tables 2-11 through 2-14.

Table 2-11. *Employee Table Data*

Employee ID	Employee Name
E1	Mike
E2	Steffi

Table 2-12. *Insert Data: Inserted New Rows from E3–E5*

Employee ID	Employee Name
E1	Mike
E2	Steffi
E3	Michelle
E4	Steve
E5	Sandy

Table 2-13. *Update Data: Updated Names for Employee ID E2 and E5*

Employee ID	Employee Name
E1	Mike
E2	Steffi Tom
E3	Michelle
E4	Steve
E5	Sandy Riddle

Table 2-14. *Delete Data:*
Deleted Employee ID E2

Employee ID	Employee Name
E1	Mike
E2	~~Steffi Tom~~
E3	Michelle
E4	Steve
E5	Sandy Riddle

Read Requests

Read requests are operations that are used for retrieving or querying the data stored within the table. See Table 2-15.

Table 2-15. *Query Data:*
Showing All Employees with
Name Starting with M

Employee ID	Employee Name
E1	Mike
E3	Michelle

Transactions

SQL (Structured Query Language) is the query language used for performing all these operations on the relational databases.

In general in relational databases, the operations of accessing and modifying data are grouped together into a logical unit of work. This logical unit of work is called a *transaction*.

You can better grasp what a transaction is with an example. Say you have a banking system. Suppose Account A has a balance of $400 and Account B has $700. Account A is transferring $100 to Account B. This is really two updates to the underlying database: First the amount in Account A needs to be reduced by $100 and then the amount in Account B needs to be increased by $100.

In relational databases, all the work is carried out in a transaction. Let's refer to it as T1.

```
T1
BEGIN
Read Account A amount from the database: 400$
Read Account B amount from the database: 700$
Subtract 100$ from Account A: Resulting to 300$
Write Output 300$ to Account A in the database
Add 100$ to Account B: Resulting to 800$
Write Output 800$ to Account B in the database
COMMIT
```

Note   BEGIN indicates the start of the operation and COMMIT indicates that the operation is complete.

Transactions in relational databases use the ACID property. ACID stands for the four guarantees any relational database provides to ensure that database modifications are saved in a consistent, safe, and robust manner. It stands for Atomicity, Consistency, Isolation, and Durability.

Atomicity is the property that ensures that either all the operations of a transaction are reflected in the database or none are.

In the previous example, say the first operation, which was to reduce Account A by $100, is completed, but the second operation fails. In that case, Account A's balance will be $300 while B's remains unchanged ($700 instead of $800). This is unacceptable, because this means a loss of $100. Instead, either the transaction should fail without executing any operations or it should process both operations. This is ensured in an RDBMS using the atomicity property.

Consistency is used to preserve the data consistency. While discussing the databases, you read about *constraints*, which are rules defined to ensure data consistency. The consistency property ensures that none of the rules are violated when a transaction completes, and any transaction trying to violate the rule will not be allowed to complete. It ensures that at all times anyone reading any data from the database will always see consistent data—i.e., data that conforms to all defined rules.

Consistency also ensures that readers don't read dirty and uncommitted changes. In the previous example, any time prior to the transaction COMMIT, a read query or a request for Account A's balance or B's balance will show the amount as [400$, 700$] and not [300$, 800$].

The *isolation* property ensures that if multiple transactions are concurrently performed on the database, individual updates of the transactions will never be interleaved in such a way as to result in bad data. The database must guarantee that updates happen in such a way that it appears as if all the transactions happened one after the other.

To understand this better, say you have one more transaction (T2) in which Account A is receiving $100 from another account, which is Account C. Account C has $500 in it. Let's further assume that the transactions run concurrently, leading to interleaving of operations between the two transactions, as follows:

```
T1:
        BEGIN
        Read Account A amount from the database: 400$
        Read Account B amount from the database: 700$
T2:     BEGIN
        Read Account A amount from the database: 400$
        Read Account C amount from the database: 500$
        Subtract 100$ from Account C: Resulting to 400$
        Write Output 400$ to Account C in the database
        Add 100$ to Account A: Resulting to 500$
        Write Output 500$ to Account A in the database
        COMMIT
T1:
        Subtract 100$ from Account A: Resulting to 300$
        Write Output 300$ to Account A in the database
        Add 100$ to Account B: Resulting to 800$
        Write Output 800$ to Account B in the database
        COMMIT
```

Note that the final balance of Account A after completing both transactions will be $300, which means the $100 addition to Account A has been lost.

RDBMS use the isolation property to guarantee that this never happens. If the transactions were to run in isolation, the second transaction would read the correct balance as $300 once the first transaction was complete.

In effect, isolation means for every pair of transactions on the same dataset, one transaction will start execution only after the other execution is done.

Durability means that any changes done when a transaction is successful are permanent, i.e., whatever happens, the transaction will not disappear.

Whenever an UPDATE statement is issued, the update first happens in memory and then the data on the disk is updated. Let's suppose the data in memory was updated but prior to the update on the disk, a power failure happens. Since memory is volatile by nature this may lead to losing the update. However, the durability guarantee of the RDBMS ensures safety against such scenarios. The recovery management component manages the transactions in such a way that the transactions remain durable and no data loss happens in any situation.

This ACID property makes relational databases best suited for transactional workloads and is the key feature that differentiates relational database systems from modern non-relational databases.

In conclusion, relational databases are best suited for structured data with known schemas and relations and that needs to be consistent. Now that you have learned about relational databases, let's begin with Cloud SQL.

Getting Started with Cloud SQL

As described earlier, Cloud SQL is Google's fully managed SQL database service. Fully managed means that the mundane but necessary and often time-consuming tasks such as applying patches and updates, managing backup, configuring replications, etc. are all handled by Google so users simply need to focus on building the application.

A Cloud SQL instance supports two open source SQL implementations (database engines): MySQL and PostgreSQL.

MySQL is

- Best suited for simple querying

- Works exceptionally well in read-heavy systems expecting high read speed

- Underperforms with heavy loads or complex queries

- Apt for requirements of high speed and ease of setting up

PostgreSQL is

- Best suited for high-volume data operations and complex queries

- Works exceptionally well with systems requiring fast read and write speeds and extensive data analysis and validation

- Supports a variety of performance enhancers as available in commercial solutions such as SQL Server

- Apt for requirements of complex processing, integration, data integrity, and intricate designs.

Put another way, if MySQL is the Honda Activa 5G, PostgreSQL is sort of like the Royal Enfield Bullet (a four-stroke motorcycle). The Royal Enfield may have more capabilities and support extreme conditions, but it's probably not necessary if you have to just go to the grocery across the road. The selection of the SQL implementation depends on your project requirements.

It's easy to get started with Cloud SQL, as no software installations are required. You just log in to GCP and create an instance, which you can access using Cloud Shell, APIs, SDKs, etc. You will learn more about accessing the database when you start working with the instance in a forthcoming chapter.

This section looks at provisioning a Cloud SQL instance using Cloud Console. You'll get started by provisioning the Cloud SQL-MySQL instance.

Provision a MySQL Instance

Navigate to the `https://console.cloud.google.com/` URL and log in using your Google account. Once you're signed in, Google will redirect to the Cloud Console.

As discussed earlier, resources belong to a project, so the first thing you need to ensure is that your project is selected.

In order to run all the exercises for Cloud SQL, there is a project named `DemoCloudSQL`. Select the project from the Project dropdown to get started. Figure 2-1 shows the project selected.

Figure 2-1. Project selection

Next you open the left-side navigation menu and click SQL underneath the storage section, as shown in Figure 2-2.

Figure 2-2. *SQL selection under the Storage section*

This takes you to the Cloud SQL page. You will see the Create Instance button, as shown in Figure 2-3.

Figure 2-3. *Cloud SQL Create Instance pop up*

Note   This is the first cloud SQL instance being created, which is why no instance is listed.

Click on Create Instance and choose MySQL from the subsequent screen. Figure 2-4 shows the database engine selection screen.

Figure 2-4. *Database engine selection*

This will take you to the page shown in Figure 2-5, where you set up the parameters of the SQL instance.

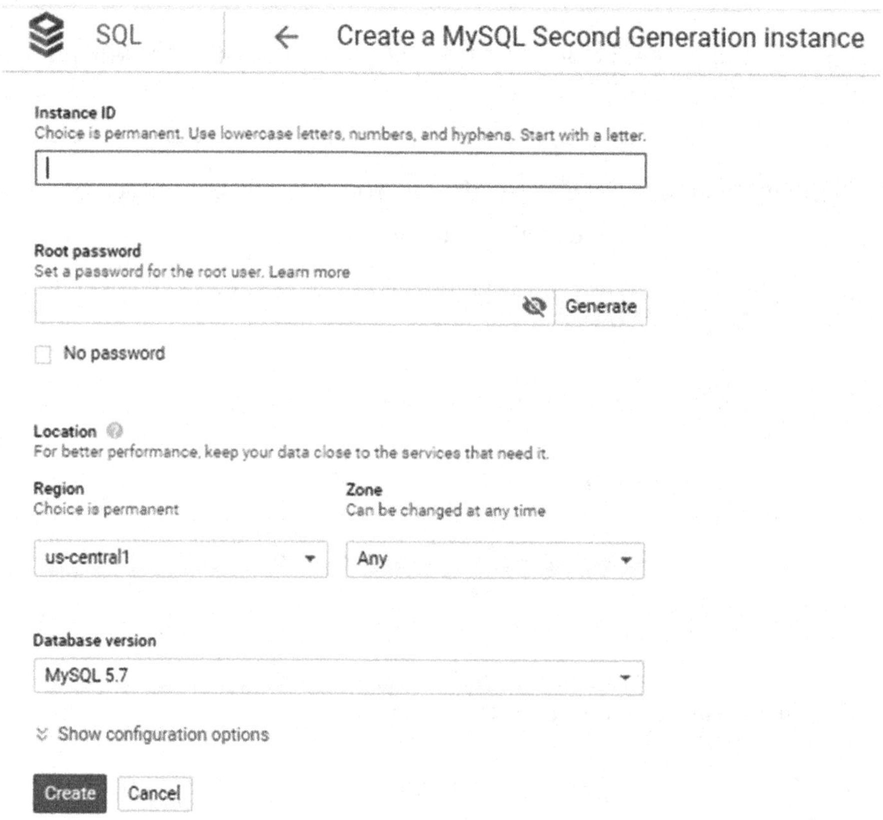

Figure 2-5. *Instance creation page*

You first specify the Instance ID. For this example, name the instance `mysqldb`.

Note   The name has to be unique within your project, which means you can have only one database with this name at a time.

Next choose a password to access the MySQL instance. The Cloud Console can automatically generate a new secure password or you can choose your own.

You also have the option to choose No Password; however, this is not a recommended option as anyone could connect to your instance with full admin privileges.

Specify your own password. Next you have to choose where, geographically, you want the instance to be located. Google has datacenters across the world, so you have various options.

For this example, choose us-central1 as the region and us-central1-a as the zone. With all details filled in, the form will look like Figure 2-6.

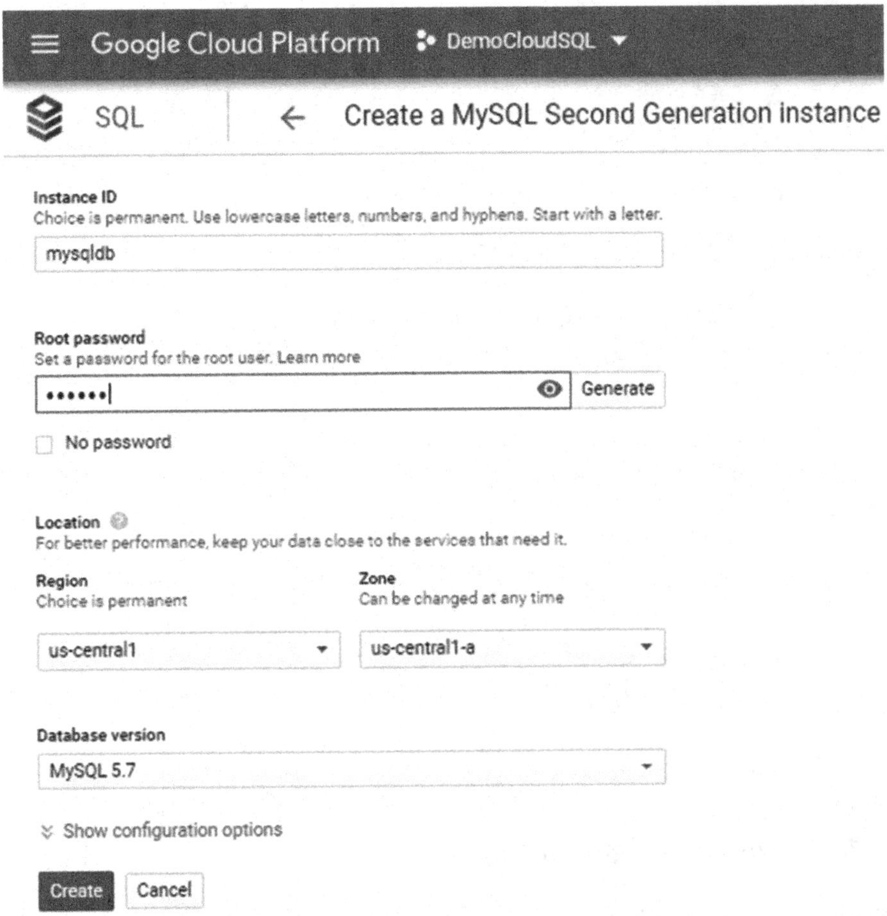

Figure 2-6. *Cloud SQL instance creation form filled in with details*

Note that the ones you specify here are the basic options; there's list of advanced options available to configure further.

You can change the options anytime later so to begin with, you will get started with the base configurations. You'll learn more about these options in the forthcoming chapter, which discusses factors that are important for setting up the Cloud SQL instance for a production environment.

Just to have a look at the option, click Show Configuration Options near the bottom of the page. This lists all the advanced options available to you. Figure 2-7 shows the options. Before you proceed, take a brief moment to familiarize yourself with the options.

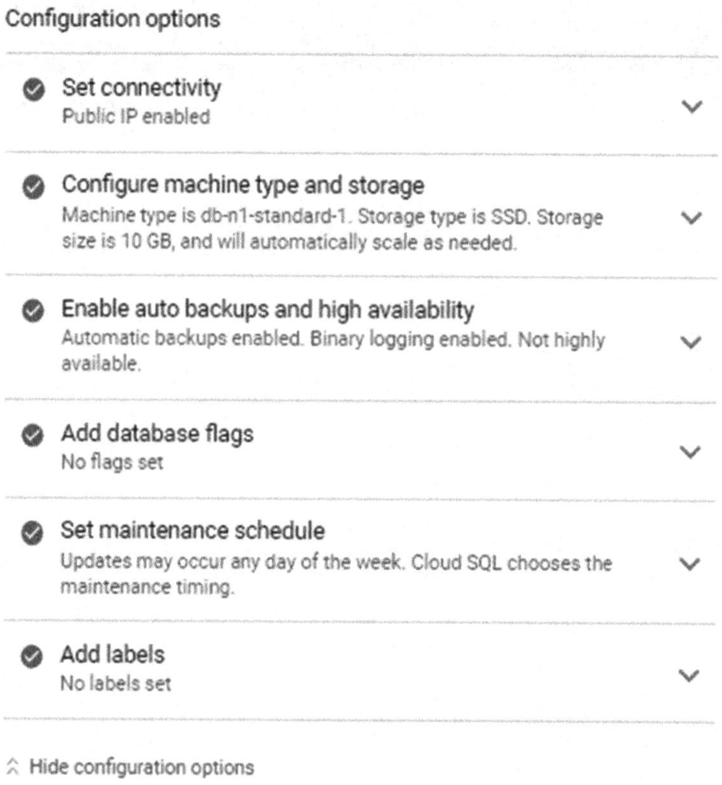

Configuration options

✅ **Set connectivity**
Public IP enabled   ⌄

✅ **Configure machine type and storage**
Machine type is db-n1-standard-1. Storage type is SSD. Storage   ⌄
size is 10 GB, and will automatically scale as needed.

✅ **Enable auto backups and high availability**
Automatic backups enabled. Binary logging enabled. Not highly   ⌄
available.

✅ **Add database flags**
No flags set   ⌄

✅ **Set maintenance schedule**
Updates may occur any day of the week. Cloud SQL chooses the   ⌄
maintenance timing.

✅ **Add labels**
No labels set   ⌄

⌃ Hide configuration options

Figure 2-7. *Advanced configuration options*

The Set Connectivity option enables you to configure access to your instance.
Figure 2-8 shows the available options.

Figure 2-8. *Set connectivity options*

You might want to change the size of the VM instance or increase the size of the associated disk, and for this you have the Configure Machine Type and Storage option. Figure 2-9 shows the available choices.

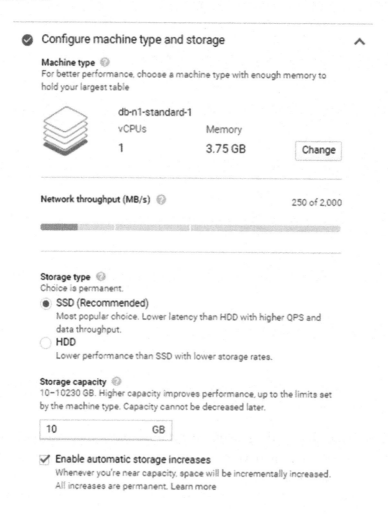

Figure 2-9. *Configure machine type and storage*

By default, the instance uses a db-n1-standard-1 type instance and starts with 10GB SSD disk with automatic storage increase enabled.

The automatic storage increase is a must when you are using the instance for your production deployment, as the data within the database constantly increases. If it exceeds the current hard disk capacity, Google will automatically add more storage to accommodate the increased data. A limit can be specified up to which you want the increase to occur. The default value is 0, which means there's no limit. Instance data is stored in the region where the instance resides.

Next for scheduling backups and enabling HA is the Enable Auto-Backups and High Availability option, as shown in Figure 2-10.

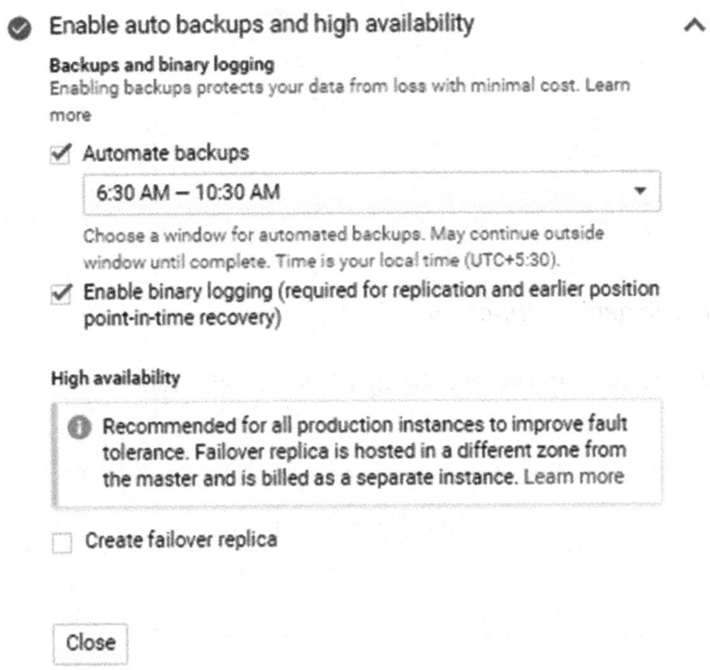

Figure 2-10. *Enable auto backups and high availability*

By default, automatic backups and binary logging are selected. Automatic backups back up the data at periodic intervals and you can specify the time at which the backup should occur.

Binary logging enables point-in-time recovery and data replication. Point-in-time recovery enables you to restore or recover your data from a time in the past. This is beneficial in transactional systems where you have frequent transactions happening. This combination of backup and binary logging keeps you safe from data loss. Backup data is stored in two regions for redundancy.

The High Availability option is used to provision a fault-tolerant instance. It is not selected by default. However, if you are working on a banking application, where the application needs to be highly available to its users, then you need a cloud SQL database that's highly available. To achieve this, you should enable High Availability.

You can also add Cloud SQL flags. These are used to adjust the database parameters and options to customize your database. Figure 2-11 shows the steps for setting the default time zone.

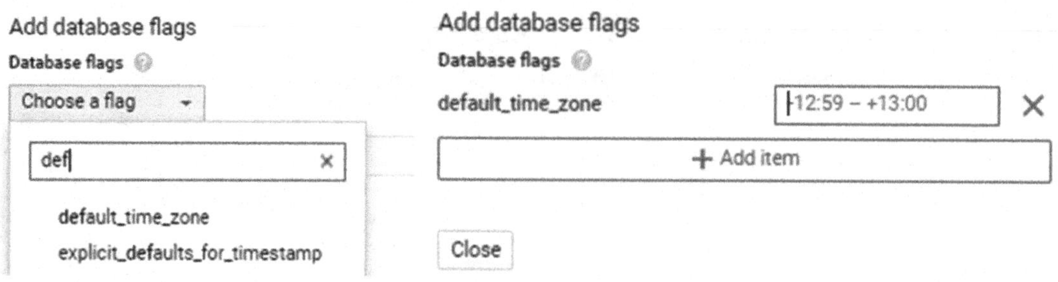

Figure 2-11. *Set the default time zone*

Figure 2-12 shows the steps for specifying the log output type.

Figure 2-12. *Specify the log output*

There are many more. These flag values are persisted as long as the instance lives.

The Set Maintenance Schedule option can be used to configure the maintenance schedule for the instance in just a few clicks. Figure 2-13 shows the options available for configuring the maintenance schedule. This is in contrast to the traditional methods, wherein prior to scheduling the maintenance, you had to take care of a complete checklist to ensure the data consistency and state.

This is a good example of the routine, time-consuming, and mundane activity that you are freed from as you move to GCP

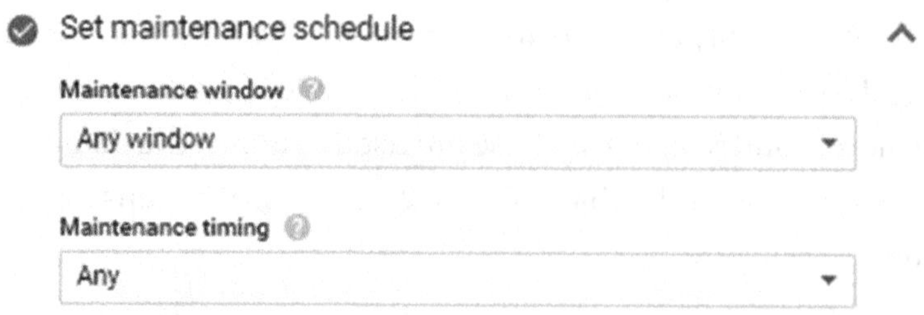

Figure 2-13. *Set maintenance schedule*

Finally, there are the Labels options, which enables you to label your instance.

All the important options from a production deployment perspective are covered in a forthcoming chapter dedicated to this topic. To get started with Cloud SQL, this section moves ahead with the basic configurations and leaves the remaining ones as they are.

Click on Create to start creating the Cloud SQL instance.

The control will be redirected to the Instance List page, as shown in Figure 2-14, where the instance appears and is greyed out while it initializes and starts. It will take some time to spin up.

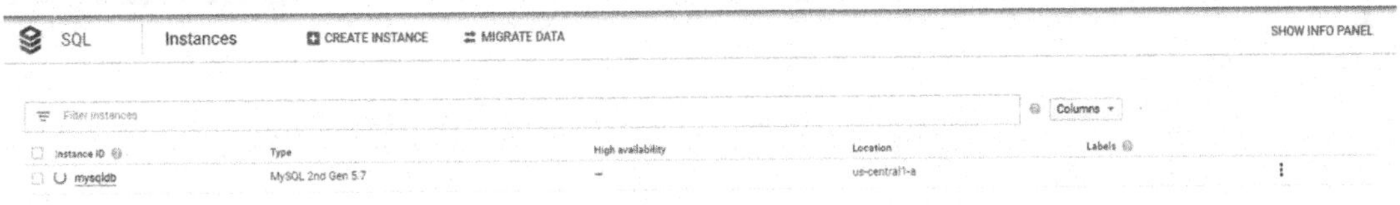

	SQL	Instances	CREATE INSTANCE	MIGRATE DATA			SHOW INFO PANEL
Filter instances						Columns ▾	
Instance ID		Type		High availability	Location	Labels	
mysqldb		MySQL 2nd Gen 5.7		–	us-central1-a		⋮

Figure 2-14. *Instance List page*

After it's done, a green tickmark will appear next to the instance name, confirming it has been created. Figure 2-15 shows the Instance List page with the newly created instance.

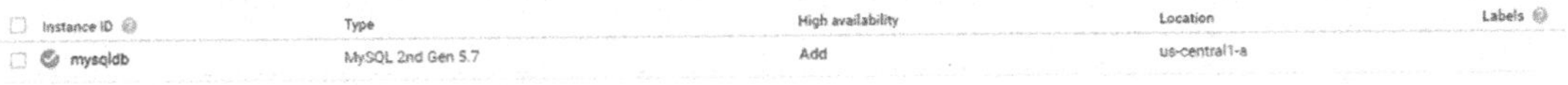

Instance ID	Type	High availability	Location	Labels
mysqldb	MySQL 2nd Gen 5.7	Add	us-central1-a	

Figure 2-15. *New instance has been created*

You also receive a notification in the notification pane confirming the creation, as shown in Figure 2-16.

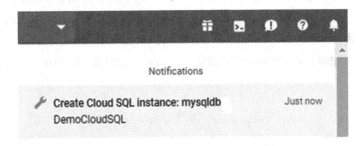

Figure 2-16. *Notification pane*

After the instance has been created, you can use the Instance Details page to show that the instance is all set. With every instance created, an Instance Details page is available and it enables you to monitor, manage, and work with your database instance using Cloud Console.

You can familiarize yourself a bit with the Instance Details page. Click on the instance name in the instance list. It takes you to the Instance Details page. Figure 2-17 shows all the options available on the Instance Details page.

Figure 2-17. *Instance Details page for mysqldb*

At the top of the Instance Details page, you'll see the Stop, Restart, Clone, and Delete options. Next to those, you also have option to Import/Export data to/from a database within the instance. The Edit option opens the configuration page with options you configured while creating the instance, thus enabling you to modify the settings.

In addition, there are various tabs available to work with the instance. For example, the Users tab manages the instance database users. Figure 2-18 shows the Users tab details.

Figure 2-18. *Users details for mysqldb*

The Database tab lists all the databases of the instance, as shown in Figure 2-19. You can use it to manage your databases, create a new database, and delete an existing user database.

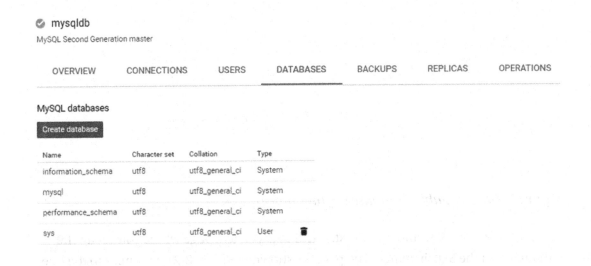

Figure 2-19. *Databases tab for mysqldb*

Note   Since this is a fresh instance, the databases displayed are the default databases that are created by MySQL whenever a new instance in created.

You can further use the Backups tab to schedule backups or create on-demand backups, the Connections tab to manage the connectivity of the database, the Replicas tab to create read replica or a failover replica, and the Operations tab to monitor the database instance operations.

Feel free to explore the details page to familiarize yourself with it. We will come back to these later as we explore a few of the options in Chapter 4. Having covered provisioning of a MySQL instance, it's time to look at provisioning the PostgreSQL instance.

Provisioning a PostgreSQL Instance

As with MySQL, you can select the SQL option under the Storage section. It will take you to the Cloud SQL instance list, where you should select Create Instance. Figure 2-20 lists the database engine choices.

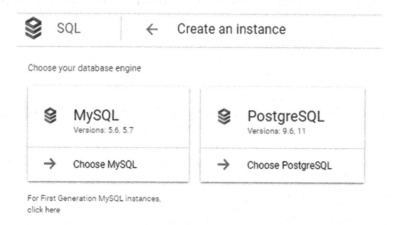

Figure 2-20. *Available database engine choices*

Choose PostgreSQL and click Next. It will take you to a page where you set up the parameters of the SQL instance. The page, as shown in Figure 2-21, is similar to the one you saw when creating a MySQL instance.

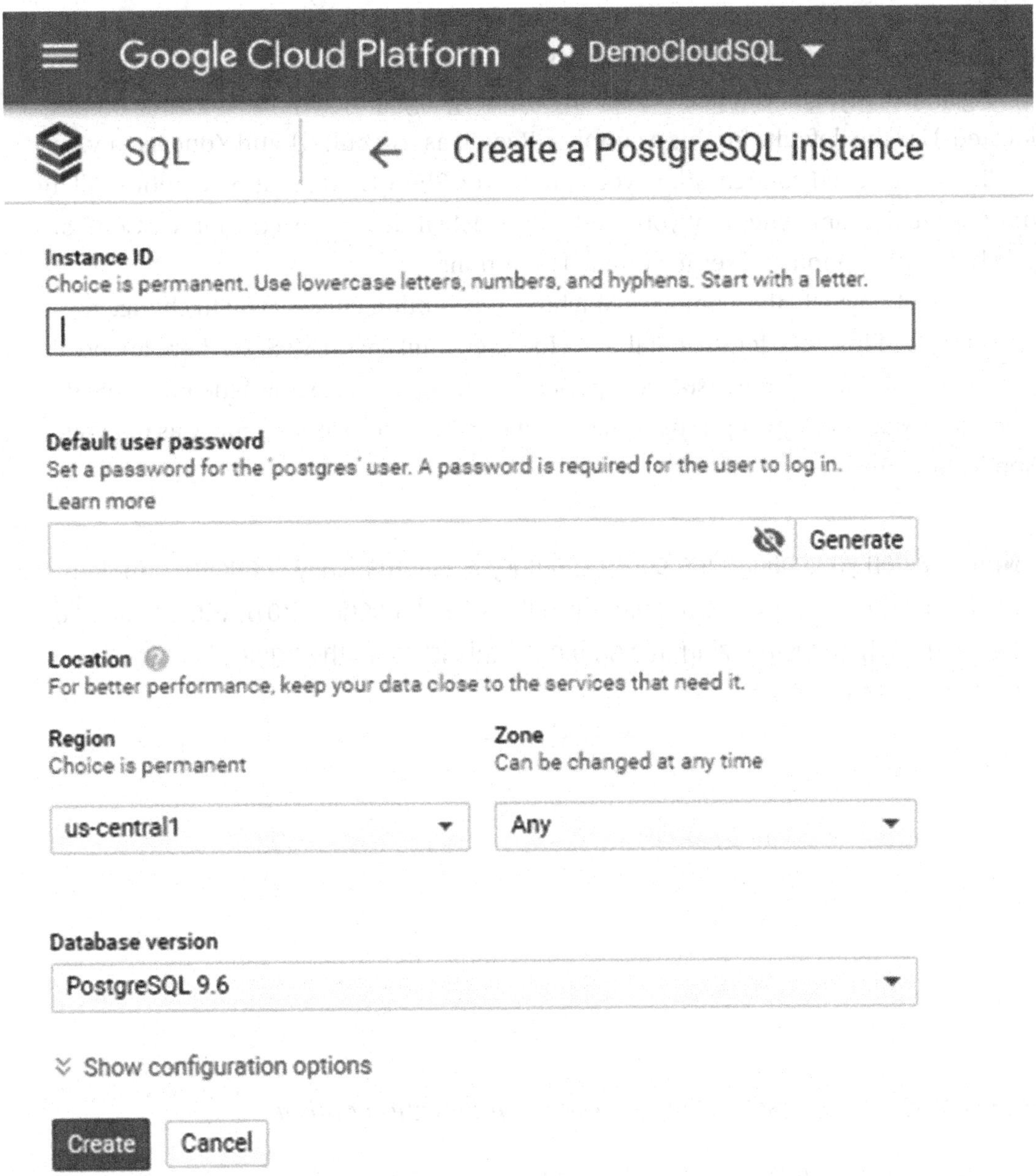

Figure 2-21. *Create PostgreSQL instance*

Like with MySQL, you need to provide an instance ID. For this example, let's name the instance test-ps. Next, choose the default user (postgres) password. Like MySQL, Cloud Console can generate a password or you can choose your own. However, unlike MySQL, there's no option to not set the password. It's mandatory to specify a password. The password here is set for the default user `postgres`, which is different from the default user `root` in MySQL.

Again like MySQL, you need to specify where, geographically, the instance is to be located. Use the defaults for this example—Region as us-central1 and Zone as Any.

To do advanced configuration, you can use the Show Configuration Options. All the options are the same ones that you used in the MySQL section, except for the Configure Machine Type option and setting up the HA options.

Like with MySQL, the Configure Machine Type option enables you to change the size of the VM instance for the database. However, unlike with MySQL, there are no predefined options for the instance type selection. Figure 2-22 shows the PostgreSQL Configure Machine Type options. You can set the vCPU core and memory as per your application needs.

Note   When you change the cores, memory is automatically changed to match the core settings, but you can customize it further if needed. However, you should be careful when customizing this option, as this impacts the pricing and the sustained use discounts.

Figure 2-22. *PostgreSQL Machine Type Configuration option*

While enabling the backup, unlike MySQL, you don't have the binary logging option available, and High Availability is configured using regional instances. With regional instances, you have persistent disks used for replication.

As mentioned, these are discussed in a later section. From a user perspective, it provides safety against primary instance failure. As with MySQL, you retain the default settings for advanced configuration. With all the details filled in, the provisioning page looks like Figure 2-23.

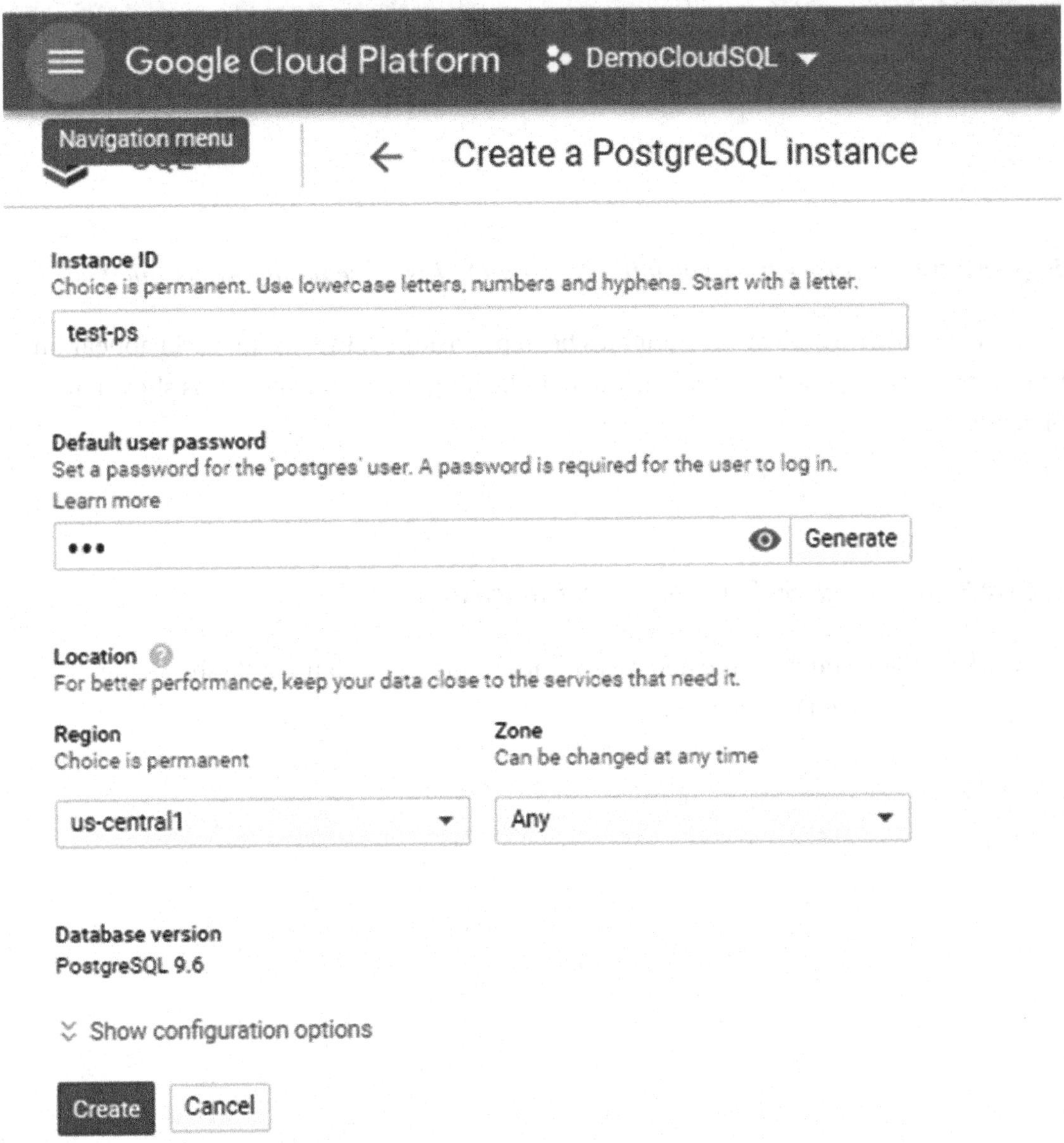

Figure 2-23. *Configured PostgreSQL new instance creation form*

Click on Create to provision the PostgreSQL. It takes a few minutes to provision the machine. Figure 2-24 shows the instance list page with the PostgreSQL instance listed.

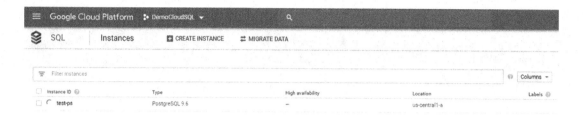

Figure 2-24. *Instance list page with PostgreSQL instance being provisioned*

As with the MySQL instance, after it's been provisioned, the instance will appear on the instance list page with a green tickmark indicating it's been enabled, as shown in Figure 2-25.

Figure 2-25. *PostgreSQL instance provisioned and listed*

Click on the instance name and review the details page. Figure 2-26 shows the PostgreSQL Instance Details page.

Figure 2-26. *PostgreSQL Instance Details page*

As with the MySQL Instance Details page, all the options are as is. However, the content in the tabs is database specific. So, for example, the Users tab in PostgreSQL lists the default user as `postgres`, which is different from the `root` user in MySQL. The options and activities on each tab using the console are the same. For example, you can use the Database tab to create new databases and the Users tab to add new users.

Summary

This chapter introduced you to relational databases and Cloud SQL, Google's fully managed relational database. It covered instance provisioning using Cloud Console.

The next chapter explains how to start working with the Cloud SQL (MySQL) instance using Cloud Shell and how to use the database instance to build a sample application using Python code.

CHAPTER 3

Working with CloudSQL

Now that we have provisioned our CloudSQL instance, let's get started working with it. In this chapter we will work with the MySQL instance *mysqldb* which we provisioned in the previous chapter. In the previous chapter we also used Instance detail page to manage our instance, we looked at various options available; these options enable us to work with the Instance and its databases using Cloud Console.

Let's now look at accessing the instance and working with it using Cloud Shell first and then we will develop a small program in Python where we will access the instance and its data using Python APIs. Let's get started working with Cloud Shell.

This chapter covers

- Working with CloudSQL using Cloud Shell
- Create a Python program with CloudSQL

Getting Started in Cloud Shell

This walkthrough will connect to the *mysqldb* instance, create database and tables, load data in the table created and run few example queries.

Navigate to https://console.cloud.google.com/. Login with your Google Account and select the project which we created in the last chapter for working with CloudSQL *DemoCloudSQL*. Now it's time to switch to the Cloud Shell. Activate the Cloud Shell.

```
Welcome to Cloud Shell! Type "help" to get started.
Your Cloud Platform project in this session is set to democloudsql-248408.
Use "gcloud config set project [PROJECT_ID]" to change to a different
project.
architectbigdata@cloudshell:~ (democloudsql-248408)$
```

For all the following command line operations we will be using *gcloud* utility.

57

© Navin Sabharwal, Shakuntala Gupta Edward 2020
N. Sabharwal and S. G. Edward, *Hands On Google Cloud SQL and Cloud Spanner*,
https://doi.org/10.1007/978-1-4842-5537-7_3

Connect to the Database

Let's start by checking whether we can see our CloudSQL instance using the following command gcloud sql instances list

```
architectbigdata@cloudshell:~ (democloudsql-248408)$ gcloud sql instances list
NAME      DATABASE_VERSION  LOCATION      TIER            PRIMARY_ADDRESS
PRIVATE_ADDRESS  STATUS
mysqldb  MYSQL_5_7          us-central1-a  db-n1-standard-1  35.193.44.13
-                RUNNABLE
architectbigdata@cloudshell:~ (democloudsql-248408)$
```

We can be sure now that our instance is up and running, look at the Status field, it is showing ***RUNNABLE***. Let's now start with connecting to it. We will use the command gcloud sql connect [Instance_Name] –user=[User]

Where *[Instance_Name]* is the instance to which we want to connect to and *[User]* is the user with which we want to connect to MySQL. In this case our instance is *mysqldb* and we have only one user specified while creating the instance which is the *root* user. The command with all inputs in place looks as below

```
architectbigdata@cloudshell:~ (democloudsql-248408)$ gcloud sql connect
mysqldb --user=root
```

It will ask for the root user password before the connection is successful. Specify the password and press enter. On successful connection MySQL prompt will be visible.

```
architectbigdata@cloudshell:~ (democloudsql-248408)$ gcloud sql connect
mysqldb --user=root
Whitelisting your IP for incoming connection for 5 minutes...done.
Connecting to database with SQL user [root].Enter password:
Welcome to the MariaDB monitor.  Commands end with ; org.
Your MySQL connection id is 809
Server version: 5.7.14-google-log (Google)

Copyright (c) 2000, 2018, Oracle, MariaDB Corporation Ab and others.

Type 'help;' or '\h' for help. Type '\c' to clear the current input
statement.

MySQL [(none)]>
```

In order to allow Cloud Shell to connect to the specified database instance MySQL whitelists the IP address of your cloud shell instance temporarily.

The Cloud shell instances are ephemeral when we reconnect to cloud shell the session changes and the IP address might change as well. This white listing is temporary for that reason.

Alternative Way to Connect to the Instance

Once logged in to the Google Web console, navigate to the CloudSQL instance list. Go to the instance detail page by selecting the instance from the list. Once you are there on the instance detail page, in the Overview tab there's a *Connect to this instance* card as shown in Figure 3-1 with various options listed. One of the options is to Connect using Cloud Shell.

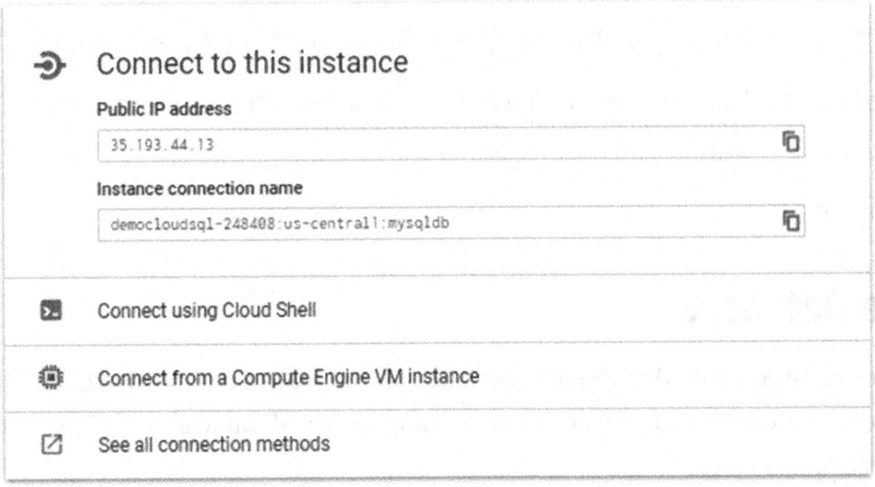

Figure 3-1. *Connect to the instance card*

Click on Connect using Cloud Shell. It opens the Cloud shell window with the command typed in the connect to the instance

```
Welcome to Cloud Shell! Type "help" to get started.
Your Cloud Platform project in this session is set to democloudsql-248408.
architectbigdata@cloudshell:~ (democloudsql-248408)$ gcloud sql connect
mysqldb --user=root --quiet
```

Like the first option on pressing enter it whitelists the Cloud Shell IP and prompts for the password. Specify the password and press enter. Like before on successful connection MySQL prompt will be enabled.

```
Welcome to Cloud Shell! Type "help" to get started.
Your Cloud Platform project in this session is set to democloudsql-248408.
architectbigdata@cloudshell:~ (democloudsql-248408)$ gcloud sql connect
mysqldb --user=root --quiet
Whitelisting your IP for incoming connection for 5 minutes...done.
Connecting to database with SQL user [root].Enter password:
Welcome to the MariaDB monitor.  Commands end with ; org.
Your MySQL connection id is 848
Server version: 5.7.14-google-log (Google)

Copyright (c) 2000, 2018, Oracle, MariaDB Corporation Ab and others.

Type 'help;' or '\h' for help. Type '\c' to clear the current input
statement.

MySQL [(none)]>
```

Create Database

Now that we are connected to the instance. Let's next create a database *classof97* using *Create Database* command. On successful creation of the database the following will be prompted.

```
MySQL [(none)]> CREATE DATABASE classof97;
Query OK, 1 row affected (0.19 sec)

MySQL [(none)]>
```

Let's change to the database using *USE* command.

```
use classof97;
```

Once the database is changed successfully the MySQL prompt changes reflecting the database name in the prompt.

```
MySQL [(none)]> use classof97;
Database changed
MySQL [classof97]>
```

Show tables command is used to show tables that exist within this database. Since this is a newly created database that's the reason no table exists right now.

```
MySQL [classof97]> show tables;
Empty set (0.20 sec)

MySQL [classof97]>
```

Create Table

Let's go ahead and create table *students* in the *classof97* database. The Create table command is same as any MySQL create table command, specify the names and the datatype of the columns and then we specify the primary key. In this case the students table has two columns *id* and *name*. *Id* is the primary key for the table.

This translates into the MySQL create statement as shown below

```
CREATE TABLE students(
    id INT NOT NULL AUTO_INCREMENT,
    Name VARCHAR(100) NOT NULL,
    PRIMARY KEY (id)
);
```

Run that against the database *classof97* as shown below

```
MySQL [classof97]> CREATE TABLE students(
    -> id INT NOT NULL AUTO_INCREMENT,
    -> Name VARCHAR(100) NOT NULL,
    -> PRIMARY KEY (id)
    -> );
Query OK, 0 rows affected (0.23 sec)

MySQL [classof97]>
```

Now Run *Show Tables* command. It will show the table which we recently created.

```
MySQL [classof97]> show tables;
+---------------------+
| Tables_in_classof97 |
+---------------------+
| students            |
+---------------------+
1 row in set (0.21 sec)

MySQL [classof97]>
```

Insert and Select

Now that we have the table in place let's next load some sample data in the table, as shown below using the *insert* commands.

```
MySQL [classof97]> INSERT INTO students values(1,"s1"), (2,"s2"), (3,"s3"),
(4,"s4"), (5,"s5");
Query OK, 5 rows affected (0.21 sec)
Records: 5  Duplicates: 0  Warnings: 0

MySQL [classof97]>
```

Next we can do things like show all the students data as shown below to validate whether the data is loaded or not.

```
MySQL [classof97]> select * from students;
+----+------+
| id | Name |
+----+------+
|  1 | s1   |
|  2 | s2   |
|  3 | s3   |
|  4 | s4   |
|  5 | s5   |
+----+------+
5 rows in set (0.21 sec)

MySQL [classof97]>
```

The CloudSQL MySQL commands are same as any MySQL.

Note   Learn more about the MySQL commands `https://dev.mysql.com/doc/refman/5.7/en/sql-syntax.htm`

Type *exit* to exit from the MySQL instance.

```
MySQL [classof97]> exit
Bye
architectbigdata@cloudshell:~ (democloudsql-248408)$
```

Note   The method to connect to the PostgreSQL instance and the basic querying are same across all SQL databases however there might be some differences in the more complex queries. To learn more about the PostgreSQL commands refer `https://www.postgresql.org/docs/9.6/sql-commands.html`

CloudSQL supports most common features of MySQL or PostgreSQL however there's few differences, for the list of the differences please refer to `https://cloud.google.com/sql/docs/features#differences` and `https://cloud.google.com/sql/docs/postgres/features#differences-pg` respectively for MySQL and PostgreSQL.

Load and Query Sample Dataset

Now that we know how to create database, tables and insert data into it, let's use a sample dataset from the official MySQL site to run queries.

In the Cloud Shell window use the following command to download the sample dataset.

```
wget https://codeload.github.com/datacharmer/test_db/zip/master -O testsql.zip
```

The cloud shell looks as below,

```
architectbigdata@cloudshell:~ (democloudsql-248408)$ wget https://codeload.
github.com/datacharmer/test_db/zip/master -O testsql.zip
--2019-08-03 15:22:13--  https://codeload.github.com/datacharmer/test_db/
zip/master
Resolving codeload.github.com (codeload.github.com)... 13.250.162.133
Connecting to codeload.github.com (codeload.github.
com)|13.250.162.133|:443... connected.
HTTP request sent, awaiting response... 200 OK
Length: unspecified [application/zip]
Saving to: 'testsql.zip'

testsql.zip            [            <=>                ] 34.99M  3.54MB/s  in 1.9s

2019-08-03 15:22:24 (3.54 MB/s) - 'testsql.zip' saved [36687757]

architectbigdata@cloudshell:~ (democloudsql-248408)$
```

At the end of this download we will have a zipped file named *testsql.zip*. Use command ls -l to validate.

```
architectbigdata@cloudshell:~ (democloudsql-248408)$ ls -l
total 143316
-rw-r--r-- 1 architectbigdata architectbigdata 36687757 Aug  1 17:28 master
-rw-r--r-- 1 architectbigdata architectbigdata 36687757 Aug  1 17:29
master.1
-rw-r--r-- 1 architectbigdata architectbigdata 36687757 Aug  1 17:34
master.2
lrwxrwxrwx 1 architectbigdata architectbigdata       38 Aug  1 16:58
README-cloudshell.txt -> /google/devshell/README-cloudshell.txt
drwxr-xr-x 4 architectbigdata architectbigdata     4096 Aug  1 17:49 test_
db-master
-rw-r--r-- 1 architectbigdata architectbigdata 36687757 Aug  3 15:22
testsql.zip
architectbigdata@cloudshell:~ (democloudsql-248408)$
```

Next we unzip the file using command unzip testsql.zip

```
architectbigdata@cloudshell:~ (democloudsql-248408)$ unzip testsql.zip
Archive:  testsql.zip
0b66c2338736779e3b150c7d125b1012d95a961f
   Creating: test_db-master/
  inflating: test_db-master/Changelog
  inflating: test_db-master/README.md
  inflating: test_db-master/employees.sql
  inflating: test_db-master/employees_partitioned.sql
  inflating: test_db-master/employees_partitioned_5.1.sql
  inflating: test_db-master/images/employees.gif
  inflating: test_db-master/images/employees.jpg
  inflating: test_db-master/images/employees.png
  inflating: test_db-master/load_departments.dump
  inflating: test_db-master/load_dept_emp.dump
  inflating: test_db-master/load_dept_manager.dump
  inflating: test_db-master/load_employees.dump
  inflating: test_db-master/load_salaries1.dump
  inflating: test_db-master/load_salaries2.dump
  inflating: test_db-master/load_salaries3.dump
  inflating: test_db-master/load_titles.dump
  inflating: test_db-master/objects.sql
  inflating: test_db-master/sakila/README.md
  inflating: test_db-master/sakila/sakila-mv-data.sql
  inflating: test_db-master/sakila/sakila-mv-schema.sql
  inflating: test_db-master/show_elapsed.sql
  inflating: test_db-master/sql_test.sh
  inflating: test_db-master/test_employees_md5.sql
  inflating: test_db-master/test_employees_sha.sql
architectbigdata@cloudshell:~ (democloudsql-248408)$
```

This creates a *test_db-master* directory in your current working directory. Change to the *test_db-master* directory using **cd** command.

```
architectbigdata@cloudshell:~ (democloudsql-248408)$ cd test_db-master
architectbigdata@cloudshell:~/test_db-master (democloudsql-248408)$
```

List the content of the directory using *ls –l* command, we will see a file named ***employees.sql***.

```
architectbigdata@cloudshell:~/test_db-master (democloudsql-248408)$ ls -l
total 168344
-rw-r--r-- 1 architectbigdata architectbigdata       964 Apr 10 00:43
Changelog
-rw-r--r-- 1 architectbigdata architectbigdata      7948 Apr 10 00:43
employees_partitioned_5.1.sql
-rw-r--r-- 1 architectbigdata architectbigdata      6276 Apr 10 00:43
employees_partitioned.sql
-rw-r--r-- 1 architectbigdata architectbigdata      4193 Apr 10 00:43
employees.sql
drwxr-xr-x 2 architectbigdata architectbigdata      4096 Aug  3 15:25 images
-rw-r--r-- 1 architectbigdata architectbigdata       250 Apr 10 00:43
load_departments.dump
-rw-r--r-- 1 architectbigdata architectbigdata  14159880 Apr 10 00:43
load_dept_emp.dump
-rw-r--r-- 1 architectbigdata architectbigdata      1090 Apr 10 00:43
load_dept_manager.dump
-rw-r--r-- 1 architectbigdata architectbigdata  17722832 Apr 10 00:43
load_employees.dump
-rw-r--r-- 1 architectbigdata architectbigdata  39806034 Apr 10 00:43
load_salaries1.dump
-rw-r--r-- 1 architectbigdata architectbigdata  39805981 Apr 10 00:43
load_salaries2.dump
-rw-r--r-- 1 architectbigdata architectbigdata  39080916 Apr 10 00:43
load_salaries3.dump
-rw-r--r-- 1 architectbigdata architectbigdata  21708736 Apr 10 00:43
load_titles.dump
-rw-r--r-- 1 architectbigdata architectbigdata      4568 Apr 10 00:43
objects.sql
-rw-r--r-- 1 architectbigdata architectbigdata      4325 Apr 10 00:43
README.md
```

```
drwxr-xr-x 2 architectbigdata architectbigdata      4096 Aug  3 15:25 sakila
-rw-r--r-- 1 architectbigdata architectbigdata       272 Apr 10 00:43
show_elapsed.sql
-rwxr-xr-x 1 architectbigdata architectbigdata      1800 Apr 10 00:43
sql_test.sh
-rw-r--r-- 1 architectbigdata architectbigdata      4878 Apr 10 00:43
test_employees_md5.sql
-rw-r--r-- 1 architectbigdata architectbigdata      4882 Apr 10 00:43
test_employees_sha.sql
architectbigdata@cloudshell:~/test_db-master (democloudsql-248408)$
```

Let's examine the content of the *employees.sql* file using *vi*

```
architectbigdata@cloudshell:~/test_db-master (democloudsql-248408)$ vi
employees.sql
```

The file contains SQL statements for creating the *employees* database and all its relevant tables with load data statements to insert data in the tables created. Figure 3-2 shows the file content.

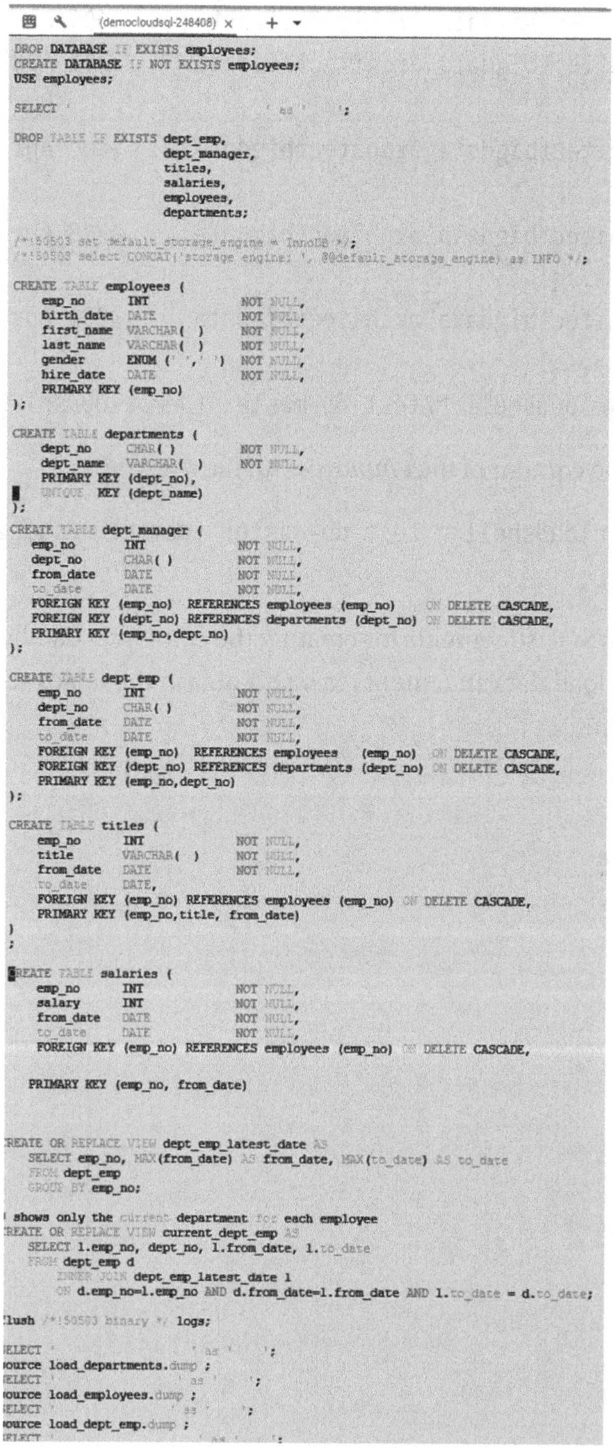

Figure 3-2. *employees.sql*

Now that we have examined the content of the file, let's now execute the SQL scripts contained in the file *employees.sql*. Use the command to connect to our MySQL instance and execute the contents of the file.

```
gcloud sql connect mysqldb --user=root < employees.sql
```

Like when we connect to the instance, whitelisting is automatically handled by google cloud and we will be prompted to specify the root user password.

```
architectbigdata@cloudshell:~/test_db-master (democloudsql-248408)$ gcloud
sql connect mysqldb --user=root < employees.sql
Whitelisting your IP for incoming connection for 5 minutes...
.....done.
Connecting to database with SQL user [root].Enter password:
```

Once the authentication is successful we will be able to see status messages being displayed as the commands in the file are executed.

```
architectbigdata@cloudshell:~/test_db-master (democloudsql-248408)$ gcloud
sql connect mysqldb --user=root < employees.sql
Whitelisting your IP for incoming connection for 5 minutes...
.....done.
Connecting to database with SQL user [root].Enter password:
INFO
CREATING DATABASE STRUCTURE
INFO
storage engine: InnoDB
INFO
LOADING departments
INFO
LOADING employees
INFO
LOADING dept_emp
INFO
LOADING dept_manager
INFO
```

```
LOADING titles
INFO
LOADING salaries
data_load_time_diff
00:01:13
architectbigdata@cloudshell:~/test_db-master (democloudsql-248408)$
```

Now that we have the database created with schema and data in place, lets connect back to our SQL instance using *gcloud sql connect* command.

```
architectbigdata@cloudshell:~/test_db-master (democloudsql-248408)$ gcloud
sql connect mysqldb --user=root
Whitelisting your IP for incoming connection for 5 minutes...done.
Connecting to database with SQL user [root].Enter password:
Welcome to the MariaDB monitor.  Commands end with ; or \g.
Your MySQL connection id is 7741
Server version: 5.7.14-google-log (Google)

Copyright (c) 2000, 2018, Oracle, MariaDB Corporation Ab and others.

Type 'help;' or '\h' for help. Type '\c' to clear the current input
statement.

MySQL [(none)]>
```

Switch to the employees database. Next run the show tables command to list all tables. We can see all tables created as there in the script file.

```
MySQL [(none)]> use employees;
Reading table information for completion of table and column names
You can turn off this feature to get a quicker startup with -A
```

```
Database changed
MySQL [employees]> show tables;
+-----------------------+
| Tables_in_employees   |
+-----------------------+
| current_dept_emp      |
| departments           |
| dept_emp              |
| dept_emp_latest_date  |
| dept_manager          |
| employees             |
| salaries              |
| titles                |
+-----------------------+
8 rows in set (0.19 sec)

MySQL [employees]>
```

Run the *describe* commands on the tables to view the table structure.

```
MySQL [employees]> describe employees;
+------------+---------------+------+-----+---------+-------+
| Field      | Type          | Null | Key | Default | Extra |
+------------+---------------+------+-----+---------+-------+
| emp_no     | int(11)       | NO   | PRI | NULL    |       |
| birth_date | date          | NO   |     | NULL    |       |
| first_name | varchar(14)   | NO   |     | NULL    |       |
| last_name  | varchar(16)   | NO   |     | NULL    |       |
| gender     | enum('M','F') | NO   |     | NULL    |       |
| hire_date  | date          | NO   |     | NULL    |       |
+------------+---------------+------+-----+---------+-------+
6 rows in set (0.19 sec)
```

```
MySQL [employees]> describe salaries;
+------------+----------+------+-----+---------+-------+
| Field      | Type     | Null | Key | Default | Extra |
+------------+----------+------+-----+---------+-------+
| emp_no     | int(11)  | NO   | PRI | NULL    |       |
| salary     | int(11)  | NO   |     | NULL    |       |
| from_date  | date     | NO   | PRI | NULL    |       |
| to_date    | date     | NO   |     | NULL    |       |
+------------+----------+------+-----+---------+-------+
4 rows in set (0.19 sec)

MySQL [employees]> describe dept_manager;
+------------+----------+------+-----+---------+-------+
| Field      | Type     | Null | Key | Default | Extra |
+------------+----------+------+-----+---------+-------+
| emp_no     | int(11)  | NO   | PRI | NULL    |       |
| dept_no    | char(4)  | NO   | PRI | NULL    |       |
| from_date  | date     | NO   |     | NULL    |       |
| to_date    | date     | NO   |     | NULL    |       |
+------------+----------+------+-----+---------+-------+
4 rows in set (0.19 sec)

MySQL [employees]> describe departments;
+------------+-------------+------+-----+---------+-------+
| Field      | Type        | Null | Key | Default | Extra |
+------------+-------------+------+-----+---------+-------+
| dept_no    | char(4)     | NO   | PRI | NULL    |       |
| dept_name  | varchar(40) | NO   | UNI | NULL    |       |
+------------+-------------+------+-----+---------+-------+
2 rows in set (0.20 sec)

MySQL [employees]>
```

Now that we have verified the database, let's now start querying the tables.

Query 1: Find out joining year wise average salary of all employees

```
select year(e.hire_date) joiningyear, avg(s.salary) avgsalary
from employees e, salaries s
where e.emp_no = s.emp_no
group by year(e.hire_date);
```

```
MySQL [employees]> select year(e.hire_date) joiningyear, avg(s.salary)
avgsalary
    -> from employees e, salaries s
    -> where e.emp_no = s.emp_no
    -> group by year(e.hire_date);
+-------------+------------+
| joiningyear | avgsalary  |
+-------------+------------+
|        1985 | 66966.7550 |
|        1986 | 66187.3453 |
|        1987 | 65199.4887 |
|        1988 | 64205.4734 |
|        1989 | 63658.8510 |
|        1990 | 62736.4975 |
|        1991 | 61765.4281 |
|        1992 | 60962.9784 |
|        1993 | 60393.9920 |
|        1994 | 59372.7106 |
|        1995 | 58369.3347 |
|        1996 | 57724.8363 |
|        1997 | 56797.7335 |
|        1998 | 56390.4280 |
|        1999 | 55561.4406 |
|        2000 | 54084.6389 |
+-------------+------------+
16 rows in set (2.28 sec)

MySQL [employees]>
```

Query 2: Find out joining year wise maximum salary.

```
select year(e.hire_date) joiningyear, max(s.salary) avgsalary
from employees e, salaries s
where e.emp_no = s.emp_no
group by year(e.hire_date);
```

```
MySQL [employees]> select year(e.hire_date) joiningyear, max(s.salary)
avgsalary
    -> from employees e, salaries s
    -> where e.emp_no = s.emp_no
    -> group by year(e.hire_date);
+-------------+-----------+
| joiningyear | avgsalary |
+-------------+-----------+
|        1985 |    158220 |
|        1986 |    156286 |
|        1987 |    155513 |
|        1988 |    152220 |
|        1989 |    149440 |
|        1990 |    153715 |
|        1991 |    142638 |
|        1992 |    135960 |
|        1993 |    142914 |
|        1994 |    137369 |
|        1995 |    133731 |
|        1996 |    130956 |
|        1997 |    123935 |
|        1998 |    125014 |
|        1999 |    124516 |
|        2000 |     80596 |
+-------------+-----------+
16 rows in set (1.68 sec)

MySQL [employees]>
```

Query 3: Find department wise employees count

```
select d.dept_name, count(de.emp_no) empcount
from departments d, current_dept_emp de
where d.dept_no = de.dept_no
group by d.dept_name
```

```
MySQL [employees]> select d.dept_name, count(de.emp_no) empcount
    -> from departments d, current_dept_emp de
    -> where d.dept_no = de.dept_no
    -> group by d.dept_name
    -> ;
+--------------------+----------+
| dept_name          | empcount |
+--------------------+----------+
| Customer Service   |    21813 |
| Development        |    76958 |
| Finance            |    15579 |
| Human Resources    |    16071 |
| Marketing          |    18426 |
| Production         |    66675 |
| Quality Management |    18295 |
| Research           |    19285 |
| Sales              |    46922 |
+--------------------+----------+
9 rows in set (1.41 sec)

MySQL [employees]>
```

Query 4: Find month wise employees count hired in Year 1997.

```
select month(hire_date) hiremonth, count(emp_no) empcount
from employees
where year(hire_date) = 1997
group by month(hire_date);
```

```
MySQL [employees]> select month(hire_date) hiremonth, count(emp_no) empcount
    -> from employees
    -> where year(hire_date) = 1997
    -> group by month(hire_date);
+-----------+----------+
| hiremonth | empcount |
+-----------+----------+
|         1 |      669 |
|         2 |      600 |
|         3 |      638 |
|         4 |      588 |
|         5 |      576 |
|         6 |      630 |
|         7 |      549 |
|         8 |      513 |
|         9 |      506 |
|        10 |      515 |
|        11 |      435 |
|        12 |      450 |
+-----------+----------+
12 rows in set (0.25 sec)

MySQL [employees]>
```

Query 5: Find maximum salary of female employees hired across different months of year 1997.

```
select month(e.hire_date) hiremonth, max(s.salary) maxsalary
from employees e, salaries s
where e.emp_no = s.emp_no AND year(e.hire_date) = 1997
and e.gender = 'f'
group by month(e.hire_date);
```

```
MySQL [employees]> Select month(e.hire_date) hiremonth, max(s.salary) maxsalary
    -> from employees e, salaries s
    -> where e.emp_no = s.emp_no AND year(e.hire_date) = 1997
    -> and e.gender =
    -> 'f' group by month(e.hire_date);
```

```
+-----------+-----------+
| hiremonth | maxsalary |
+-----------+-----------+
|         1 |    107008 |
|         2 |    102914 |
|         3 |    111068 |
|         4 |    123169 |
|         5 |    115945 |
|         6 |    107287 |
|         7 |    113252 |
|         8 |    107117 |
|         9 |    115781 |
|        10 |    110198 |
|        11 |    100732 |
|        12 |    114356 |
+-----------+-----------+
12 rows in set (0.27 sec)

MySQL [employees]>
```

Now that we are familiar in working with our CloudSQL instance using Cloud Shell, let's next get started with programming with CloudSQL.

Python Program - Feast Out

The Feast Out program is a sample written in Python which will show how we can use CloudSQL from Python.

The Feast Out sample program will have list of restaurants registered and as the users visit the restaurants it captures the feedback on the restaurants on various parameters along with the user details. And finally, it will enable to find out best restaurants on specific parameters, and also enables to find out users to share offers based on the details captured e.g. Birth Month discounts etc. The sample program lets users:

- Register a new Restaurant

- Capture user's feedback for the visiting Restaurant

- Capture User details

- Update user details

- Unregister an existing Restaurant

- Find out best rated restaurant

- Find out top 2 restaurants basis on the specified parameter e.g. Food Quality

- Find out Users with Birth date within a week of the date specified

- Find out users with any of their special day falling in the month specified

Before we get started with programming our application, the first thing which we have to do is create a database for our application.

We will use the *DemoCloudSQL* project and *mysqldb* instance which we provisioned earlier for creating the database.

Database Schema

Activate the cloud shell, connect to the instance. Use the following command to create our database *eatout*.

```
MySQL [(none)]> CREATE DATABASE eatout;
Query OK, 1 row affected (0.19 sec)
```

With the database created, let's switch to the database using *use* command as shown below.

```
MySQL [(none)]> use eatout;
Database changed
```

Let's now create the tables. First, we will create a table to store details of the restaurants which will be registered with our application. This will look something like the below table.

Table 3-1. *Restaurant Master*

Restaurant Id	Name	Cuisine	Region	Location
R1	Pirates of Grill	BBQ	Noida	Sec 18
R2	Barbeque Nation	BBQ	Noida	Sec 18
R3	Pizza Hut	Fast Food	Ghaziabad	Vaishali
R4	Dominos	Fast Food	Ghaziabad	Kaushambi
R5	Haldiram	Multi-cuisine	Ghaziabad	Kaushambi
R6	Bikaner	Multi-cuisine	Noida	Sec 18
R7	Taj	Multi-cuisine	Delhi	CP

This translates into the MySQL create statement as shown below

```
CREATE TABLE Restaurant(
    id VARCHAR(10) NOT NULL,
    Name VARCHAR(50) NOT NULL,
    Cuisine VARCHAR(50) NOT NULL,
    Region VARCHAR(50) NOT NULL,
    Location VARCHAR(50) NOT NULL,
    PRIMARY KEY (id)
    );
```

Run that against the database created as shown below

```
MySQL [eatout]> CREATE TABLE Restaurant(
    -> id VARCHAR(10) NOT NULL,
    -> Name VARCHAR(50) NOT NULL,
    -> Cuisine VARCHAR(50) NOT NULL,
    -> Region VARCHAR(50) NOT NULL,
    -> Location VARCHAR(50) NOT NULL,
    -> PRIMARY KEY (id)
    -> );
Query OK, 0 rows affected (0.21 sec)
```

Next, we will create a table to store user details. This will look something like the below table.

Table 3-2. *Users*

User Id	Name	Phone Number	EMailId	Birthday	Spouse Birthday	Anniversary
U1	Steve	9876543210	steve@gmail.com	01-Sep	31-Dec	13-June
U2	Michelle	9765432180	michelle@hotmail.com	08-Jan	09-July	07-Aug

This translates into the MySQL create statement as shown below

```
CREATE TABLE UserDetails(
    id VARCHAR(10) NOT NULL,
    Name VARCHAR(50) NOT NULL,
    PhoneNumber VARCHAR(50) NOT NULL,
    EmailId VARCHAR(50),
    Birthday DATE,
    SpouseBirthday DATE,
    Anniversary DATE,
    PRIMARY KEY (id),
    UNIQUE KEY (PhoneNumber)
    );
```

Run that against the database *eatout* as shown below

```
MySQL [eatout]> CREATE TABLE UserDetails(
    -> id VARCHAR(10) NOT NULL,
    -> Name VARCHAR(50) NOT NULL,
    -> PhoneNumber VARCHAR(50) NOT NULL,
    -> EmailId VARCHAR(50),
    -> Birthday DATE,
    -> SpouseBirthday DATE,
    -> Anniversary DATE,
    -> PRIMARY KEY (id),
```

```
    -> UNIQUE KEY (PhoneNumber)
    -> );
Query OK, 0 rows affected (0.21 sec)
```

Finally, we will create the Feedback table to capture the ratings. The table looks like below.

Table 3-3. *Feedback*

User Id	Restaurant Id	Visit Date	Food Quality	Service Quality	Ambience
U1	R1	12-Jun-2019	5	4	3
U2	R2	13-Aug-2019	4	4	4

Live music	Value for Money	Cleanliness	Food Variety
3	5	4	2
5	4	3	2

This translates into the MySQL create statement as shown below

```
CREATE TABLE UserFeedback(
    UserId VARCHAR(10) NOT NULL,
    RestaurantId VARCHAR(10) NOT NULL,
    VisitDate DATE NOT NULL,
    FoodQuality INT DEFAULT 5,
    ServiceQuality INT DEFAULT 5,
    Ambience INT DEFAULT 5,
    LiveMusic INT DEFAULT 5,
    ValueForMoney INT DEFAULT 5,
    Cleanliness INT DEFAULT 5,
    FoodVariety INT DEFAULT 5,
    FeedbackId INT NOT NULL AUTO_INCREMENT,
    PRIMARY KEY (FeedbackId)
    );
```

Run that against the database created as shown below

```
MySQL [eatout]> CREATE TABLE UserFeedback(
    -> UserId VARCHAR(10) NOT NULL,
    -> RestaurantId VARCHAR(10) NOT NULL,
    -> VisitDate DATE NOT NULL,
    -> FoodQuality INT DEFAULT 5,
    -> ServiceQuality INT DEFAULT 5,
    -> Ambience INT DEFAULT 5,
    -> LiveMusic INT DEFAULT 5,
    -> ValueForMoney INT DEFAULT 5,
    -> Cleanliness INT DEFAULT 5,
    -> FoodVariety INT DEFAULT 5,
    -> FeedbackId INT NOT NULL AUTO_INCREMENT,
    -> PRIMARY KEY (FeedbackId)
    -> );
Query OK, 0 rows affected (0.21 sec)

MySQL [eatout]>
```

Now that we have the database schema in place, let's now begin with environment readiness. We will first provision our VM instance where we will be writing and executing our Python program.

Provision Compute Instance

In the Cloud Console, open the left side Navigation menu, navigate to Compute Engine underneath the Compute section and select VM instances option as shown in Figure 3-3.

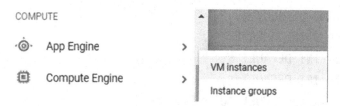

Figure 3-3. *Left Side Navigation Menu for Creating a VM instance*

Figure 3-4 shows the Create VM Instance popup. Click on Create.

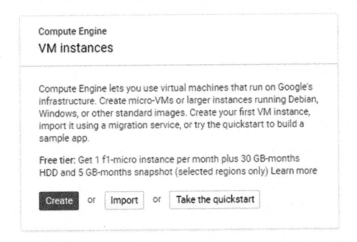

Figure 3-4. *Create Instance pop-up*

In the subsequent page, we select option New VM instance and specify name for the instance. For this example, let's name the instance *feasting*. Figure 3-5 shows the Boot disk selected. Click on ***change*** button next to Boot Disk.

Figure 3-5. *Change Boot Disk*

Figure 3-6 shows the available images. Select ***Ubuntu 18.04 LTS*** in the list displayed underneath *OS images* section, and click on ***SELECT*** button.

Boot disk

Select an image or snapshot to create a boot disk; or attach an existing disk

OS images   Application images   Custom images   Snapshots   Existing disks

☐ Show images with Shielded VM features ⓘ

○ **Debian GNU/Linux 10 (buster)**
  amd64 built on 20190729
○ **Debian GNU/Linux 9 (stretch)**
  amd64 built on 20190729
○ **CentOS 6**
  x86_64 built on 20190729
○ **CentOS 7**
  x86_64 built on 20190729
○ **CoreOS alpha 2219.0.0**
  amd64-usr published on 2019-08-01
○ **CoreOS beta 2191.2.0**
  amd64-usr published on 2019-08-01
○ **CoreOS stable 2135.6.0**
  amd64-usr published on 2019-08-01
○ **Ubuntu 14.04 LTS**
  amd64 trusty image built on 2019-05-14
○ **Ubuntu 16.04 LTS**
  amd64 xenial image built on 2019-06-28
◉ **Ubuntu 18.04 LTS**
  amd64 bionic image built on 2019-07-22
○ **Ubuntu 19.04**
  amd64 disco image built on 2019-07-24
○ **Ubuntu 16.04 LTS Minimal**
  amd64 xenial minimal image built on 2019-06-28
○ **Ubuntu 18.04 LTS Minimal**
  amd64 bionic minimal image built on 2019-07-23

Can't find what you're looking for? Explore hundreds of VM solutions in Marketplace

Boot disk type ⓘ   Size (GB) ⓘ

| Standard persistent disk   ▼ | | 10 |

[Select] [Cancel]

Figure 3-6. *Image or snapshot for creating a boot disk*

Leave the remaining configurations as is. With all the inputs the form look like Figure 3-7.

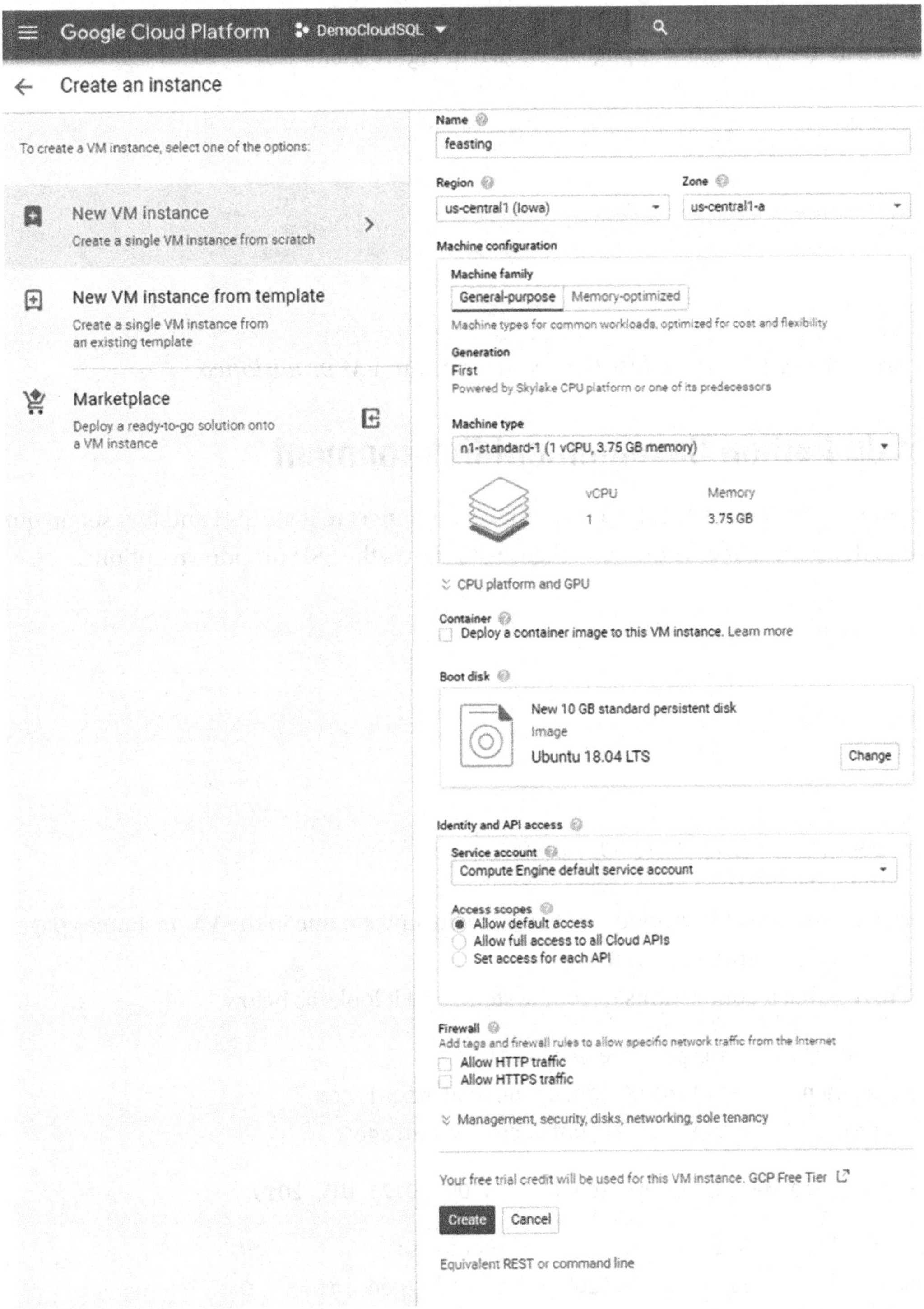

Figure 3-7. *Configured New VM instance*

Click on *Create* to start creating the VM instance. Once the VM is provisioned it will be listed in the VM instances page as shown in Figure 3-8.

Figure 3-8. *VM Instance List Page with the new VM provisioned*

Set Up Python Development Environment

Now that we have our VM up and running, let's connect to it via SSH and first set up our python development environment. Figure 3-9 shows the SSH dropdown options.

Figure 3-9. *SSH Dropdown Options*

Navigate to the SSH dropdown next to the instance name in the VM instances page and select Open in browser window.

This establish connections to your system, and it looks as below

```
* Documentation:  https://help.ubuntu.com
 * Management:     https://landscape.canonical.com
 * Support:        https://ubuntu.com/advantage

  System information as of Mon Aug  5 09:40:21 UTC 2019

  System load:  0.1           Processes:           91
  Usage of /:   11.7% of 9.52GB  Users logged in:    0
  Memory usage: 5%            IP address for ens4: 10.128.0.3
  Swap usage:   0%
```

0 packages can be updated.
0 updates are security updates.

The programs included with the Ubuntu system are free software;
the exact distribution terms for each program are described in the
individual files in /usr/share/doc/*/copyright.

Ubuntu comes with ABSOLUTELY NO WARRANTY, to the extent permitted by
applicable law.

architectbigdata@feasting:~$

We will now install packages and libraries using the following commands.

```
architectbigdata@feasting:~$ sudo apt-get update
architectbigdata@feasting:~$ sudo apt-get install python3-pip
architectbigdata@feasting:~$ pip3 install pymysql
```

Wherever prompted, type Y (for Yes) and press Enter to confirm. With our development environment ready, let's next follow steps for using proxy to connect to our CloudSQL instance

Enable APIs

To begin with we will first enable the Cloud SQL APIs using Cloud Console. Navigate to Cloud Console, open the left side Navigation menu and click APIs & Services as shown in Figure 3-10.

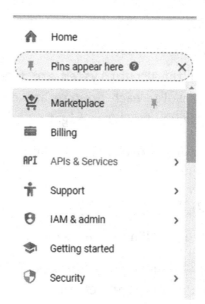

Figure 3-10. *APIs & Services option in the Left Navigation Menu*

This takes us to the Dashboard page of APIs & Services. Figure 3-11 shows the Dashboard page. You will see Enable APIs & Services button.

Figure 3-11. *APIs & Services Dashboard*

Click on Enable APIs & Services. This will take us to the API library page as shown in Figure 3-12.

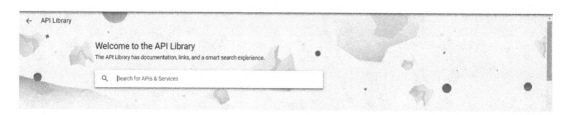

Figure 3-12. *API Library Page*

Enter *CloudSQL* in the textbox. Figure 3-13 shows the results. Select Cloud SQL Admin API from the results displayed.

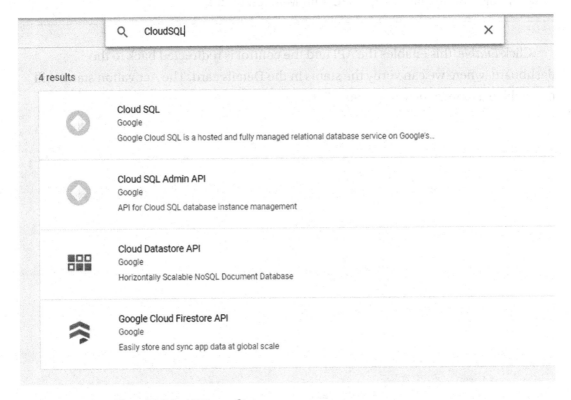

Figure 3-13. *CloudSQL API results*

This takes us to the Cloud SQL Admin API page as shown in Figure 3-14. You will see the ***Enable*** button.

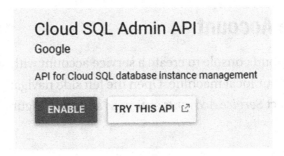

Figure 3-14. *Cloud SQL Admin API*

> **Note**   If the API is already enabled, we will see a green icon stating API is enabled, and enable button will be replaced with Manage button.

Click *Enable*, this enables the API and the control is redirected back to the dashboard, where we can verify the status in the Details card. The Activation status will be Enabled as shown below in Figure 3-15.

Figure 3-15. *Details Card*

Create Service Account

Next, we will use the cloud console to create a service account with key which we will be using to connect from our local machine. Open the left side navigation menu, navigate to *IAM & Admin* and select *Service Accounts* option as shown in Figure 3-16.

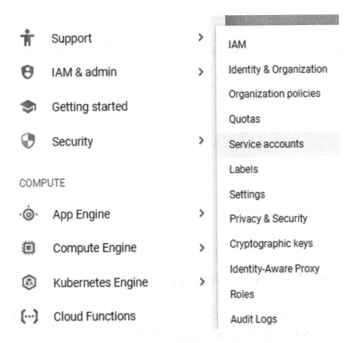

Figure 3-16. *Service Accounts Option in Left Navigation Menu*

This takes us to the service account for our selected project DemoCloudSQL.

Figure 3-17 shows the Service accounts. You will see a Compute Engine default service account, and a Create Service Account link as shown below.

| Service accounts | + CREATE SERVICE ACCOUNT | 🗑 DELETE | | | | | | SHOW INFO PANEL |

Service accounts for project "DemoCloudSQL"

A service account represents a Google Cloud service identity, such as code running on Compute Engine VMs, App Engine apps, or systems running outside Google. Learn more

	Email	Status	Name ↑	Description	Key ID	Key creation date	Actions
☐	62743598792-compute@developer.gserviceaccount.com	✅	Compute Engine default service account		No keys		⋮

Figure 3-17. *Default Service Accounts for DemoCloudSQL project*

Click on **Create Service Account** and follow the below steps to Create a service account with a key. Figure 3-18 shows the first step for providing the service account details. For this example, we will create service account *tutorialservice*. Enter name, id will be auto generated. Click on *Create*.

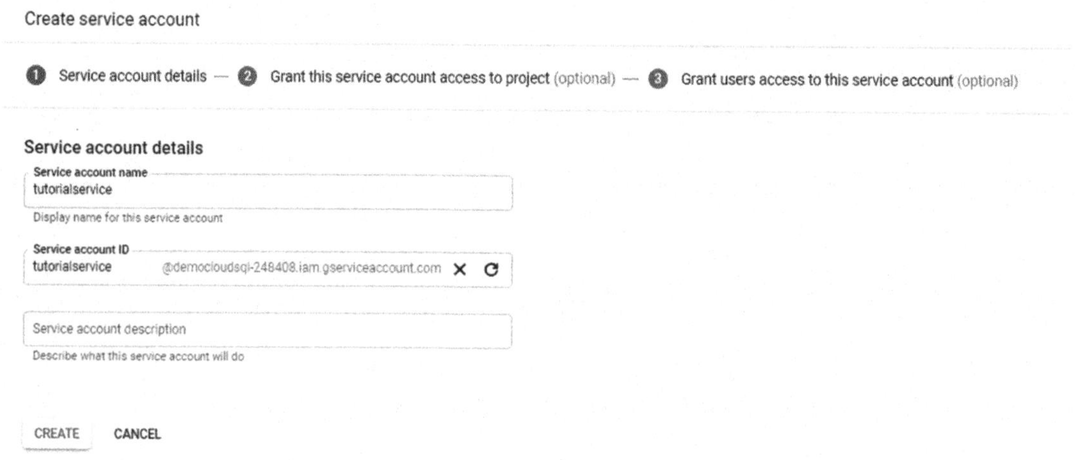

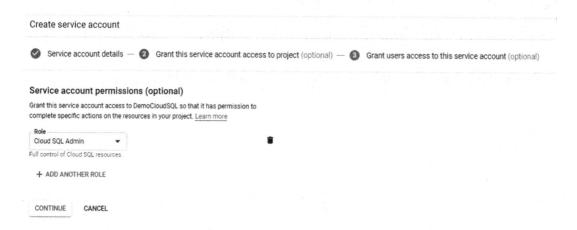

Figure 3-18. *Service Account Details page*

It takes us to the Role access screen as shown in Figure 3-19. In this screen, select **Cloud SQL admin** in *Role* and click on *Continue*.

Figure 3-19. *Assign Roles to the Service Account*

This takes us to the next screen from where we will create the Key. Figure 3-20 shows the screen. Click on *Create Key* button.

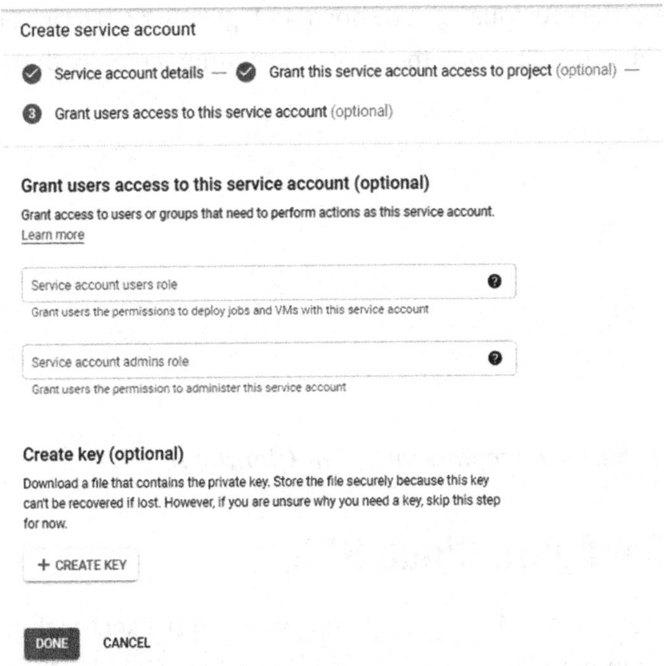

Create service account

✓ Service account details — ✓ Grant this service account access to project (optional) —

③ Grant users access to this service account (optional)

Grant users access to this service account (optional)

Grant access to users or groups that need to perform actions as this service account.
Learn more

Service account users role	❓

Grant users the permissions to deploy jobs and VMs with this service account

Service account admins role	❓

Grant users the permission to administer this service account

Create key (optional)

Download a file that contains the private key. Store the file securely because this key
can't be recovered if lost. However, if you are unsure why you need a key, skip this step
for now.

+ CREATE KEY

DONE   CANCEL

Figure 3-20. Create Key Option

This opens the Create Key form as shown in Figure 3-21. This prompts for the key
type. Click on *Create* button to download the file containing the private key using the
recommended key type (JSON).

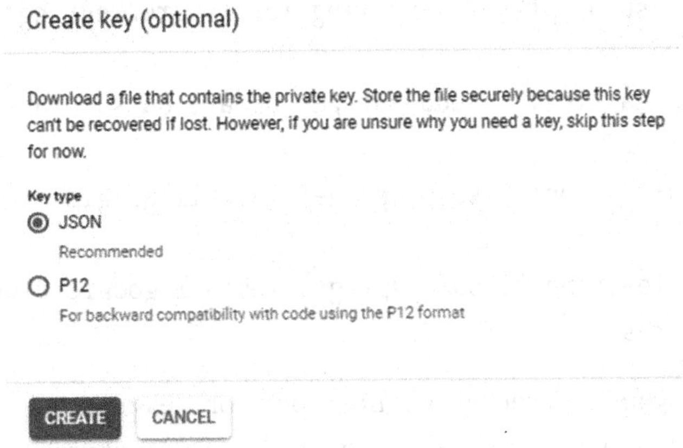

Create key (optional)

Download a file that contains the private key. Store the file securely because this key
can't be recovered if lost. However, if you are unsure why you need a key, skip this step
for now.

Key type
◉ JSON
  Recommended
○ P12
  For backward compatibility with code using the P12 format

CREATE   CANCEL

Figure 3-21. Create Key Form

Click on *Done* in the previous screen shown in Figure 3-22. Service account with key file is created. Figure 3-22 shows the Service accounts screen with the new service account created.

Service accounts for project "DemoCloudSQL"

A service account represents a Google Cloud service identity, such as code running on Compute Engine VMs, App Engine apps, or systems running outside Google. Learn more

	Email	Status	Name ↑	Description	Key ID	Key creation date	Actions
	62743598792-compute@developer.gserviceaccount.com	✓	Compute Engine default service account		No keys		⋮
	tutorialservice@democloudsql-248408.iam.gserviceaccount.com	✓	tutorialservice		fbf98d129be3a58adbd6392bedc31166b789f1b4	Aug 2, 2019	⋮

Figure 3-22. *New Service Account for DemoCloudSQL*

Install and Configure Cloud SDK

Connect to our provisioned VM as shown in the above step. Execute the following commands on the command line to install the Cloud SDK. Cloud SDK contains tools which we will use to work with our GCP products and services from our command line.

```
architectbigdata@feasting:~$ echo "deb [signed-by=/usr/share/keyrings/
cloud.google.gpg] https://packages.cloud.google.com/apt cloud-sdk main" |
sudo tee -a /etc/apt/sources.list.d/google-cloud-sdk.list
architectbigdata@feasting:~$ curl https://packages.cloud.google.com/apt/
doc/apt-key.gpg | sudo apt-key --keyring /usr/share/keyrings/cloud.google.
gpg add -
architectbigdata@feasting:~$ sudo apt-get update && sudo apt-get install
google-cloud-sdk
architectbigdata@feasting:~$ sudo apt-get install google-cloud-sdk-app-
engine-python
architectbigdata@feasting:~$ sudo apt-get install google-cloud-sdk-app-
engine-python-extras
```

Ensure to verify you don't see any warnings or error messages before proceeding to the next command. Wherever prompted, type Y (for Yes) and press Enter to confirm. With Cloud SDK installed, let's run through the commands for configuration of gcloud. Enter command

```
architectbigdata@feasting:~$ gcloud init
```

This will provide us with options to configure. It starts with network diagnostics. Post completion of the network diagnostic checks, it prompts to choose the Google Account as shown below.

```
architectbigdata@feasting:~$ gcloud init
Welcome! This command will take you through the configuration of gcloud.

Your current configuration has been set to: [default]

You can skip diagnostics next time by using the following flag:
  gcloud init --skip-diagnostics

Network diagnostic detects and fixes local network connection issues.
Checking network connection...done.
Reachability Check passed.
Network diagnostic (1/1 checks) passed.

Choose the account you would like to use to perform operations for
this configuration:
 [1] 62743598792-compute@developer.gserviceaccount.com
 [2] Log in with a new account
Please enter your numeric choice:   2
```

We choose to *Log in with a new account*. When prompted, type Y and press enter. It will generate a link for us to get the verification code, which need to be entered as the next step. Follow the link. The first sceen prompts to selet your google account. Post login you will be redirected to the screen as shown in Figure 3-23.

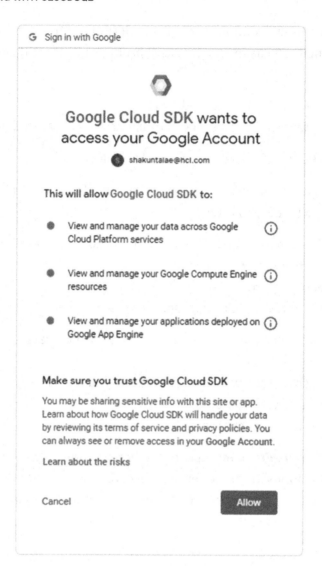

Figure 3-23. *Click Allow to generate the verfication code*

Select Allow. The control will be redirected to the screen as shown in Figure 3-24.

Figure 3-24. *Verfication code*

Get the verification code from there and paste it against *Enter Verification code* prompt. Post verification it will confirm your login as shown below and prompt us to pick the cloud project to use.

```
You are running on a Google Compute Engine virtual machine.
It is recommended that you use service accounts for authentication.

You can run:

  $ gcloud config set account `ACCOUNT`

to switch accounts if necessary.

Your credentials may be visible to others with access to this
virtual machine. Are you sure you want to authenticate with
your personal account?

Do you want to continue (Y/n)?  Y

Go to the following link in your browser:
```

```
https://accounts.google.com/o/oauth2/auth?redirect_uri=urn%3Aietf%3
Awg%3Aoauth%3A2.0%3Aoob&prompt=select_account&response_type=code&client_
id=32555940559.apps.googleusercontent.com&scope=https%3A%2F%2Fwww.
googleapis.com%2Fauth%2Fuserinfo.email+https%3A%2F%2Fwww.googleapis.
com%2Fauth%2Fcloud-platform+https%3A%2F%2Fwww.googleapis.
com%2Fauth%2Fappengine.admin+https%3A%2F%2Fwww.googleapis.com%2Fa
uth%2Fcompute+https%3A%2F%2Fwww.googleapis.com%2Fauth%2Faccounts.
reauth&access_type=offline
```

```
Enter verification code: 4/rgEnOtcGFJtJqucsoEe4ax627v4yMo4VdV4UTLxPzTksE_
9LyFxOpI8
You are logged in as: [architectbigdata@gmail.com].
```

```
Pick cloud project to use:
 [1] democloudsql-248408
 [2] examplegettingstarted-248810
 [3] igneous-future-248210
 [4] Create a new project
Please enter numeric choice or text value (must exactly match list
item):  1
```

We choose our CloudSQL project *democloudsql*. This sets our project and prompts to configure a default compute region and zone, specify N, and we are done with the configuration of our cloud SDK as shown below

```
Your current project has been set to: [democloudsql-248408].
```

```
Do you want to configure a default Compute Region and Zone? (Y/n)?  n
```

```
Created a default .boto configuration file at [/home/architectbigdata/.
boto]. See this file and
[https://cloud.google.com/storage/docs/gsutil/commands/config] for more
information about configuring Google Cloud Storage.
Your Google Cloud SDK is configured and ready to use!
```

```
* Commands that require authentication will use architectbigdata@gmail.com
by default
```

```
* Commands will reference project `democloudsql-248408` by default
Run `gcloud help config` to learn how to change individual settings

This gcloud configuration is called [default]. You can create additional
configurations if you work with multiple accounts and/or projects.
Run `gcloud topic configurations` to learn more.

Some things to try next:

* Run `gcloud --help` to see the Cloud Platform services you can interact
with. And run `gcloud help COMMAND` to get help on any gcloud command.
* Run `gcloud topic -h` to learn about advanced features of the SDK like
arg files and output formatting
architectbigdata@feasting:~$
```

Now that we have the Cloud SDK configured, lets next generate the application default credentials. Enter the command

```
architectbigdata@feasting:~$ gcloud auth application-default login
```

Wherever prompted, type Y (Yes) and press enter. This will generate a link for us to fetch the verification code, follow the URL, enter the verification code against the prompt and that's it. The credentials will be saved to a file as shown below.

```
architectbigdata@feasting:~$ gcloud auth application-default login

You are running on a Google Compute Engine virtual machine.
The service credentials associated with this virtual machine
will automatically be used by Application Default
Credentials, so it is not necessary to use this command.

If you decide to proceed anyway, your user credentials may be visible
to others with access to this virtual machine. Are you sure you want
to authenticate with your personal account?

Do you want to continue (Y/n)?   Y
```

Go to the following link in your browser:

> https://accounts.google.com/o/oauth2/auth?redirect_uri=urn%3
> Aietf%3Awg%3Aoauth%3A2.0%3Aoob&prompt=select_account&response_
> type=code&client_id=764086051850-6qr4p6gpi6hn506pt8ejuq83di341h
> ur.apps.googleusercontent.com&scope=https%3A%2F%2Fwww.googleapis.
> com%2Fauth%2Fuserinfo.email+https%3A%2F%2Fwww.googleapis.
> com%2Fauth%2Fcloud-platform&access_type=offline

Enter verification code: 4/nQGLQbUqCrGT4DpjfxzWfDx3-IvS7dtBT5Tww60SD6oVeD_KjgyRN2s

Credentials saved to file: [/home/architectbigdata/.config/gcloud/application_default_credentials.json]

These credentials will be used by any library that requests Application Default Credentials.

To generate an access token for other uses, run:
  gcloud auth application-default print-access-token
architectbigdata@feasting:~$

Next we will install a local copy of the proxy. Use the following command to download the proxy

architectbigdata@feasting:~$ wget https://dl.google.com/cloudsql/cloud_sql_proxy.linux.amd64 -O cloud_sql_proxy

This saves the *cloud_sql_proxy* to your current working directory.

architectbigdata@feasting:~$ wget https://dl.google.com/cloudsql/cloud_sql_proxy.linux.amd64 -O cloud_sql_proxy
--2019-08-05 10:49:39-- https://dl.google.com/cloudsql/cloud_sql_proxy.linux.amd64
Resolving dl.google.com (dl.google.com)... 172.217.212.136,
172.217.212.190, 172.217.212.91, ...
Connecting to dl.google.com (dl.google.com)|172.217.212.136|:443...
connected.
HTTP request sent, awaiting response... 200 OK
Length: 13068633 (12M) [application/octet-stream]

Saving to: 'cloud_sql_proxy'

cloud_sql_proxy   100%[==>]
12.46M --.-KB/s   in 0.06s

2019-08-05 10:49:40 (225 MB/s) - 'cloud_sql_proxy' saved
[13068633/13068633]

architectbigdata@feasting:~$

Use the following command to make the proxy executable.

architectbigdata@feasting:~$ chmod +x cloud_sql_proxy

Let's finally, start the Cloud SQL proxy. Prior to this we will create a directory in our current working directory for storing the proxy client details using the following command

architectbigdata@feasting:~$ mkdir tutorialcloudsql

And upload the key file we generated for our service account, using Upload file option as shown below in Figure 3-25.

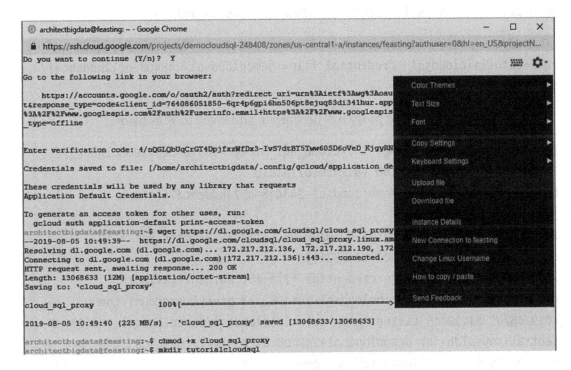

Figure 3-25. *Upload File to VM*

Navigate to your local directory where the key file was downloaded and upload it. Post the upload completion you will see notification as shown in Figure 3-26.

File Transfer		Close
democloudsql-248408-d272bddebc47.json	Finished	
File upload destination: /home/architectbigdata		

Figure 3-26. *File Uploaded*

Now, use the following command to start the proxy

```
./cloud_sql_proxy -instances=<Instance Connection Name>
-dir=tutorialcloudsql -credential_file= <KEY File> &
```

With all the details in place the command looks as follows.

```
./cloud_sql_proxy -instances=democloudsql-248408:us-central1:mysqldb
-dir=tutorialcloudsql -credential_file= democloudsql-248408-d272bddebc47.
json &
```

Enter the command. The proxy will be started, and it will look as below

```
architectbigdata@feasting:~$ ./cloud_sql_proxy -instances=democloudsql-
248408:us-central1:mysqldb -dir=tutorialclo
udsql -credential_file=democloudsql-248408-d272bddebc47.json &
[2] 21549
architectbigdata@feasting:~$ 2019/08/05 11:12:15 Rlimits for file
descriptors set to {&{8500 1048576}}
2019/08/05 11:12:15 using credential file for authentication;
email=tutorialservice@democloudsql-248408.iam.gserviceaccount.com
2019/08/05 11:12:15 Listening on tutorialcloudsql/democloudsql-248408:us-
central1:mysqldb for democloudsql-248408:us-central1:mysqldb
2019/08/05 11:12:15 Ready for new connections
```

With our environment ready and the proxy enabled, let's look at the python code next. For this we assume that you are familiar with Python programming.

Python Program

To start with we will first import the following libraries

```
import pymysql
import json
import random as r
import sys
```

Next, we set the following connection variables

```
db_user = "root"
db_pass = *******"
db_name = "eatout"
socket_path="/home/adminuser/tutorialcloudsql/democloudsql-248408:us-
central1:mysqldb"
```

db_user/db_pass is our MySQL database user credentials. For this example, we use root user. ***db_name*** is the database (*eatout*) which we created to work with. ***socket_path*** is the file created while starting the proxy in the previous step.

With the variables set, we next establish connection within the main function, and open cursor to work with our database in the subsequent methods.

```
db_conn = pymysql.connect(unix_socket=socket_path, user=db_user,
password=db_pass, db=db_name)
cursor = db_conn.cursor()
```

Following this we list all available options for the user to act with. Against each option we create a method.

```
print("Select the operations to perform:")
print("1. Register Restaurant")
print("2. Load User Feedback")
print("3. Fetch the top rated restaurant")
print("4. Top 2 basis on my input")
```

```python
print("5. List users with birthdays in next 7 days from the
date specified")
print("6. List users with any of there occasion in given month")
print("7. Delete Restaurant")
print("0. Exit")
operation = input()
# print(operation)
if(operation=='1' or operation == 1):
    print("Selected: Register Restaurant")
    register_restaurant()
if(operation == '2' or operation == 2):
    print("Selected: Load User Feedback")
    user_input()
if(operation == '3' or operation== 3):
    print("Selected: Fetch top rated restaurant")
    query_1()
if (operation == '4' or operation == 4):
    print("Selected: Top 2 on the basis of input")
    query_2()
if (operation == '5' or operation == 5):
    print("Selected: List users with birthday")
    query_3()
if (operation == '6' or operation == 6):
    print("Selected: List users with any occassion")
    query_4()
if (operation == '7' or operation == 7):
    print("Selected: Delete Restaurant")
    delete_restaurant()
if( operation == '0' or operation == 0):
    print("Thank You")
```

Finally, in the main post we close the connection using

```python
cursor.close()
db_conn.close()
```

With all this in place the main looks as below.

```python
if __name__ == "__main__":
    try:
        db_conn = pymysql.connect(unix_socket=socket_path, user=db_user,
        password=db_pass, db=db_name)
        cursor = db_conn.cursor()
        while True:
            print("Select the operations to perform:")
            print("1. Register Restaurant")
            print("2. Load User Feedback")
            print("3. Fetch the top rated restaurant")
            print("4. Top 2 basis on my input")
            print("5. List users with birthdays in next 7 days from the
            date specified")
            print("6. List users with any of there occasion in given month")
            print("7. Delete Restaurant")
            print("0. Exit")
            operation = input()
            # print(operation)
            if(operation=='1' or operation == 1):
                print("Selected: Register Restaurant")
                register_restaurant()
            if(operation == '2' or operation == 2):
                print("Selected: Load User Feedback")
                user_input()
            if(operation == '3' or operation== 3):
                print("Selected: Fetch top rated restaurant")
                query_1()
            if (operation == '4' or operation == 4):
                print("Selected: Top 2 on the basis of input")
                query_2()
            if (operation == '5' or operation == 5):
                print("Selected: List users with birthday")
                query_3()
```

```
            if (operation == '6' or operation == 6):
                print("Selected: List users with any occassion")
                query_4()
            if (operation == '7' or operation == 7):
                print("Selected: Delete Restaurant")
                delete_restaurant()
            if( operation == '0' or operation == 0):
                print("Thank You")
                cursor.close()
                db_conn.close()
                print (db_conn.ping())
                break

    except Exception as e:
        db_conn.close()
        print(e)
```

Next, we will look at individual method. Let's start with register restaurant method. This takes a file input, and load the data in the restaurant table.

```
def register_restaurant():
    "'function to upload restaurant data from file in json format"'
    try:
        f_name=input("Enter File name to upload Restaurant Data       ")

        with open(f_name,'r') as json_file:
            line=json_file.readline()
            count=1
            while line:
                input_json1 = json.loads(line)
                print(input_json1)
                uid = generate_uuid() # function called to generate unique id.
                cursor.execute("""INSERT INTO Restaurant VALUES ("%s",
                "%s", "%s", "%s", "%s")""" % (uid, (input_json1["name"]),
                (input_json1["cuisine"]), (input_json1["region"]),(input_
                json1["location"])))
                db_conn.commit()
```

```
            print("Record No - "+ str(count)+ "   Insertion Successful
            for Restaurant name -- " + (input_json1["name"]))
            count += 1
            line=json_file.readline()

    except Exception as e:
        print(e)
```

We can see reference to a function to generate a unique identifier. This looks like below; we generate a 5-character random identifier.

```
def generate_uuid():
    "'Function generating random unique id of 5 digit"'
    random_string = "
    random_str_seq = "0123456789abcdefghijklmnopqrstuvwxyzABCDEFGHIJKLMNOPQ
    RSTUVWXYZ"
    uuid_format = 5
    for n in range(uuid_format):
        random_string += str(random_str_seq[r.randint(0, len(random_str_
        seq) - 1)])
    return random_string
```

We will be using the same function for generating UserId as well while creating a new user, which we will see in a while.

We next look at methods for loading the user feedback data. Phone number is unique for our user data. We use phone number to first check for the user existence. If the user is already there, we update the Name, Email, Date of Birth, Spouse Date of Birth and anniversary detail and fetch its user id. If the user is new, we insert the data and generate a new user id. With the user id detail, we next load the feedback data in the User Feedback table.

```
def user_input():
    "' Function to upload User detail/Feedback data in json "'
    try:
        f_name = input("Enter File name to upload User Detail and Feedback
        Data      ")
        with open(f_name, 'r') as json_file:
            line = json_file.readline()
```

```
            count = 1
            while line:
                input_user = json.loads(line)
                #pno = str(input_user["pno"])
                rows_count = cursor.execute("""SELECT id FROM UserDetails
                WHERE phonenumber='%s'""" % (input_user["pno"]))
                records = cursor.fetchone()
                for i in records:
                    ud_id = i[0]
                if rows_count: # in case user already exists
                    user_update(input_user) # Calling user_update function
                    to update user detail
                    user_feedback(input_user, ud_id) # Calling user_
                    feedback to insert feedback data
                else: # in case of new user
                    ud_id = generate_uuid()
                    user_details(input_user, ud_id) # Calling user_details
                    function to insert user details
                    user_feedback(input_user, ud_id)  # Calling user_
                    feedback to insert feedback data
                print(str(count) + " Record Successfully Inserted/Updated")
                count += 1
                line = json_file.readline()

    except Exception as e:
        print(e)

def user_update(input_json):
    "'function to update user information incase user already exists"'
    try:
        cursor.execute(
            """update UserDetails set Name = '%s' , Emailid='%s',
            Birthday='%s', SpouseBirthday='%s', Anniversary='%s' where
            phonenumber='%s'""" % (
            input_json["name"], input_json["emailid"], input_
            json["selfdob"], input_json["spousedob"], input_
            json["anniversary"], input_json["pno"],))
```

```
        db_conn.commit()
        print("User Record Updated successfully ")
    except Exception as e:
        print(e)

def user_details(input_json=None, ud_id=None):
    "'function to insert user information incase of new user"'
    try:
        user_id = ud_id
        cursor.execute("""INSERT into UserDetails VALUES ("%s", "%s", "%s",
        "%s", "%s","%s","%s")""" % (
        user_id, input_json["name"], input_json["pno"], input_
        json["emailid"], input_json["selfdob"], input_json["spousedob"],
        input_json["anniversary"]))
        db_conn.commit()
        print("User Detail Record Insertion Successful")

    except Exception as e:
        print(e)

def user_feedback(input_json=None, us_id=None):
    "'function to insert feedback information"'
    try:
        cursor.execute("""INSERT INTO UserFeedback (`UserId`, `VisitDate`,
        `RestaurantId`, `FoodQuality`,`ServiceQuality`,`Ambience`,
        `LiveMusic`,`ValueForMoney`,`Cleanliness`,`FoodVariety`) VALUES
        ("%s", "%s", "%s", "%s", "%s","%s","%s","%s","%s","%s")""" % (
        us_id, input_json["dateofvisit"], input_json["restid"], input_
        json["foodquality"], input_json["servicequality"], input_
        json["ambience"], input_json["music"], input_json["valueformoney"],
        input_json["cleanliness"], input_json["foodvariety"]))
        db_conn.commit()

        print("Feedback Record Insertion Successful")

    except Exception as e:
        print(e)
```

The next method deletes the restaurants; like with other options we take file with restaurant ids to be deleted.

```
def delete_restaurant():
    "' function to delete restaurant data from database based on
    restaurantid"'
    try:
        f_name = input("Enter File name to Delete Restaurant Data        ")
        with open(f_name, 'r') as json_file:
            line = json_file.readline()
            while line:
                input_json1 = json.loads(line)
                restid = str(input_json1["id"])
                data = (restid,)
                query = "delete from Restaurant where id= %s"
                rows_count = cursor.execute("""SELECT id FROM Restaurant
                WHERE id='%s'""" % restid)
                if rows_count > 0:
                    cursor.execute(query, data)
                    db_conn.commit()
                    print(" Restaurant Successfully Deleted")
                else:
                    print("Restaurant doesnt exists")
                line = json_file.readline()
    except Exception as e:
        print(e)
```

With all data manipulation methods in place, let's next look at the methods provisioned for querying.

First query fetches the Top-rated restaurant. In this we average out all parameters rating data and then we take an average across all the user inputs received.

```
def query_1():
    "' Fetch top rated restaurant "'
    try:
        cursor.execute("select r1.name from (select restaurantid,
        avg(((foodquality+servicequality+ambience+livemusic+valueform
        oney+cleanliness+foodvariety)*1.0)/7) avgratingacrossall from
        UserFeedback group by restaurantid order by 1 desc limit 1)tbla,
        Restaurant r1 where tbla.restaurantid=r1.id")
        rows=cursor.fetchall()
        for i in rows:
            print(i)
    except Exception as e:
        print(e)
```

Second query is to fetch a restaurant basis two factors which will be provided by the user: food quality and quality of service.

```
def query_2():
    "'Query to fetch top 2 records on the basis of foodquality or
    servicequality entered as input"'
    try:
        print("Enter parameter on which restaurants has to be compared  :")
        parameter = input('Please enter either foodquality or servicequality')
        if parameter.lower()== 'foodquality':
            cursor.execute("""select r1.name from (select restaurantid,
            avg(foodquality) avgratingselected from UserFeedback group by
            restaurantid order by 1 desc limit 2)tbla, Restaurant r1 where
            tbla.restaurantid=r1.id;""")
        if parameter.lower()=='servicequality':
            cursor.execute("""select r1.name from (select restaurantid,
            avg(servicequality) avgratingselected from UserFeedback group
            by restaurantid order by 1 desc limit 2)tbla, Restaurant r1
            where tbla.restaurantid=r1.id;""")
```

```
        rows=cursor.fetchall()
        for i in rows:
            print(i)
    except Exception as e:
        print(e)
```

Third and fourth query is from restaurant perspective, where the third query enables to find out users with date of birth in 7 days.

```
def query_3():
    "'Query to fetch list of users with birthday on date entered as input"'
    try:
        print("Enter the date for which the birthday has to be checked :")
        date_input = input()
        cursor.execute("""select Name, PhoneNumber, emailId from
        UserDetails where month(birthday)=month('%s') and day(birthday)
        between day('%s') and day('%s')+7"""%(date_input,date_input,
        date_input))
        rows = cursor.fetchall()
        for i in rows:
            print(i)
    except Exception as e:
        print(e)
```

And the fourth query returns user with any occasion date in the month of the date specified.

```
def query_4():
    "'Query to fetch list of users with any occassion on date entered as
    input "'
    try:
        print("Enter the date for which occassion has to checked :")
        date_input = input()
        cursor.execute("""select Name, PhoneNumber, emailId from UserDetails
        where month(birthday)=month('%s') or month(spousebirthday)=mont
        h('%s') and month(anniversary)=month('%s')"""%(date_input,date_
        input,date_input))
```

```
    rows = cursor.fetchall()
    for i in rows:
        print(i)
  except Exception as e:
    print(e)
```

The columns, database names and credentials are hardcoded for simplicity. With everything combined, the complete code is available for download at `https://github. com/architectbigdata/cloudsql`.

Now that we have the code in place, let's execute and validate.

Run and Verify

Prior to executing let's connect to our database and check all the tables using CloudShell. The database shows our tables with no data as shown below.

```
architectbigdata@cloudshell:~ (democloudsql-248408)$ gcloud sql connect
mysqldb --user=root
Whitelisting your IP for incoming connection for 5 minutes...done.
Connecting to database with SQL user [root].Enter password:
Welcome to the MariaDB monitor.  Commands end with ; or \g.
Your MySQL connection id is 7276
Server version: 5.7.14-google-log (Google)

Copyright (c) 2000, 2018, Oracle, MariaDB Corporation Ab and others.

Type 'help;' or '\h' for help. Type '\c' to clear the current input statement.

MySQL [(none)]> use eatout;
Reading table information for completion of table and column names
You can turn off this feature to get a quicker startup with -A
```

```
Database changed
MySQL [eatout]> show tables;
+------------------+
| Tables_in_eatout |
+------------------+
| Restaurant       |
| UserDetails      |
| UserFeedback     |
+------------------+
3 rows in set (0.19 sec)

MySQL [eatout]> SELECT * FROM Restaurant;
Empty set (0.19 sec)

MySQL [eatout]> SELECT * FROM UserDetails;
Empty set (0.19 sec)

MySQL [eatout]> SELECT * FROM UserFeedback;
Empty set (0.19 sec)

MySQL [eatout]>
```

Let's begin the execution of our program.

Note   The above code is to be saved in cloud_sql_python directory on the VM by the name of tutorial.py. So, prior to executing ensure the code is saved and directory is set.

In the Ubuntu prompt enter the following command

```
python3 tutorial.py
```

This will display the options as shown below

```
architectbigdata@feasting:~/cloud_sql_python$ python3 tutorial.py
Select the operations to perform:
1. Register Restaurant
2. User Feedback
3. Fetch the top rated restaurant
```

114

4. Top 2 basis on my input

5. List users with birthdays in next 7 days from the date specified

6. List users with any of there occasion in given month

7. Delete Restaurant

0. Exit

Since we don't have any data, we start with registering the restaurants. We choose option 1.

```
architectbigdata@feasting:~/cloud_sql_python$ python3 tutorial.py
Select the operations to perform:
1. Register Restaurant
2. User Feedback
3. Fetch the top rated restaurant
4. Top 2 basis on my input
5. List users with birthdays in next 7 days from the date specified
6. List users with any of there occasion in given month
7. Delete Restaurant
0. Exit
1
Selected: Register Restaurant
Enter File name to upload Restaurant Data      restaurants.txt
```

It prompts for the file name, which we have specified as *restaurants.txt*. The content of the file is as shown below.

```
{"name":"Pirates of Grill","cuisine":"BBQ","region":"noida","location":
"sector 18"}
{"name":"Barbeque Nation","cuisine":"BBQ","region":"noida","location":
"sector 18"}
{"name":"Pizza Hut","cuisine":"Fast Food","region":"Ghaziabad","location":
"vaishali"}
{"name":"Dominos","cuisine":"Fast Food","region":"Ghaziabad","location":
"Kaushambi"}
{"name":"Haldiram","cuisine":"Multi-cuisine","region":"Ghaziabad",
"location":"Kaushambi"}
```

{"name":"Bikaner","cuisine":"Multi-cuisine","region":"Ghaziabad",
"location":"Kaushambi"}
{"name":"Bikaner","cuisine":"Multi-cuisine","region":"Noida","location":
"sector 18"}
{"name":"Taj","cuisine":"Multi-cuisine","region":"Delhi","location":"CP"}

As the program executes, it displays the status, post successful completion, it again displays the choice of actions.

```
Selected: Register Restaurant
Enter File name to upload Restaurant Data       restaurants.txt
Record No - 1  Insertion Successful for Restaurant name -- Pirates of Grill
Record No - 2  Insertion Successful for Restaurant name -- Barbeque Nation
Record No - 3  Insertion Successful for Restaurant name -- Pizza Hut
Record No - 4  Insertion Successful for Restaurant name -- Dominos
Record No - 5  Insertion Successful for Restaurant name -- Haldiram
Record No - 6  Insertion Successful for Restaurant name -- Bikaner
Record No - 7  Insertion Successful for Restaurant name -- Bikaner
Record No - 8  Insertion Successful for Restaurant name -- Taj
Select the operations to perform:
1. Register Restaurant
2. User Feedback
3. Fetch the top rated restaurant
4. Top 2 basis on my input
5. List users with birthdays in next 7 days from the date specified
6. List users with any of there occasion in given month
7. Delete Restaurant
0. Exit
```

Let's validate the data in our CloudSQL instance. We run the select on Restaurant table and the data is as below.

```
MySQL [eatout]> SELECT * FROM Restaurant;
+-------+-----------------+---------------+-----------+-----------+
| id    | Name            | Cuisine       | Region    | Location  |
+-------+-----------------+---------------+-----------+-----------+
| 4wHrP | Barbeque Nation | BBQ           | noida     | sector 18 |
| CRncG | Bikaner         | Multi-cuisine | Ghaziabad | Kaushambi |
```

116

```
| ieFWQ | Haldiram        | Multi-cuisine | Ghaziabad | Kaushambi |
| KR5Vq | Pirates of Grill | BBQ          | noida     | sector 18 |
| MlWwK | Taj             | Multi-cuisine | Delhi     | CP        |
| OHUvB | Bikaner         | Multi-cuisine | Noida     | sector 18 |
| x1gIm | Pizza Hut       | Fast Food     | Ghaziabad | vaishali  |
| X9gWS | Dominos         | Fast Food     | Ghaziabad | Kaushambi |
+-------+-----------------+---------------+-----------+-----------+
8 rows in set (0.20 sec)
```

We can see, all the file data is loaded. Let's next load the user feedback. We select option 2.

```
Select the operations to perform:
1. Register Restaurant
2. User Feedback
3. Fetch the top rated restaurant
4. Top 2 basis on my input
5. List users with birthdays in next 7 days from the date specified
6. List users with any of there occasion in given month
7. Delete Restaurant
0. Exit
2
Selected: User Feedback
Enter File name to upload User Detail and Feedback Data   userfeedback1.txt
```

Just like above, it prompts for the filename which in this case we specify as *userfeedback1.txt*. The following shows the content of the file *userfeedback1.txt*.

```
{"name":"Kishore Kumar","pno":"8974563421","emailid":"kishore_k@gmail.com",
"selfdob":"1980-01-01","spousedob":"1982-08-10","anniversary":"1996-06-08",
"dateofvisit":"2019-08-01","restid":"M4OaD","foodquality":3,"servicequality":4,
"ambience":5,"music":1,"valueformoney":3,"cleanliness":3,"foodvariety":4}
{"name":"Radhey Shyam","pno":"8774563421","emailid":"ak@gmail.com",
"selfdob":"1934-03-18","spousedob":"1938-08-18","anniversary":"1961-08-16",
"dateofvisit":"2019-03-18","restid":"CLnjx","foodquality":5,"servicequality":4,
"ambience":5,"music":5,"valueformoney":3,"cleanliness":4,"foodvariety":4}
{"name":"Natasha","pno":"8674563421","emailid":"nat@gmail.com","selfdob":
"1984-03-28","spousedob":"1980-03-18","anniversary":"2006-08-18",
```

117

"dateofvisit":"2019-03-18","restid":"RbwsK","foodquality":4,"servicequality":4,
"ambience":5,"music":1,"valueformoney":3,"cleanliness":3,"foodvariety":4}
{"name":"Chivi","pno":"8574563421","emailid":"schivi@gmail.com","selfdob":
"1990-04-15","spousedob":"1985-02-10","anniversary":"2010-08-01",
"dateofvisit":"2019-08-01","restid":"RbwsK","foodquality":5,"servicequality":5,"
ambience":5,"music":5,"valueformoney":4,"cleanliness":5,"foodvariety":4}
{"name":"Michie","pno":"8474563421","emailid":"michie@gmail.com","selfdob":
"2009-06-08","spousedob":"1999-03-15","anniversary":"2019-01-01",
"dateofvisit":"2019-06-08","restid":"M40aD","foodquality":3,
"servicequality":4,"ambience":5,"music":1,"valueformoney":3,
"cleanliness":3,"foodvariety":4}

As the program executes the state is being displayed.

```
Select the operations to perform:
1. Register Restaurant
2. User Feedback
3. Fetch the top rated restaurant
4. Top 2 basis on my input
5. List users with birthdays in next 7 days from the date specified
6. List users with any of there occasion in given month
7. Delete Restaurant
0. Exit
2
Selected: User Feedback
Enter File name to upload User Detail and Feedback Data    userfeedback1.txt
User Detail Record Insertion Successful
Feedback Record Insertion Successful
1 Record Successfully Inserted/Updated
User Detail Record Insertion Successful
Feedback Record Insertion Successful
2 Record Successfully Inserted/Updated
User Detail Record Insertion Successful
Feedback Record Insertion Successful
3 Record Successfully Inserted/Updated
User Detail Record Insertion Successful
Feedback Record Insertion Successful
```

4 Record Successfully Inserted/Updated
User Detail Record Insertion Successful
Feedback Record Insertion Successful
5 Record Successfully Inserted/Updated
Select the operations to perform:
1. Register Restaurant
2. User Feedback
3. Fetch the top rated restaurant
4. Top 2 basis on my input
5. List users with birthdays in next 7 days from the date specified
6. List users with any of there occasion in given month
7. Delete Restaurant
0. Exit

Let's validate *UserDetails* and *UserFeedback* table. We can see all data loaded.

```
MySQL [eatout]> SELECT * FROM UserDetails
    -> ;
+-------+---------------+-------------+---------------------+------------+
----------------+-------------+
| id    | Name          | PhoneNumber | EmailId             | Birthday   |
 SpouseBirthday | Anniversary |
+-------+---------------+-------------+---------------------+------------+
----------------+-------------+
| 7Dtzj | Natasha       | 8674563421  | nat@gmail.com       | 1984-03-28 |
 1980-03-18     | 2006-08-18  |
| AZDBP | Kishore Kumar | 8974563421  | kishore_k@gmail.com | 1980-01-01 |
 1982-08-10     | 1996-06-08  |
| DtTbT | Chivi         | 8574563421  | schivi@gmail.com    | 1990-04-15 |
 1985-02-10     | 2010-08-01  |
| iSmwG | Michie        | 8474563421  | michie@gmail.com    | 2009-06-08 |
 1999-03-15     | 2019-01-01  |
| xaJSA | Radhey Shyam  | 8774563421  | ak@gmail.com        | 1934-03-18 |
 1938-08-18     | 1961-08-16  |
+-------+---------------+-------------+---------------------+------------+
----------------+-------------+
```

```
5 rows in set (0.20 sec)

MySQL [eatout]> SELECT * FROM UserFeedback;
+--------+--------------+------------+-------------+-----------------+----------+
-----------+--------------+-------------+-------------+------------+
| UserId | RestaurantId | VisitDate  | FoodQuality | ServiceQuality | Ambience |
 LiveMusic | ValueForMoney | Cleanliness | FoodVariety | FeedbackId |
+--------+--------------+------------+-------------+-----------------+----------+
-----------+--------------+-------------+-------------+------------+
| AZDBP  | 4wHrP        | 2019-08-01 |           3 |              4 |        5 |
         1 |            3 |           3 |           4 |         10 |
| xaJSA  | KR5Vq        | 2019-03-18 |           5 |              4 |        5 |
         5 |            3 |           4 |           4 |         11 |
| 7Dtzj  | KR5Vq        | 2019-03-18 |           4 |              4 |        5 |
         1 |            3 |           3 |           4 |         12 |
| DtTbT  | KR5Vq        | 2019-08-01 |           5 |              5 |        5 |
         5 |            4 |           5 |           4 |         13 |
| iSmwG  | 4wHrP        | 2019-06-08 |           3 |              4 |        5 |
         1 |            3 |           3 |           4 |         14 |
+--------+--------------+------------+-------------+-----------------+----------+
-----------+--------------+-------------+-------------+------------+
5 rows in set (0.20 sec)

MySQL [eatout]>
```

Let's again choose option 2 with a different file name *userfeedback2.txt*.

```
Select the operations to perform:
1. Register Restaurant
2. User Feedback
3. Fetch the top rated restaurant
4. Top 2 basis on my input
5. List users with birthdays in next 7 days from the date specified
6. List users with any of there occasion in given month
7. Delete Restaurant
0. Exit
```

2

```
Selected: User Feedback
Enter File name to upload User Detail and Feedback Data       userfeedback2.
txt
```

The following is the content of the file userfeedback2.txt.

```
{"name":"Kishore Kumar","pno":"8974563421","emailid":"kishore_kumar@gmail.
com","selfdob":"1970-01-01","spousedob":"1980-08-10","anniversary":"1994-
06-08","dateofvisit":"2019-08-01","restid":"CRncG","foodquality":3,"service
quality":4,"ambience":5,"music":1,"valueformoney":3,"cleanliness":3,"foodva
riety":4}
{"name":"Mickey Sharma","pno":"9999993421","emailid":"mickey@gmail.
com","selfdob":"1945-08-17","spousedob":"1938-08-18","anniversary":"1960-
05-16","dateofvisit":"2019-08-01","restid":"X9gWS","foodquality":5,"service
quality":4,"ambience":5,"music":5,"valueformoney":3,"cleanliness":4,"foodva
riety":4}
```

The output of the python program for option 2 is as below

```
Enter File name to upload User Detail and Feedback Data   userfeedback2.txt
User Record Updated successfully
Feedback Record Insertion Successful
1 Record Successfully Inserted/Updated
User Detail Record Insertion Successful
Feedback Record Insertion Successful
2 Record Successfully Inserted/Updated
Select the operations to perform:
```

Let's validate the tables,

```
MySQL [eatout]> SELECT * FROM UserDetails;
+-------+---------------+-------------+------------------------+
-------------+---------------+-------------+
| id    | Name          | PhoneNumber | EmailId                |
 Birthday   | SpouseBirthday | Anniversary |
+-------+---------------+-------------+------------------------+
-------------+---------------+-------------+
| 7Dtzj | Natasha       | 8674563421  | nat@gmail.com          |
 1984-03-28 | 1980-03-18     | 2006-08-18  |
| AZDBP | Kishore Kumar | 8974563421  | kishore_kumar@gmail.com |
 1970-01-01 | 1980-08-10     | 1994-06-08  |
| DtTbT | Chivi         | 8574563421  | schivi@gmail.com       |
 1990-04-15 | 1985-02-10     | 2010-08-01  |
| iSmwG | Michie        | 8474563421  | michie@gmail.com       |
 2009-06-08 | 1999-03-15     | 2019-01-01  |
| LZZId | Mickey Sharma | 9999993421  | mickey@gmail.com       |
 1945-08-17 | 1938-08-18     | 1960-05-16  |
| xaJSA | Radhey Shyam  | 8774563421  | ak@gmail.com           |
 1934-03-18 | 1938-08-18     | 1961-08-16  |
+-------+---------------+-------------+------------------------+
-------------+---------------+-------------+
6 rows in set (0.19 sec)

MySQL [eatout]> SELECT * FROM UserFeedback;
+--------+--------------+-------------+-------------+----------------+-----------+
-----------+---------------+-------------+-------------+------------+
| UserId | RestaurantId | VisitDate   | FoodQuality | ServiceQuality | Ambience |
 LiveMusic | ValueForMoney | Cleanliness | FoodVariety | FeedbackId |
+--------+--------------+-------------+-------------+----------------+-----------+
-----------+---------------+-------------+-------------+------------+
| AZDBP  | 4wHrP        | 2019-08-01  |           3 |              4 |        5 |
         1 |             3 |           3 |           4 |         10 |
| xaJSA  | KR5Vq        | 2019-03-18  |           5 |              4 |        5 |
         5 |             3 |           4 |           4 |         11 |
```

7Dtzj	KR5Vq	2019-03-18	4	4	5
	1	3	3	4	12
DtTbT	KR5Vq	2019-08-01	5	5	5
	5	4	5	4	13
iSmwG	4wHrP	2019-06-08	3	4	5
	1	3	3	4	14
AZDBP	CRncG	2019-08-01	3	4	5
	1	3	3	4	15
LZZId	X9gWS	2019-08-01	5	4	5
	5	3	4	4	16

```
+--------+--------------+------------+-------------+----------------+----------+
-----------+--------------+------------+-------------+-----------+
7 rows in set (0.19 sec)

MySQL [eatout]>
```

We can see *Kishore Kumar* was an existing user, data is updated for him and the new user data is created. Feedback of both users is also saved.

With the data in place, let's run the querying part. We first choose Option 5 to display the top-rated restaurant, the output is as below.

```
Select the operations to perform:
1. Register Restaurant
2. User Feedback
3. Fetch the top rated restaurant
4. Top 2 basis on my input
5. List users with birthdays in next 7 days from the date specified
6. List users with any of there occasion in given month
7. Delete Restaurant
0. Exit
3
Selected: Fetch the top rated restaurant
('Dominos',)
```

Next we choose option 6, specify parameter as Food Quality. Output is as below

```
Select the operations to perform:
1. Register Restaurant
```

```
2. User Feedback
3. Fetch the top rated restaurant
4. Top 2 basis on my input
5. List users with birthdays in next 7 days from the date specified
6. List users with any of there occasion in given month
7. Delete Restaurant
0. Exit
4
Selected: Top 2 basis on my input
foodquality
('Dominos',)
('Pirates of Grill',)
```

We next choose query to display users with their birthday within 7 days from the date 2019-08-12, the output is as below

```
Select the operations to perform:
1. Register Restaurant
2. User Feedback
3. Fetch the top rated restaurant
4. Top 2 basis on my input
5. List users with birthdays in next 7 days from the date specified
6. List users with any of there occasion in given month
7. Delete Restaurant
0. Exit
5
Selected: List users with birthdays in next 7 days from the date specified
2019-08-12
('Mickey Sharma', '9999993421', 'mickey@gmail.com')
```

Let's next list users whose any of the special days falls in the month of August. The output is as below

```
Select the operations to perform:
1. Register Restaurant
2. User Feedback
3. Fetch the top rated restaurant
4. Top 2 basis on my input
```

5. List users with birthdays in next 7 days from the date specified

6. List users with any of there occasion in given month

7. Delete Restaurant

0. Exit

6

Selected: List users with any of there occasion in given month

2019-08-01

('Mickey Sharma', '9999993421', 'mickey@gmail.com')

('Radhey Shyam', '8774563421', 'ak@gmail.com')

Finally let's unregister restaurants Taj and Pizza Hut. We choose option 7 and specify file *delete.txt*.

Select the operations to perform:

1. Register Restaurant

2. User Feedback

3. Fetch the top rated restaurant

4. Top 2 basis on my input

5. List users with birthdays in next 7 days from the date specified

6. List users with any of there occasion in given month

7. Delete Restaurant

0. Exit

7

Selected: Delete Restaurant

Enter File name to Delete Restaurant Data   delete.txt

The following is the content of the file *delete.txt* where the id's are the restaurant ids to be deleted.

{"id":"FYGvI"}

{"id":"wEekQ"}

As the data is deleted we get the output of the program as shown below.

Enter File name to Delete Restaurant Data   delete.txt

  Restaurant Successfully Deleted

  Restaurant Successfully Deleted

Let's validate, the CloudSQL output is as shown

```
MySQL [eatout]> SELECT * FROM Restaurant;
+-------+-----------------+---------------+----------+-----------+
| id    | Name            | Cuisine       | Region   | Location  |
+-------+-----------------+---------------+----------+-----------+
| 4wHrP | Barbeque Nation | BBQ           | noida    | sector 18 |
| CRncG | Bikaner         | Multi-cuisine | Ghaziabad | Kaushambi |
| ieFWQ | Haldiram        | Multi-cuisine | Ghaziabad | Kaushambi |
| KR5Vq | Pirates of Grill | BBQ          | noida    | sector 18 |
| OHUvB | Bikaner         | Multi-cuisine | Noida    | sector 18 |
| X9gWS | Dominos         | Fast Food     | Ghaziabad | Kaushambi |
+-------+-----------------+---------------+----------+-----------+
6 rows in set (0.20 sec)

MySQL [eatout]>
```

Let's enter 0 to exit the program

```
Select the operations to perform:
1. Register Restaurant
2. User Feedback
3. Fetch the top rated restaurant
4. Top 2 basis on my input
5. List users with birthdays in next 7 days from the date specified
6. List users with any of there occasion in given month
7. Delete Restaurant
0. Exit
0
Thank You
```

With all the fun working with CloudSQL, it's time to wrap up now.

Wrap Up

We need to ensure to clean up for saving precious resources and money because we will be paying for this instance based on the time it runs. This is a pretty easy step. Let's first delete the Compute instance.

Open the left navigation menu, move to Compute Engine underneath the Compute section and select VM instances. It lists all the provisioned instances. Just go to your VM instance details page by clicking on the instance name. Figure 3-27 shows the instance details page. Click on Delete.

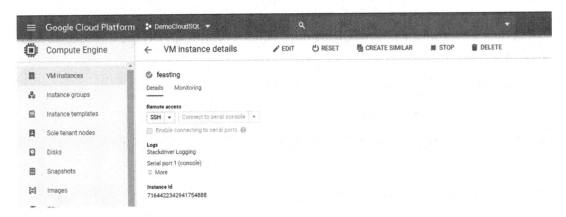

Figure 3-27. *VM instance details page*

Figure 3-28 shows the Delete VM instance prompt. Click Delete for confirmation.

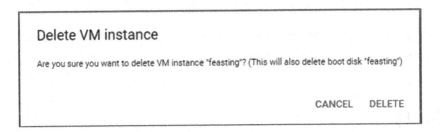

Figure 3-28. *Delete VM Instance Prompt*

Within seconds the VM will be deleted and all associated resources will be freed and cleared.

Let's next delete our CloudSQL instance. Navigate to the Instance detail page, by selecting SQL underneath Storage section and clicking on your instance name from the list displayed. Figure 3-29 shows the CloudSQL instance detail page. Click on delete.

Figure 3-29. *CloudSQL Instance Detail Page.*

Figure 3-30 shows the CloudSQL instance delete prompt. Specify the instance id, and hit delete.

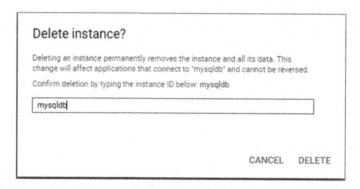

Figure 3-30. *CloudSQL Instance Delete Prompt*

Like compute, within seconds the CloudSQL instance will be deleted as well, and all associated resources will be freed and cleared.

Summary

Now that we have worked with CloudSQL instance using Cloud Shell and also used the database instance to build our python application Feast Out, in the next chapter let's look at things we will need to do to set up the Cloud SQL instance for production environment.

CHAPTER 4

Administering CloudSQL

With our sample application ready, we are now familiar with working with CloudSQL and using it from a python application. Let's now look at the activities which are important when we migrate our database instance to a live (production) environment. Most administrators would be involved in the below activities on a day to day basis:

- Authorizing access to database using a secure connection

- Enabling backups for data recovery

- Running maintenance activities to ensure that the instance is up-to-date with version upgrades and security patching.

- Managing instance resources

- Tuning the database parameters for performance optimization

- Ensuring that the instance remains highly available.

- Analyzing logs for diagnosing issues with the instance

CloudSQL being a fully managed database, handles all these activities for us. The administrative functions in a fully managed cloud service are handled very differently from the databases that are managed by enterprises themselves. Figure 4-1 shows difference between activities handled in on premise database versus a fully managed database.

© Navin Sabharwal, Shakuntala Gupta Edward 2020
N. Sabharwal and S. G. Edward, *Hands On Google Cloud SQL and Cloud Spanner*,
https://doi.org/10.1007/978-1-4842-5537-7_4

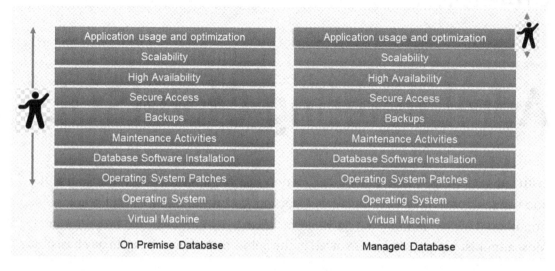

Figure 4-1.   *On-premise database vs. Managed database*

The administrative activities are configurable and Google enables us to manage the configurations using Advanced Configuration options while provisioning the instance itself or from the *Instance Detail* page.

Many of these comes with default options pre-configured. Let's run through each activity and look at the configuration.

Note   All the activities discussed below are common for both the database engines of CloudSQL – MySQL and PostgreSQL. If there are differences, we will highlight as we proceed.

Prior to beginning with the configuration activities, let's first create a SQL instance. For the examples in this chapter let's create *mysqllive* instance using the base configuration in the DemoCloudSQL project as shown below in Figure 4-2.

Figure 4-2. *mysqllive instance configuration page*

In this chapter we will cover:

- Instance access management

- High Availability and Scalability configuration options

- Backup and restores

- Maintenance and resource management.

- Logs for diagnosing

Let's first start with securing access to the instance.

Authorization and Security

Securing access to the database instance is of utmost importance. In some situations, when we are dealing with development or testing an environment, we can temporarily ignore security and allow open access to the instance; however, when we move to a live (production) environment and start dealing with actual data, then the insecure configuration can be risky, e.g. consider an application handling Credit Card details. Leaving the database open to all will result in a disaster by compromising the database.

Let's look at ways of securing access to our CloudSQL instance. This depends on the ways of accessing.

Authorized Network

If the application VMs accessing the CloudSQL instance are spread across varied networks (across multiple providers) but have static IP addresses assigned, then we can use the *Connections* section to authorize the network, limiting connectivity from the configured networks only. Navigate to the instance detail page. Select *Connections* Tab. Figure 4-3 shows the *Connections* tab.

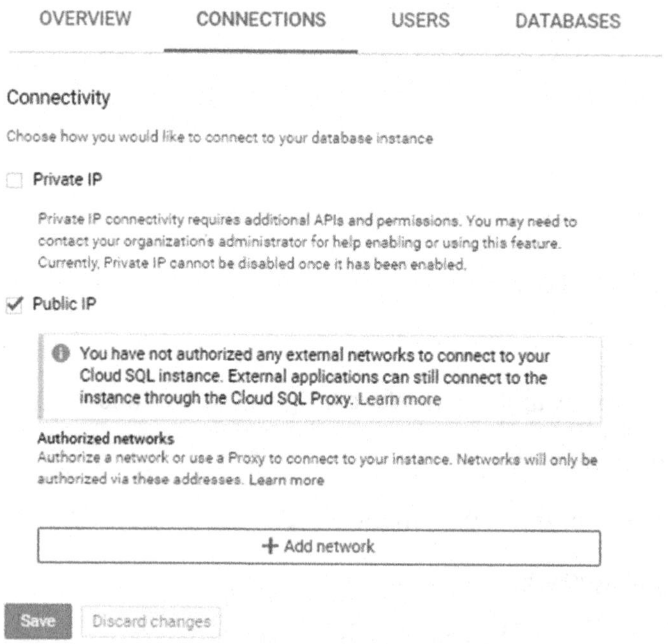

Figure 4-3. *Connections Tab*

Click on *Add Network* button. This enables us to add a new network for authorization as shown in Figure 4-4.

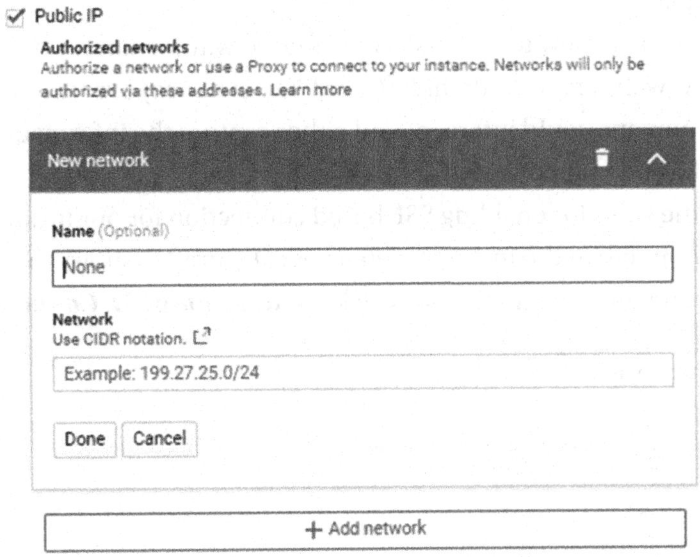

Figure 4-4. Add New Network

Add networks using **CIDR** notations. Let's look at few examples of CIDR notation. If we have a single instance e.g. 199.27.25.21 from where we need to restrict access, we should specify CIDR notation as 199.27.25.21/32. Using /32 implies that the IP is an exact IP.

If we have a range of instances following a pattern e.g. instances with IP addresses from 199.27.25.1 to 199.27.25.24 follows a pattern where only the last number is varying. In this case we can add network using the CIDR notation 199.27.25.0/24. Using /24 implies that the first three numbers are fixed and only the last number varies.

Once we are done with the configuration, Click Save. This updates the list of authorized networks. This configuration limits access at the network level. This will make the instance invisible to networks.

Though the above configuration restricts the access to our CloudSQL instance but the communication from the authorized network remains unencrypted (this is the default nature of CloudSQL). This default setting can possibly lead to data being intercepted when in transit leading to data breach.

When working with sensitive data e.g. Credit Card Details, Bank Account details, PIDs, securing data in transit is extremely important. Let's next look at the CloudSQL configuration for securing the data in transit.

Data in Transit

SSL (Secure Socket Layer) is recommended to be used with authorized networks to secure data in transit.

For the ones who are new to SSL, SSL is a standard way for safely sending sensitive data from point A (web server) to Point B (CloudSQL instance) over unsecured public network where someone could intercept and either capture the information or act as man in the middle and maneuver the data while in transit.

Let's look at the steps for enabling SSL based connection for our instance *mysqllive*. Click on *Connections* tab in the Instance detail page. Figure 4-5 shows the SSL Connections section underneath the tab. Click on ***Allow only SSL Connections***.

Figure 4-5. *SSL Connections*

In few seconds the settings will be updated to allow only secured connections and the section will look as shown in Figure 4-6.

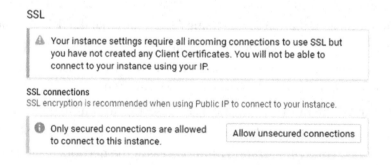

Figure 4-6. *SSL Connections Enabled*

To establish a secure connection from the client, we will be requiring the following:

- Server CA's certificate
- Client certificate and
- Client Private Key

Let's generate all the three. We will start with generating the server CA certificate first. Figure 4-7 shows the Configure SSL server certificates section. Click `Create new certificate` button.

Configure SSL server certificates
The server Certificate Authority (CA) certificate is required in SSL connections.

| Create new certificate | Rotate certificate | Rollback certificate |

Figure 4-7. *Configure SSL Server Certificates*

Once the certificate is generated it appears in the console as shown in Figure 4-8.

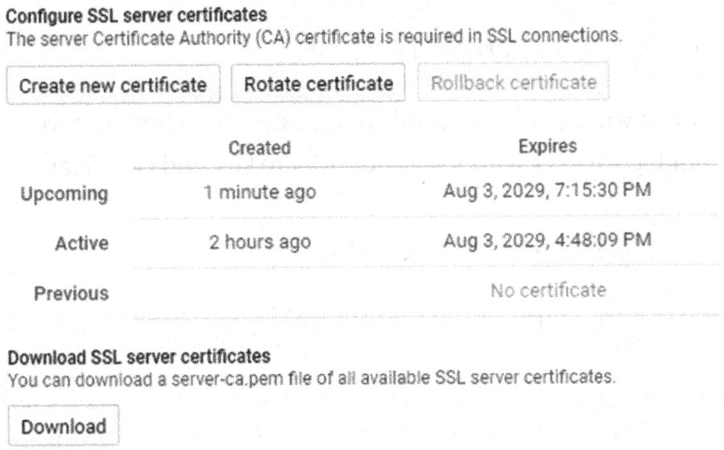

Configure SSL server certificates
The server Certificate Authority (CA) certificate is required in SSL connections.

| Create new certificate | Rotate certificate | Rollback certificate |

	Created	Expires
Upcoming	1 minute ago	Aug 3, 2029, 7:15:30 PM
Active	2 hours ago	Aug 3, 2029, 4:48:09 PM
Previous		No certificate

Download SSL server certificates
You can download a server-ca.pem file of all available SSL server certificates.

| Download |

Figure 4-8. *SSL Server Certificate Generated*

Click on ***Download*** button. It downloads the certificate as *server-ca.pem* file.

Next we will generate the Client certificate. Figure 4-9 shows the Configure SSL Client Certificates section. Click on *Create a Client Certificate* button.

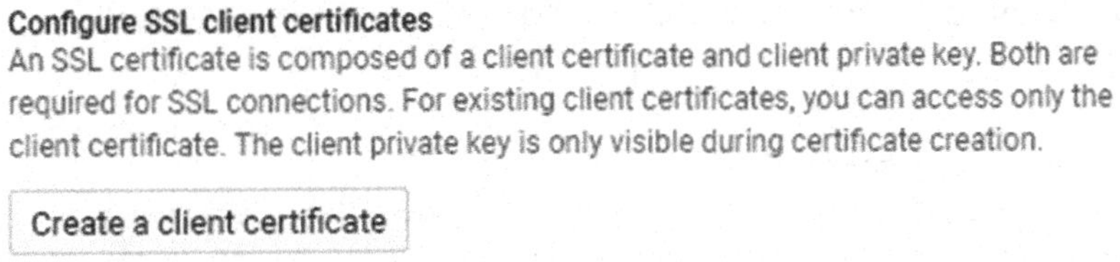

Configure SSL client certificates
An SSL certificate is composed of a client certificate and client private key. Both are required for SSL connections. For existing client certificates, you can access only the client certificate. The client private key is only visible during certificate creation.

| Create a client certificate |

Figure 4-9. *Generate SSL Client Certificates*

It prompts for name as shown in Figure 4-10. We should have a naming convention in place, it helps to better manage the keys. E.g. Naming based on the environment used, keys used for application development can be named as *app-dev*. For this example, let's name it *mysqlliveclient*.

Create a client certificate

Name
A unique identifier for your SSL certificate.

| mysqlliveclient |

CLOSE   CREATE

Figure 4-10. *Provide Client Certificate Name*

Click on Create. It will take few seconds to update. Once updated, you will see a popup as shown in Figure 4-11 with the client private key and certificate.

New SSL certificate created

To connect using this certificate, get the contents of the 3 files below.

ⓘ Before you can close this dialog, you must download the **client-key.pem** file. The file will not be accessible after this dialog is closed.

Download client-key.pem
```
-----BEGIN RSA PRIVATE KEY-----
MIIEowIBAAKCAQEAgu8N5I+jXBbiHKQG6fKSYvjd7BnJSpykf0gluW22qMoCPPHk
sJBLH1KLKWystA4MvKSGKH7Ucj0K8/19/jvVMzUQeA1gBG38haKX2LsDnMgCEIGa
```

Download client-cert.pem
```
-----BEGIN CERTIFICATE-----
MIIDbDCCA1SgAwIBAgIETI9R2zANBgkqhkiG9w0BAQsFADCBhzEtMCsGA1UELhMk
Yzc1MDA2MzktNDJhMi00MmI2LWI3ZTUtMWI0NDAwN2YzMTJhMTMwMQYDVQQDEypH
```

Download server-ca.pem
```
-----BEGIN CERTIFICATE-----
MIIDfzCCAmegAwIBAgIBADANBgkqhkiG9w0BAQsFADB3MS0wKwYDVQQuEyR1MDJ1
OGQzMi02N2E5LTQzZTQtOGJhMS02MGN1NzQxODEyMWIxIzAhBgNVBAMTGkdvb2ds
```

Figure 4-11. *New SSL Client Certificate and Private Key created*

Download the files as *client-key.pem* and *client-cert.pem*. Upload all the *.pem* files to the client environment. Use the below command to check connectivity to your instance

```
  mysql -uroot -p -h 35.226.72.252 --ssl-ca=server-ca.pem --ssl-
cert=client-cert.pem
  --ssl-key=client-key.pem
```

35.226.72.252 is our CloudSQL public IP. On successful connectivity MySQL prompt will be displayed as shown below.

```
adminuser@airo0002:~$ mysql -uroot -p -h 35.224.169.212 --ssl-ca=./SSL/server-
ca.pem --ssl-cert=./SSL/client-cert.pem --ssl-key=./SSL/client-key.pem
Enter password:
Welcome to the MySQL monitor.  Commands end with ; or \g.
Your MySQL connection id is 578
Server version: 5.7.14-google-log (Google)

Copyright (c) 2000, 2019, Oracle and/or its affiliates. All rights reserved.

Oracle is a registered trademark of Oracle Corporation and/or its
affiliates. Other names may be trademarks of their respective
owners.

Type 'help;' or '\h' for help. Type '\c' to clear the current input statement.

mysql>
```

In order to verify that the connection is encrypted, use the command SHOW STATUS, the output of the command is as follows. It displays the algorithm used for encryption.

```
mysql> SHOW STATUS LIKE 'Ssl_cipher';
+---------------+------------+
| Variable_name | Value      |
+---------------+------------+
| Ssl_cipher    | AES256-SHA |
+---------------+------------+
1 row in set (0.27 sec)
```

Also note, if SSL is enabled on the CloudSQL instance and when we try to connect to the instance without specifying the certificates, it will not let us connect to the instance. We can validate using the command

```
mysql -uroot -p -h 35.226.72.252
```

The output will be as follows

```
adminuser@airo0002:~$ mysql -uroot -p -h 35.224.169.212
Enter password:
ERROR 1045 (28000): Access denied for user 'root'@'192.8.160.188' (using password: YES)
adminuser@airo0002:~$
```

Though authorized networks with SSL encryption provide a secure method for establishing connection however this model will not fit very well if we have a dynamic environment.

Such environments have no static IPs available, they are dynamic in nature, clients may live for a short period and the environment may rapidly scale to large numbers.

In order to address this CloudSQL provides the ***Cloud SQL proxy***. The Cloud SQL Proxy provides secure access without having to authorize (whitelist) individual IP addresses of the instances. It doesn't even require SSL configuration.

Cloud Proxy

Cloud proxy is a preferable option to securely connect to your Cloud SQL instance, no matter from where it is accessed. Security and easier connection management are general features of proxies.

- **Secure connections**: The proxies help shield the real IP addresses of your instances. It automatically encrypts traffic to and from the database.

- **Easier connection management**: Proxy handles the authentication with Google Cloud SQL, removing the need to provide static IP addresses for authorizing the network.

Let's take a very quick look at how a cloud proxy works. Figure 4-12 illustrates how a client application running on a client machine communicates with Cloud SQL via a TCP secure tunnel.

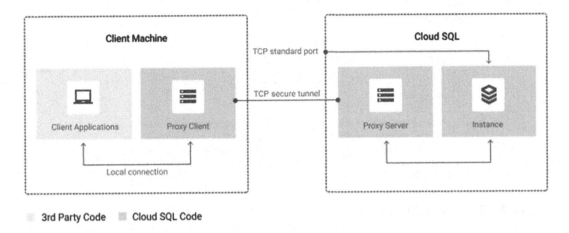

3rd Party Code   Cloud SQL Code

Figure 4-12.   Cloud Proxy Communication

The Cloud SQL proxy works by having a proxy client running on the client machine in the local environment. The client application communicates with the proxy client using standard database protocol e.g. JDBC/ODBC. The client does not directly talk to CloudSQL as a result bringing in great deal of additional security. The proxy client in turn uses a secure TCP tunnel to communicate to the CloudSQL.

While setting up the proxy on client we need to provide details of the proxy server. We also need to specify where to find the credentials which will be used to authenticate the client applications. We have covered all the steps required for connecting using Cloud Proxy in the previous chapter.

In the above examples we chose Public IP addresses and Cloud Proxy to connect to our CloudSQL instance. In addition to the above two options Google also has Private Networking connectivity option. Private network also termed as Virtual Private Cloud (VPC) enables much easier, faster and secure connection to CloudSQL.

Private IP Address

For connectivity using Private IP Addresses we have to select Private IP option from the Connections Tab. Figure 4-13 shows the *Connectivity* section underneath the Connections Tab.

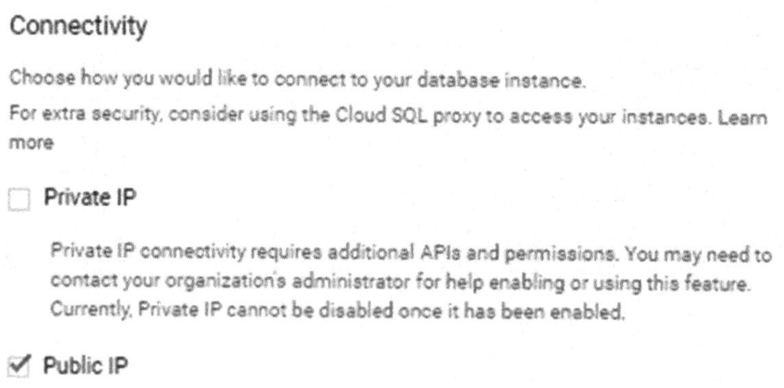

Connectivity

Choose how you would like to connect to your database instance.

For extra security, consider using the Cloud SQL proxy to access your instances. Learn more

☐ Private IP

Private IP connectivity requires additional APIs and permissions. You may need to contact your organization's administrator for help enabling or using this feature. Currently, Private IP cannot be disabled once it has been enabled.

☑ Public IP

Figure 4-13. *Enable Private IP*

Select Private IP. For Private IP enablement CloudSQL requires the Service Networking API to be enabled. Selecting Private IP prompts the pop up as shown in Figure 4-14. Select Enable API button.

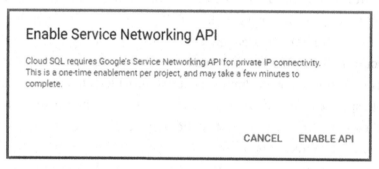

Figure 4-14. *Enable Service Networking API*

Within few seconds the API will be enabled and we will be prompted to select the network for which we need to enable the private connection as shown in Figure 4-15.

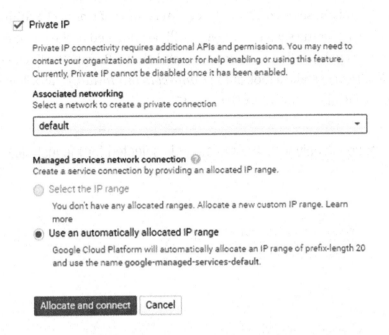

☑ Private IP

Private IP connectivity requires additional APIs and permissions. You may need to
contact your organization's administrator for help enabling or using this feature.
Currently, Private IP cannot be disabled once it has been enabled.

Associated networking
Select a network to create a private connection

default ▾

Managed services network connection ⓘ
Create a service connection by providing an allocated IP range.

○ Select the IP range
    You don't have any allocated ranges. Allocate a new custom IP range. Learn
    more

◉ Use an automatically allocated IP range
    Google Cloud Platform will automatically allocate an IP range of prefix-length 20
    and use the name google-managed-services-default.

Allocate and connect   Cancel

Figure 4-15. *Associate Network and Allocate IP*

New Networks can be created using the Networking Section from the Left Navigation
Menu as shown in Figure 4-16.

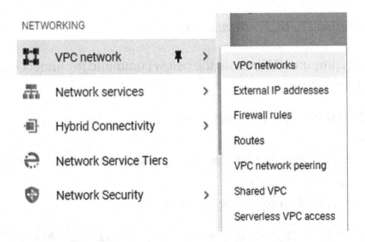

NETWORKING

VPC network   📌   >   VPC networks

Network services   >   External IP addresses

Hybrid Connectivity   >   Firewall rules

Network Service Tiers   Routes

Network Security   >   VPC network peering

                              Shared VPC

                              Serverless VPC access

Figure 4-16. *VPC Network Menu*

Note   Creation of the network is not in scope of this book.

We leave the default selection and Click on *Allocate and Connect*. Within few seconds a Private IP for the selected network will be allocated to the instance. Click *Save* for the details to be updated. In order to validate the Private IP allocated. Navigate to the *Overview* Tab and take a look at the *Connect to this instance* card. The Private IP allocated will be visible as shown in Figure 4-17.

Note   this option is only visible if private IP is selected for the instance.

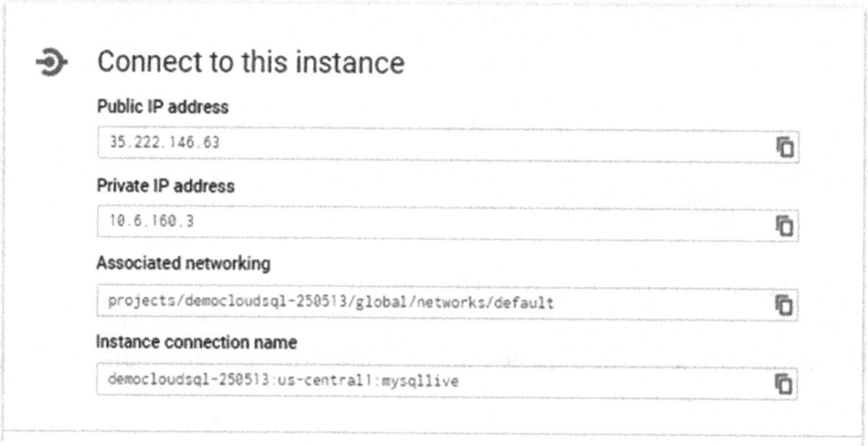

Figure 4-17.   *Connect to this instance card*

Login to your compute VM and use the below command to connect to the CloudSQL instance using Private IP.

```
architectbigdata@instance-1:~$ mysql -h 10.6.160.3 -u root -p
Enter password:
Welcome to the MySQL monitor. Commands end with ; or \g.
Your MySQL connection id is 40
Server version: 5.7.14-google-log (Google)

Copyright (c) 2000, 2019, Oracle and/or its affiliates. All rights
reserved.

Oracle is a registered trademark of Oracle Corporation and/or
itsaffiliates. Other names may be trademarks of their respective owners.
```

```
Type 'help;' or '\h' for help. Type '\c' to clear the current input
statement.

mysql>
```

That's all to it. In effect this option enables connectivity to the CloudSQL instance using GCP VPC which further facilitates private communication to our CloudSQL instance. Private IP has the following advantages as compared to Public IP and Cloud Proxy

- Enhanced Network Security as the instance is no longer exposed to the outside world.

- Reduced Network Latency

Authorization

With the access part handled it' also important to determine the control the user has on your instance. This control is divided further into

- instance management e.g. start/stop/create database etc. and

- data management e.g. ability to insert, delete, select data.

The first is controlled via the ***GCP IAM*** access control and the other is controlled via the database engine user creation. Let's first look at the IAM access control.

IAM is the identity and access management service of GCP which enables us to control actions on our resources e.g. our CloudSQL instance.

Let's begin with looking at the way we can grant instance access to a resource. Navigate to IAM in the Left Navigation panel as shown in Figure 4-18.

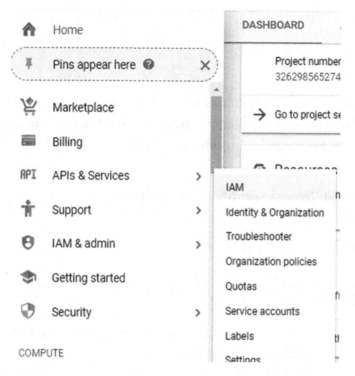

Figure 4-18. *IAM*

This takes us to a page shown in Figure 4-19 where all users of our project is listed.

Figure 4-19. *IAM Console*

We can either edit permissions of an existing user or add new user with defined roles. To edit a user access, click on *edit* icon next to its name. This opens a page as shown in Figure 4-20.

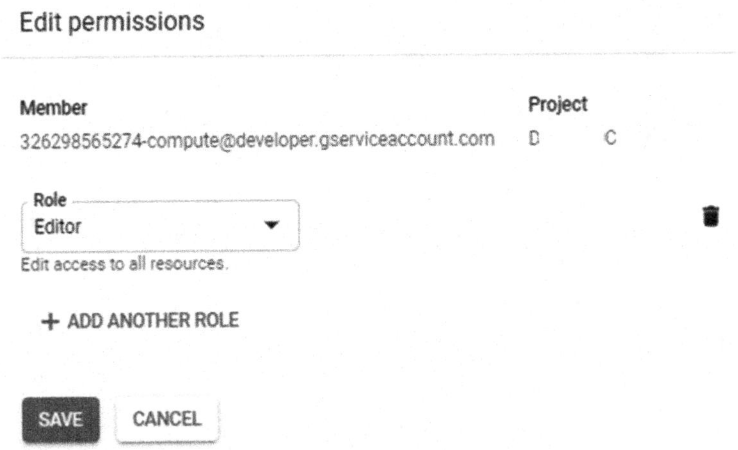

Edit permissions

Member   **Project**

326298565274-compute@developer.gserviceaccount.com   D   C

┌─ Role ─────────────────────────────────┐
│ Editor   ▼ │   🗑
└───┘
Edit access to all resources.

+ ADD ANOTHER ROLE

[SAVE]   [CANCEL]

Figure 4-20. *Edit Permission*

We can either delete the role assigned by clicking on the *delete* icon next to the role or change the role from the dropdown or add additional role to the user by clicking on *Add Another Role*. Figure 4-21 shows the roles displayed on click on the Role dropdown.

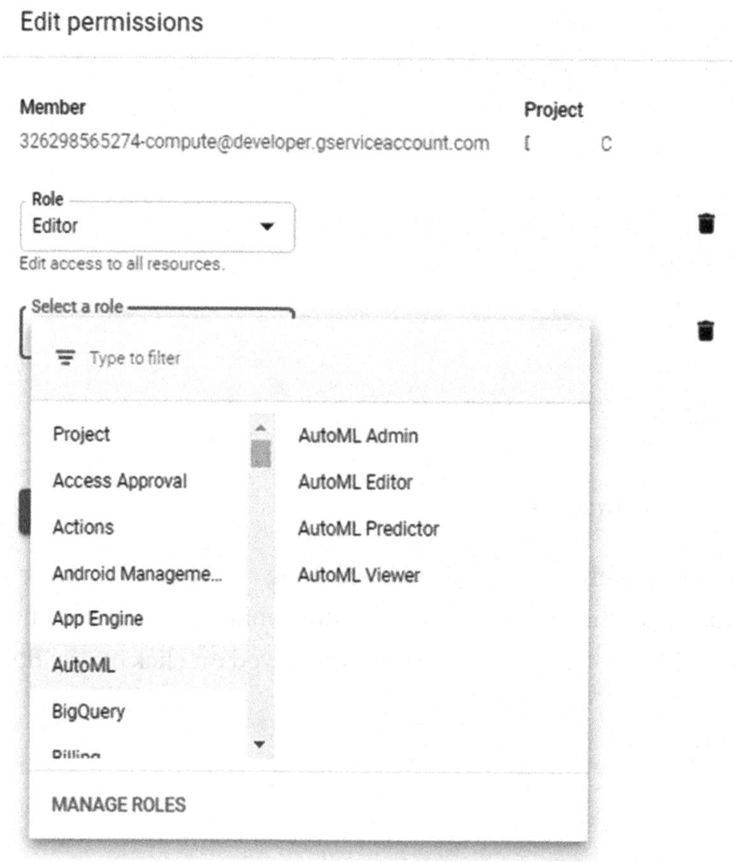

Edit permissions

Member   **Project**

326298565274-compute@developer.gserviceaccount.com   [C

Role
Editor   ▼   🗑
Edit access to all resources.

Select a role   🗑

⩸ Type to filter

Project	▲	AutoML Admin
Access Approval		AutoML Editor
Actions		AutoML Predictor
Android Manageme...		AutoML Viewer
App Engine		
AutoML		
BigQuery		
Billing	▼	

MANAGE ROLES

Figure 4-21. *Available Roles*

Figure 4-22 shows the SQL options available.

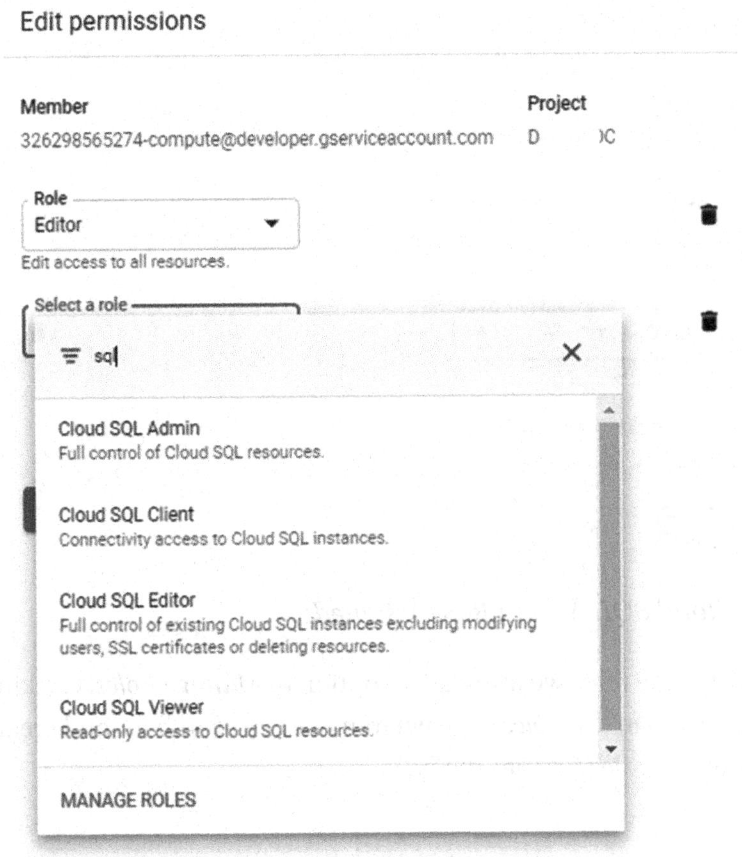

Figure 4-22. Cloud SQL Roles

Select the role. For this example, we chose *CloudSQLAdmin* role as shown in Figure 4-23. Click on *Save* for the permissions to be effective.

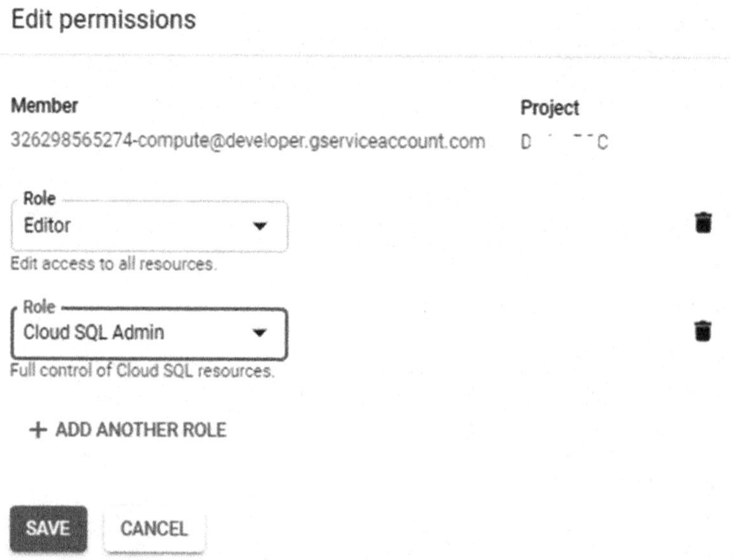

Edit permissions

Member

326298565274-compute@developer.gserviceaccount.com

Project

D ˙ ˉ ˉ C

Role

Editor ▼

Edit access to all resources.

🗑

Role

Cloud SQL Admin ▼

Full control of Cloud SQL resources.

🗑

＋ ADD ANOTHER ROLE

SAVE   CANCEL

Figure 4-23. *Cloud SQL Admin Role Assigned*

While choosing the roles we also had an option to *Manage Roles*. Clicking on *Manage Roles* takes us to the *Roles* page wherein we can search for and create new roles. Figure 4-24 shows the roles for CloudSQL.

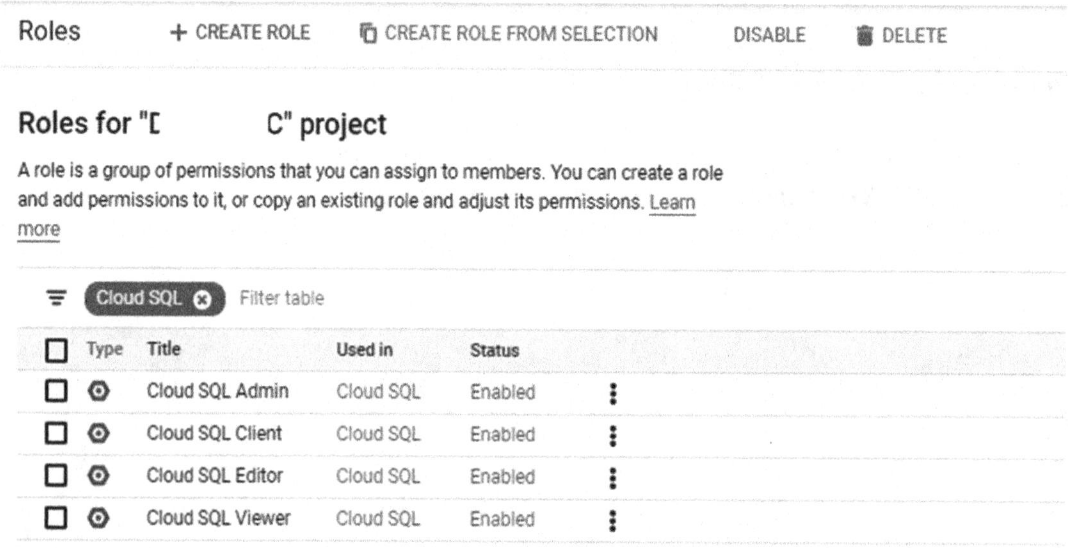

Roles   ＋ CREATE ROLE   🗐 CREATE ROLE FROM SELECTION   DISABLE   🗑 DELETE

Roles for "[C" project

A role is a group of permissions that you can assign to members. You can create a role and add permissions to it, or copy an existing role and adjust its permissions. Learn more

▼ Cloud SQL ✖ Filter table

	Type	Title	Used in	Status	
☐	⊙	Cloud SQL Admin	Cloud SQL	Enabled	⋮
☐	⊙	Cloud SQL Client	Cloud SQL	Enabled	⋮
☐	⊙	Cloud SQL Editor	Cloud SQL	Enabled	⋮
☐	⊙	Cloud SQL Viewer	Cloud SQL	Enabled	⋮

Figure 4-24. *Manage Roles View – CloudSQL Roles*

We can click on *Create Role* to merge permissions together and create roles. More on IAM access management can be referred in the Project Access Control in GCP documentation[1]. Figure 4-25 shows the screen which enables us to add a new user and grant permissions to the user.

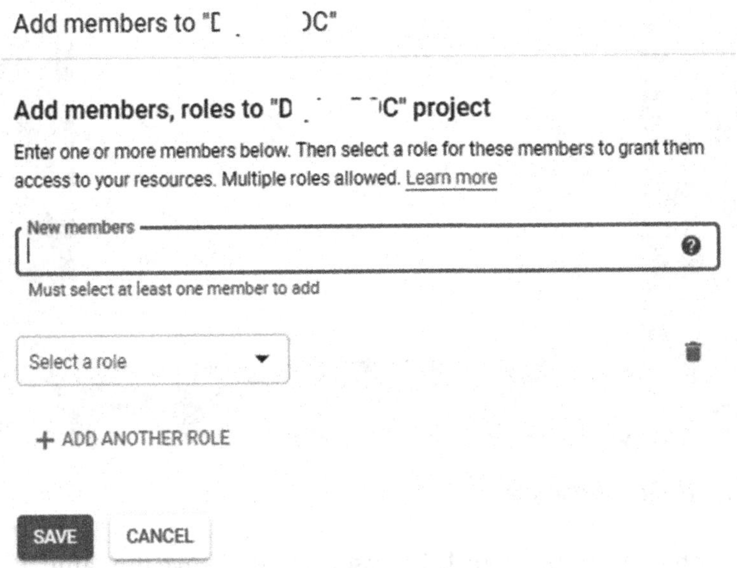

Add members to "D   )C"

Add members, roles to "D   C" project

Enter one or more members below. Then select a role for these members to grant them access to your resources. Multiple roles allowed. Learn more

New members

Must select at least one member to add

Select a role ▼

🗑

✛ ADD ANOTHER ROLE

SAVE   CANCEL

Figure 4-25. *Add new user*

In the name enter the name of the member and select the role like we did while editing. Click on *Save* to add the user with the permissions enabled.

With the IAM access controlled let's next look at the database users. Database users are created to control the access on the instance data and the operations a user can perform on the data. Navigate to the Instance detail page and click on *Users* Tab. This lists the default user created with the instance. Click on *Create User Account*. This takes us to screen as shown in Figure 4-26.

---

[1]https://cloud.google.com/sql/docs/mysql/project-access-control

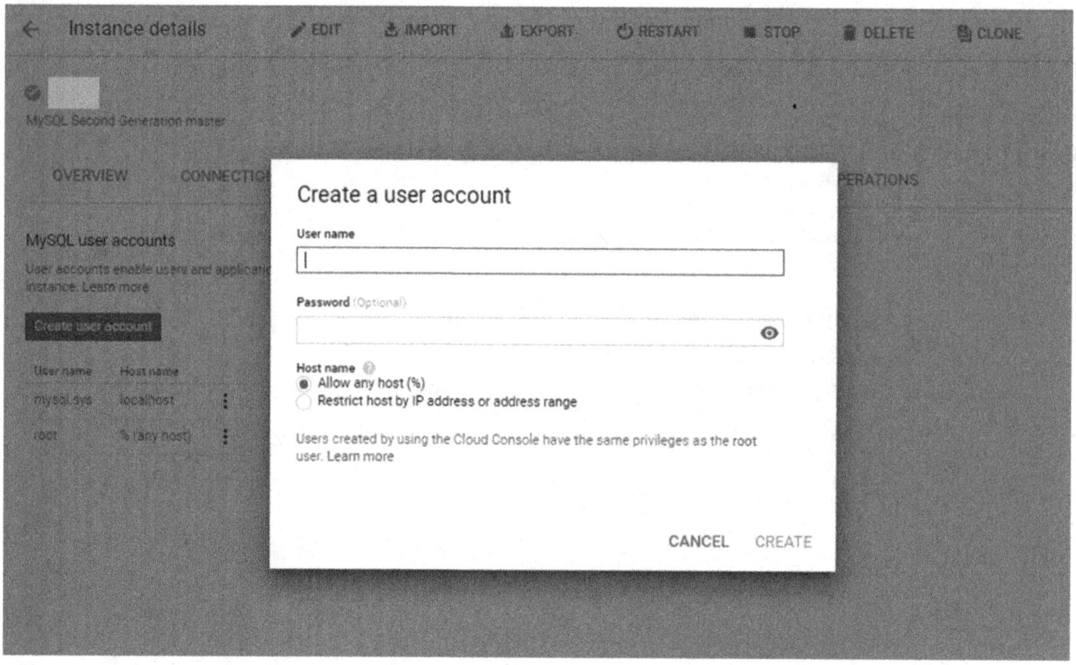

Figure 4-26. *Add Database User*

Enter the user name and password. The users created have the same privileges as the default user. To manage the access we will have to use *GRANT/REVOKE* in case of MySQL[2] and *ALTER ROLE* in case of Postgres.[3] As an admin it's important for us to provide granular controls on actions a user can perform on our instance.

With the access and authorization part handled, the next important activity is to ensure that at any point in time if our database becomes inconsistent because of accidental update or delete we are able to get our database back to a stable state.

Backups and Restores

In database world the backup & restore mechanism enables us to get our instance back to a stable state at a point in time. The trick is not in taking backups but in scheduling backups in such a way that we can restore to the latest stable data without much data loss.

---

[2]https://dev.mysql.com/doc/refman/5.7/en/access-control.html
[3]https://www.postgresql.org/docs/9.6/sql-alterrole.html

In CloudSQL automated daily backups are by default selected while provisioning the instance and they are scheduled to start in a defined period. We should change the time period which best suits our environment workload.

Navigate to the *Instance detail* page. Click on the *Backups* tab. It displays the Backup settings which was configured while creating the instance as shown in Figure 4-27.

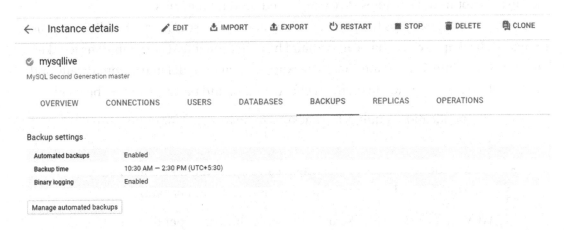

Figure 4-27. *Backups Tab*

Click *Manage automated backups* button, it opens a Pop-up as shown in Figure 4-28. Adjust the time as per your requirement.

Manage backups settings

Enabling backups protects your data from loss with minimal cost. Learn more

☑ Automate backups

| 10:30 AM — 2:30 PM | ▼ |

Choose a window for automated backups. May continue outside window until complete. Time is your local time (UTC+5:30).

Figure 4-28. *Manage Backups*

Note   The automated backups can be disabled as well. However, this is apt only when we are dealing with development environment and is not recommended in a live production environment.

Though the backups don't have any impact on write operations still it's best to choose off peak hours so that it doesn't overlap with users trying to modify data in the system.

CloudSQL retains the most recent seven automated backups per instance. These backups are incremental which means the oldest backup is a full backup and all the subsequent backups are incremental i.e. only the changed data from the previous backup are captured. This helps save storage required for backups.

The automated backups happen once daily at the time specified. In addition to this automated backup, we also have on demand backup available. This enables us to take backups at any time. Unlike automated backup these are not deleted automatically and persists till we manually delete them. In effect, on demand backups should be used if:

- Our application requires the backups to be retained for more than 7 days

- We are about to take actions which can impact the data consistency and stability and we cannot wait for the automated backup

- We want flexibility to take backups more than once per day.

Let's create on-demand backup for our *mysqllive* instance. Navigate to the instance detail page and click on the *Backups* Tab. Figure 4-29 shows the *Backups* Tab.

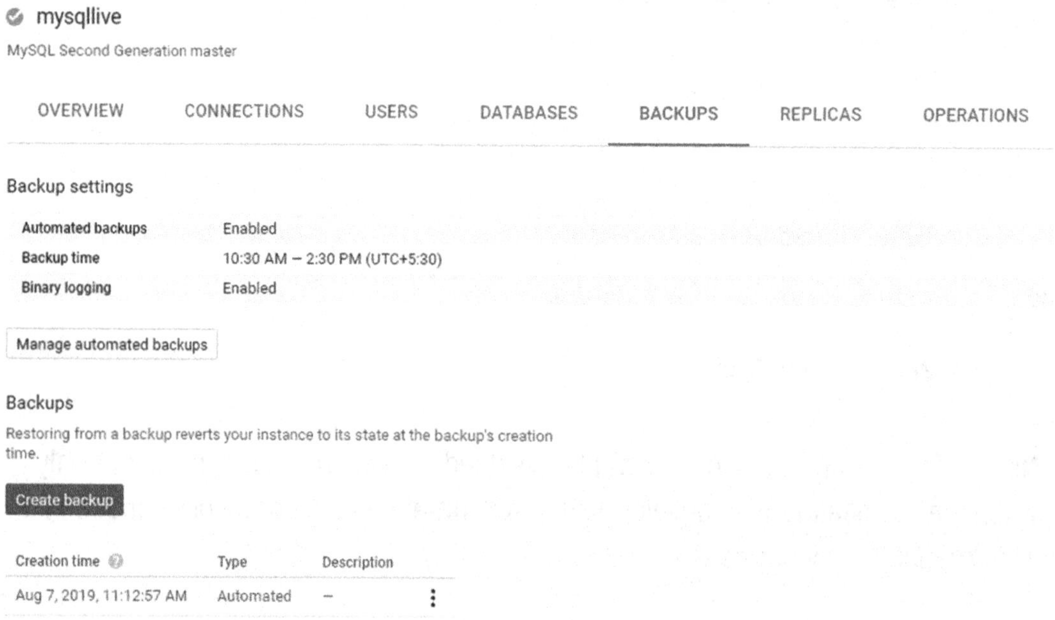

Figure 4-29. Backups Tab

Click on *Create backup* button. This opens a pop up, provide an optional description and click on *Create*. In few minutes the on-demand backup is ready and is displayed under the *Backups* tab as shown in Figure 4-30.

Figure 4-30. *On-demand Backup*

All the backups we create will be deleted when we delete the instance. CloudSQL stores the backup in two regions for redundancy to ensure safety against any disaster situations. However, if the region from where the backup was originally taken is unavailable, then we will not be able to restore from it. This limitation should be kept in mind while devising the backup and high availability strategy.

Now that we have looked at scheduling and taking backups, the next logical step is to restore the backup. In CloudSQL restoration is as simple as taking backups and involve few clicks. Navigate to the instance detail page, Click on Backups tab. This lists all the backups. Figure 4-31 lists the backups created for our instance.

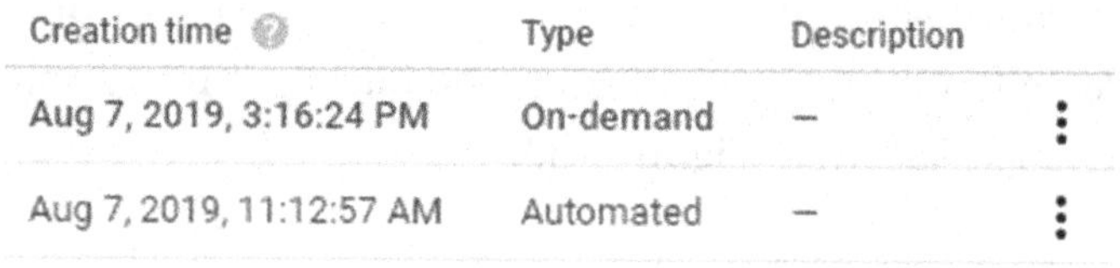

Creation time ⓘ	Type	Description	
Aug 7, 2019, 3:16:24 PM	On-demand	–	⋮
Aug 7, 2019, 11:12:57 AM	Automated	–	⋮

Figure 4-31. *Backup List*

Let's restore the On-demand backup. Click context menu next to the On-demand backup. Figure 4-32 shows the context menu options. Select restore option.

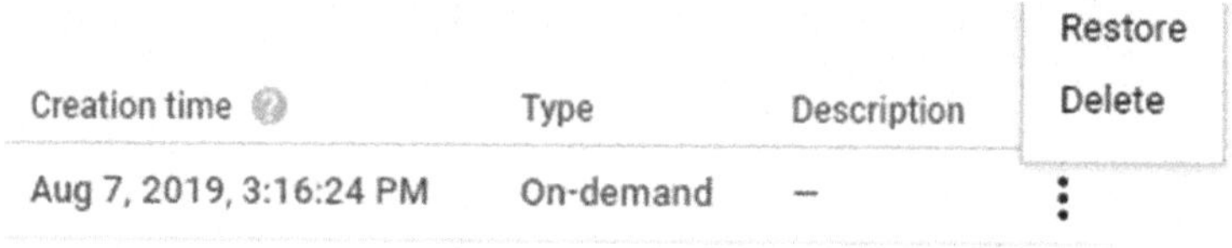

Creation time ⓘ	Type	Description	Restore
			Delete
Aug 7, 2019, 3:16:24 PM	On-demand	–	⋮

Figure 4-32. *Backup's Context Menu Options*

This opens the Restoration pop-up as shown in Figure 4-33 prompting us to specify the target instance. Restoration can be on the same instance from where the backup was taken or it can be altogether a new instance as well. Select the instance and click Ok.

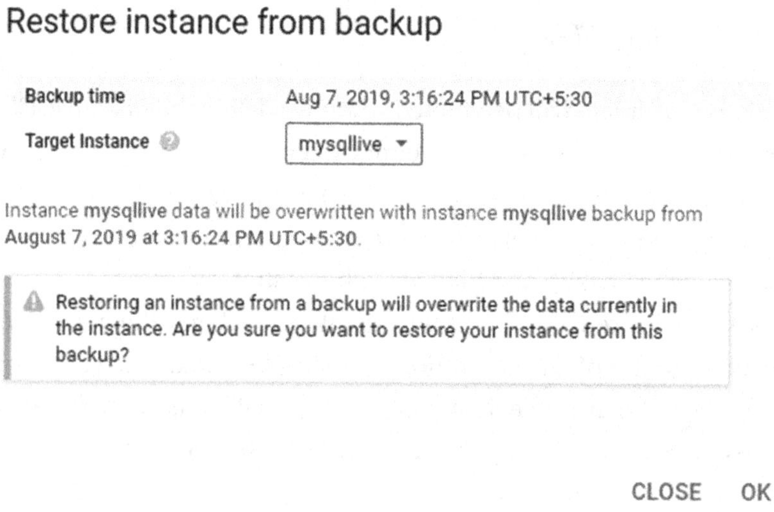

Restore instance from backup

Backup time	Aug 7, 2019, 3:16:24 PM UTC+5:30
Target Instance ⓘ	mysqllive ▾

Instance **mysqllive** data will be overwritten with instance **mysqllive** backup from August 7, 2019 at 3:16:24 PM UTC+5:30.

> ⚠ Restoring an instance from a backup will overwrite the data currently in the instance. Are you sure you want to restore your instance from this backup?

CLOSE   OK

Figure 4-33. *Specify Target Instance to be restored*

Note that while restoration is in progress the target instance remains unavailable. Within few minutes the data is restored back and the instance becomes available.

CloudSQL MySQL - Binary Logging

Binary logging is an option which is by default enabled along with automated backups while provisioning CloudSQL – MySQL instance. Binary logging records every data modification operation in an independent log post the last stable backup.

This will be helpful in situations where we accidently end up modifying some critical information. We can use the last stable backup and the log file coordinates till that operation to restore the data back to the state prior to the operation.

It is recommended to keep it on if the application deals with lots of data operations as it will be extremely helpful to restore the state back to a specific point in time. However, we need to note that since binary logging logs all operations, it impacts the write performance.

Like backups the Manage automated backup settings can be used to enable or disable binary logging. Figure 4-34 shows the binary logging enablement option.

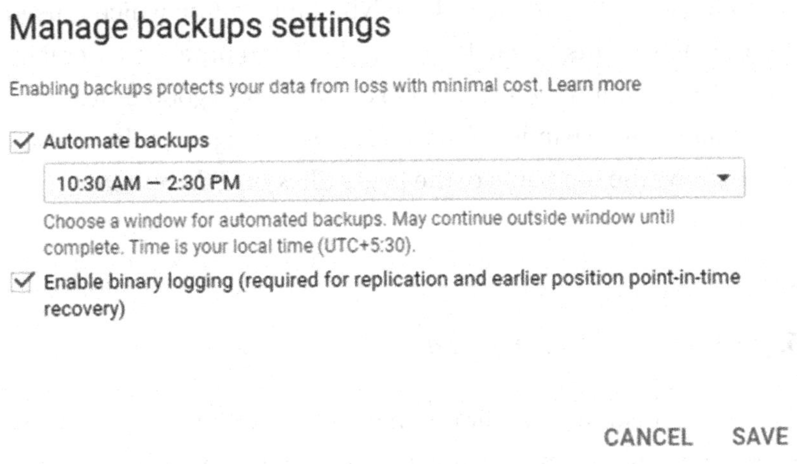

Manage backups settings

Enabling backups protects your data from loss with minimal cost. Learn more

☑ Automate backups

10:30 AM — 2:30 PM ▼

Choose a window for automated backups. May continue outside window until complete. Time is your local time (UTC+5:30).

☑ Enable binary logging (required for replication and earlier position point-in-time recovery)

CANCEL   SAVE

Figure 4-34. *Binary Logging Option*

This change restarts the instance, so a few minutes' downtime should be expected when changing this configuration.

Note   Automated backup should be enabled for enabling binary logging.

Database restores using the binary logging differ from restoring from a backup. A point in time recovery creates a new instance with the recovered data. While restoring

155

we choose the stable backup and specify the binary log file name and the position of the event till which we want to recover. If we don't specify the coordinates, then the instance is recovered up to the latest binary log coordinates.

With backups enabled and scheduled, let's next look at maintenance for our instance. Maintenance is important for proper functioning of the instance. It involves tasks such as applying security patches, upgrading the instance to newer releases so that the known bugs and issues are fixed.

Maintenance

CloudSQL handles the maintenance activities for us. It's scheduled to run any day any time by default when an instance is provisioned. We should set the maintenance window to day and time when it's acceptable to carry out the maintenance activities, so that the end users of our application are not impacted.

E.g. if the application is Reporting and Analytics application which is used by business users, then late nights on weekend start is a good time, however if it is a social networking kind of application then early weekdays will be a good time.

Let's set the maintenance window for *mysqldblive*. Navigate to the instance detail page. Figure 4-35 shows the top panel of the page. Click on *Edit* button.

Figure 4-35. *Instance details Top panel*

This takes us to the instance configuration page. Click on *Set maintenance schedule*. Figure 4-36 shows the default configurations for maintenance schedule.

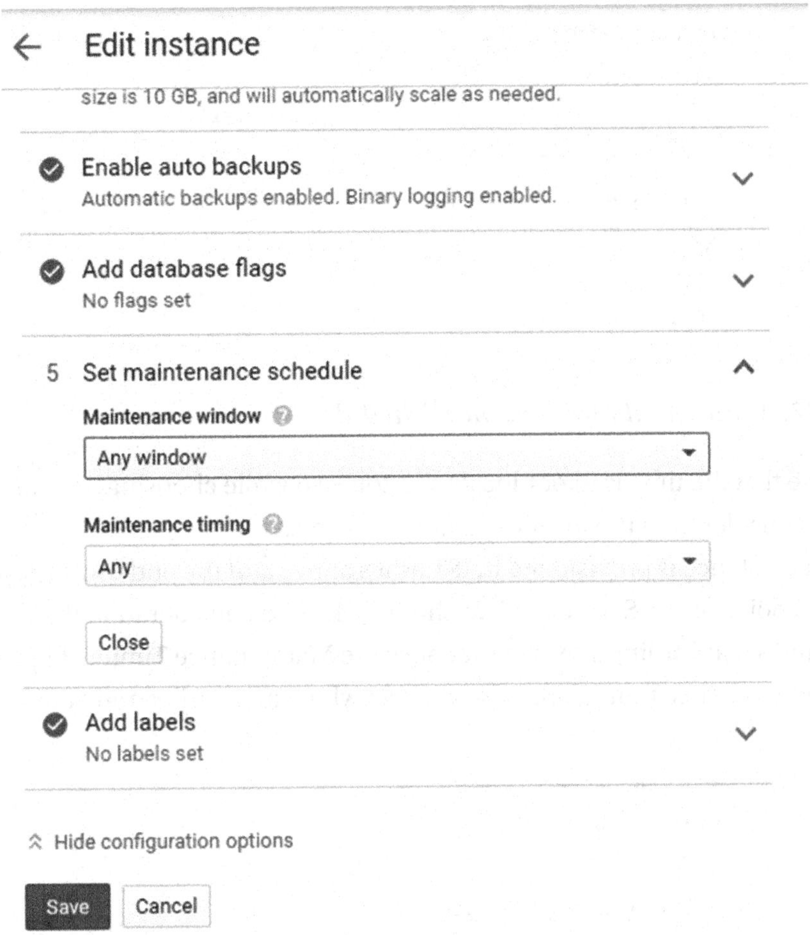

← **Edit instance**

size is 10 GB, and will automatically scale as needed.

✓ **Enable auto backups**
Automatic backups enabled. Binary logging enabled.

✓ **Add database flags**
No flags set

5   Set maintenance schedule

Maintenance window ❓
```
Any window                                    ▼
```

Maintenance timing ❓
```
Any                                           ▼
```

Close

✓ **Add labels**
No labels set

≫ Hide configuration options

Save   Cancel

Figure 4-36. *Set Maintenance Schedule*

First choose day of the week from Maintenance Window dropdown. This prompts to specify the time period. As mentioned above we should choose the window which suits our application workload. For this example, we choose Saturday, between midnight 12:00 AM – 1:00 AM. Figure 4-37 shows the configurations done.

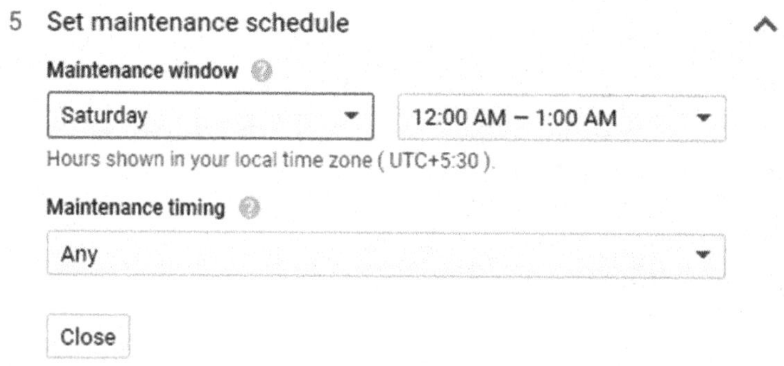

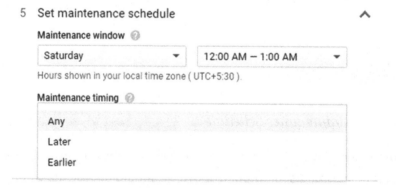

Figure 4-37. *Configured Maintenance Schedule*

Also note that the time is in our local time zone, so while choosing the time we need to take into consideration the location of our end users.

E.g. if the instance is provisioned in IST as it's above and the end users are located in US then the choice of late Saturday night should take into consideration the time zone difference and set accordingly. Next we choose the Maintenance Timing. Figure 4-38 shows the maintenance timing options available which are: Earlier and Later.

Figure 4-38. *Maintenance Timing Options*

This decides the time when the upgrades will be applied, as soon as a new release happens (earlier) or with delay (later). For this example, we choose later, which is also a recommended option.

With the selections in place, let's click on Save. This updates the schedule. It can be verified in the Maintenance Card in Overview tab of the instance detail page. Figure 4-39 shows the maintenance card.

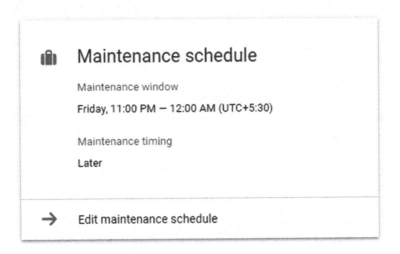

Figure 4-39. *Maintenance Card*

With the schedule set, Google takes care of the rest. With connections secured, backups and maintenance scheduled, let's look at managing resources.

As few of us might already be aware that as the load increases whether its data or end users accessing our application, the instances start to show performance issues. We have to accordingly increase the resources (Vertical scaling) for maintaining optimal performance.

Managing Resources

In CloudSQL, the instance performance is driven by the following

- Instance Type which determines the Compute - CPU, memory

- Storage capacity – this determines the disk performance

Let's first begin with instance type. Navigate to the *Instance detail* page and click *Edit* in the top panel. It takes us to the instance configuration page. Select *Configure Machine Type and storage* option. Figure 4-40 shows the Configure Machine Type and Storage section. It shows the instance type which our instance is presently running on, we can see that we started a *db-n1-standard-1* instance type which is a single core machine. Let's click on *Change* and look at the instance types available.

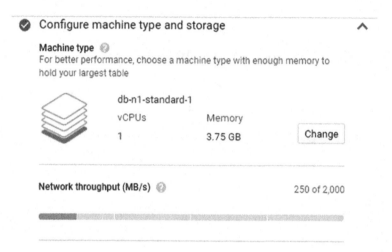

Figure 4-40. *Configure Machin Type and storage*

Figure 4-41 shows all the options available. The list is divided into three categories - Shared, Standard and High memory.

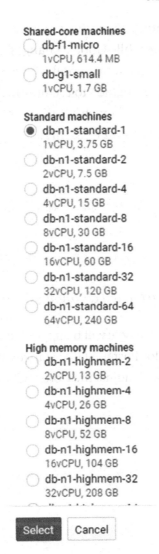

Figure 4-41. *Instance Type Options*

If our load increases (or decreases), we can choose to upgrade (or downgrade) to any of the available instance types in just a single click. The choice of the instance type will be completely dependent on your application workload.

E.g. For memory intensive applications, it's best to choose from high memory instances. These applications typically would pin a lot of data in memory so that the response time of returning results from the database is faster.

We can look at the variants *d1-n1-standard-4* and *d1-ni-highmem-4*. Though both have same cores, but they differ in the memory allocated.

Also note that this configuration change will require restart of the instance. In effect, we will have a minimal downtime while Google changes the resources of our instance. So, we should choose to upgrade in a time period which will have less impact on the end users. For this example, we simply upgrade to the next higher machine under standard – *db-n1-standard-2*, a two core standard machine. Click Select. This will show a prompt as shown in Figure 4-42. Click on *SAVE and RESTART*.

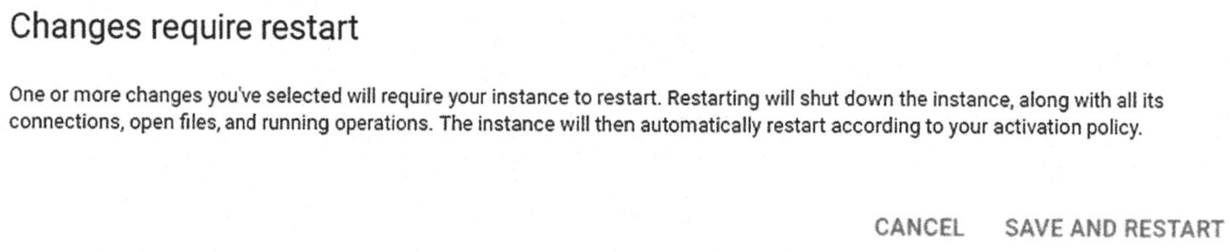

Changes require restart

One or more changes you've selected will require your instance to restart. Restarting will shut down the instance, along with all its connections, open files, and running operations. The instance will then automatically restart according to your activation policy.

CANCEL   SAVE AND RESTART

Figure 4-42. *Prompt for Restart when changing the instance type*

Within few minutes the instance type will be upgraded (or downgraded). Choice of instance type is slightly different for PostgreSQL instances, instead of a list of machine types, we have the knobs available to adjust the Core and memory as shown in Figure 4-43.

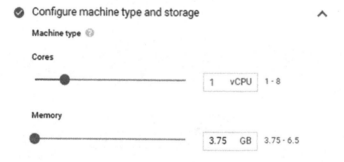

Figure 4-43. *PostgreSQL Instance Type Configuration Section*

We need to note that when we change the cores, memory is automatically changed to match the core settings, but the user can change it further to either increase or decrease as per the needs. The on demand and elasticity provided by cloud makes it a matter of few clicks to increase and decrease capacity. With the instance type upgraded, let's now look at the storage capacity. Figure 4-44 shows the choices available for Storage Capacity.

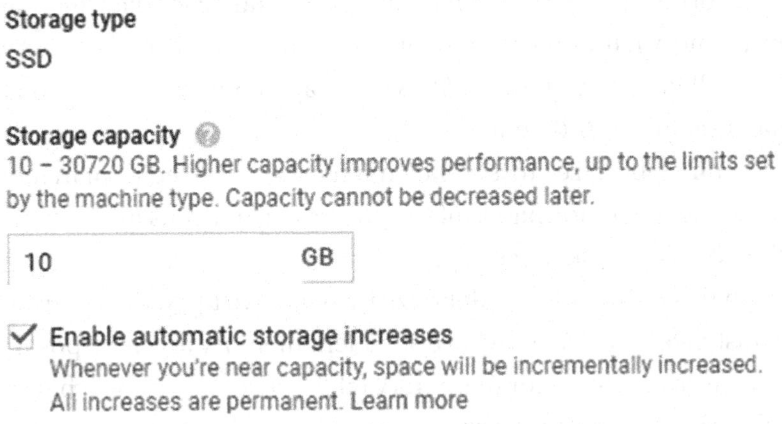

Storage type

SSD

Storage capacity ⓘ

10 – 30720 GB. Higher capacity improves performance, up to the limits set
by the machine type. Capacity cannot be decreased later.

10	GB

☑ **Enable automatic storage increases**
  Whenever you're near capacity, space will be incrementally increased.
  All increases are permanent. Learn more

Figure 4-44. *Storage Capacity Options*

By default, it is set to **10GB** and enabled for automatic storage increases to handle
the increase in data load.

In effect, in CloudSQL the probability of running into low disk space issue is rare as
it automatically increases the storage as we near the capacity. The growth factor is set to
indefinite i.e. there's no restriction.

However, as a best practice we should limit the growth. Because though increasing
the disk size is instantaneous (this change doesn't require any restart), going back is not
possible. If a temporary data fluctuation happens, we will end up with a large storage
capacity, then the actual requirement.

Though we don't require changing the disk size, however we need to note that the
size is proportional to the performance. Larger the disk size, better is the IOPS capacity
and fetches. So, if our application is doing frequent disk access then it's good to start with
a larger disk size for better disk performance.

To increase the disk size, just enter your desired size next to the storage capacity and
click save. The change is almost instantaneous as no restart is required.

As already mentioned while increasing the size is just few clicks, once increased we
will not be able to decrease the size. Keep this in mind while changing the capacity as
storage on cloud is charged on pay per use basis.

Now that we have an upgraded instance it doesn't imply that the database engine
will automatically tune to the changes. As with on-premises database, we will have
to tune the parameters to effectively utilize the resource increase for maximized
performance. Let's understand with an example.

We have a reporting application using *mysqllive* instance for data analysis. This ends up creating in-memory temporary tables for data processing. The in memory temporary table size is controlled by *max_heap_table_size* parameter of MySQL database engine. This is by default set to a 16 MB limit.

As the temporary table size crosses the limit it gets converted from in memory to on disk table, impacting the performance of the processing query as in memory processing is significantly faster than disk processing.

Let's say with this observation of data size increase, we upgrade the instance to a high memory instance type. Now we have sufficient memory at our disposal, but to reap benefit of this memory increase for temporary table processing we will have to tune the *max_heap_table_size* parameter. We choose to set it to 256 MB.

CloudSQL enables us to tune in our instance specific parameters using *Database* flags. Let's modify the *max_heap_table_size* parameter of *mysqllive*. Navigate again to *instance detail* page and click on *edit*. In the instance configuration page, expand the *Add Database Flag* section as shown in Figure 4-45.

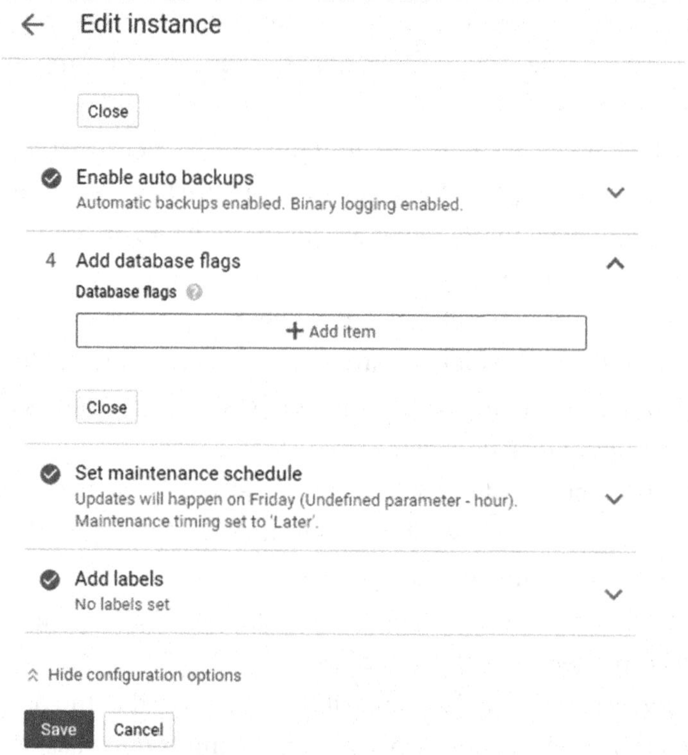

Figure 4-45. *Add Database Flags*

Click on *Add Item*. In the dropdown, search for *max_heap_table_size* and select the flag. With every flag selected, CloudSQL displays the possible value range. Figure 4-46 shows the value range for *max_heap_table_size* flag. Pay close attention to the units, here the size is to be specified in bytes.

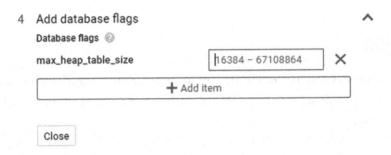

Figure 4-46. *Value range for max_heap_table_size database flag*

We choose a value in the range displayed and that's all to it. To add more, click on *Add Item* again. Once done setting all the flags, click on *Save*.

Like the instance type upgrade, this configuration change also requires instance restart. Figure 4-47 shows the prompt.

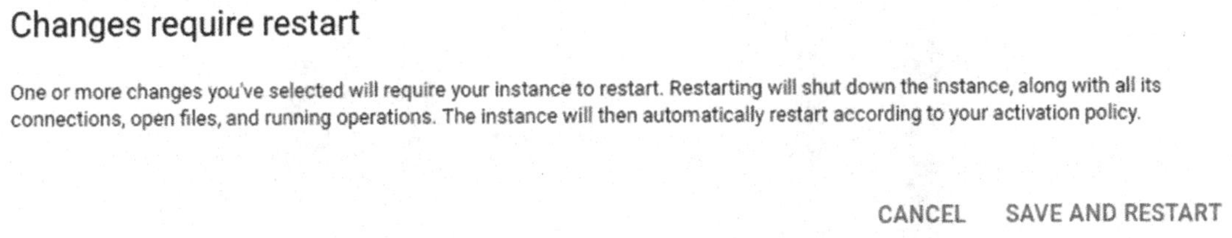

Changes require restart

One or more changes you've selected will require your instance to restart. Restarting will shut down the instance, along with all its connections, open files, and running operations. The instance will then automatically restart according to your activation policy.

CANCEL   SAVE AND RESTART

Figure 4-47. *Restart Prompt for Database Flag Configurations*

Click on *Save and Restart* and within few minutes the parameters are configured. An exhaustive list of parameters is already available in the respective database engine documentation sites.

Let's finally look at the most important activity, being highly available ensuring our instance is fault tolerant. Goal is to ensure that the instance continues to run and remain available despite component or service failures. This is extremely important if we are dealing with critical applications.

High Availability

Replication is the mechanism of replicating data across multiple instances ensuring data redundancy. This help alleviates system failures. In effect, replication enables highly available system. Let's look at replication in CloudSQL.

Replication

CloudSQL provides a clustered environment for replication comprising of a primary (or master) instance, a replica for fault tolerance and one or more read replicas. Let's first look at Read Replicas.

Read Replica

Read replica serves only Read requests to the client. It is a copy of the primary (or master) instance. It reflects changes to the primary instance in almost real time. The read replicas follow the primary (or master) instance to pull the updates. Figure 4-48 shows the process.

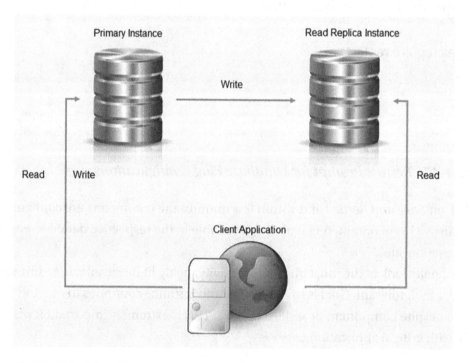

Figure 4-48. *Read Replicas*

MySQL Read Replicas sync with the Primary instance using asynchronous replication. In asynchronous replication the primary instance keeps writing the events to its binary log. But it does not track whether or when a replica has accessed and processed the events.

Note   Replication in MySQL expects binary logging to be enabled. Please refer to the section on binary logging for more details.

PostgreSQL Read Replicas use the PostgreSQL default replication methodology - write ahead log (WAL) shipping. Every transaction in PostgreSQL is written to a transaction log called WAL (write-ahead log) to achieve durability. A read replica uses these WAL segments to continuously replicate changes from its primary instance.

In effect in either of the database engine creating a read replica does not impact the performance of the primary instance as the operation doesn't have to wait for any acknowledgement from the read replicas.

Read Replicas can be used to horizontally scale our read loads and offload the read requests from the primary instance. If we have applications with more reads than writes, then turn on multiple read replica instances and route read traffic to these instances.

Fault Tolerance Replica

Replica for Fault tolerance is same as Read replica, however it's primary job is to be ready as a primary (or master) instance replacement, reducing downtime and ensuring the data continues to be available to client applications in case of any disaster e.g. either zone where the primary (or master) instance is located experiences an outage or the primary (or master) instance is unresponsive.

CloudSQL continuously checks the health of primary (or master) instance. If the instance becomes unresponsive, an automatic switch over happens to the standby fault tolerant replica for serving data. This entire process is called a failover. Let's first look at the failover process of MySQL database engine.

MySQL

In MySQL the replica for fault tolerance is called a Failover replica. Semisynchronous replication method is used to sync data between the primary instance and the failover replica. This means every write operation performed on the primary instance waits until the failover replica acknowledges that it has received and logged all events for the operations. This is to ensure that changes are never lost and the order of the operation is also maintained exactly replicating the primary instance. Using this log data, the failover replica then performs its updates. The HA enabled MySQL instance looks as shown in Figure 4-49.

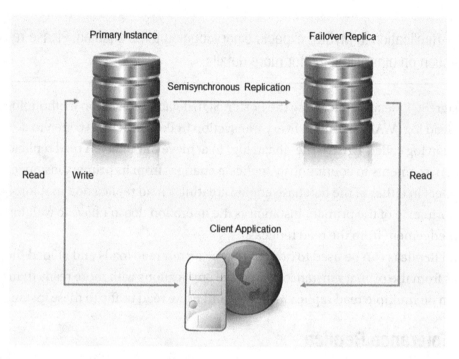

Figure 4-49. *HA Enabled MySQL Instance*

Let's look at the failover process. As we mentioned above the failover process will be initiated as the primary instance becomes unresponsive as shown in Figure 4-50.

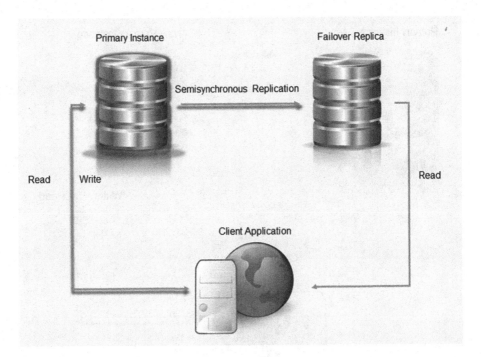

Figure 4-50. *Failover Initiated*

CloudSQL waits for the failover replica to catch up to the primary instance's state.

Note   This step is affected by replication lag. This is difference in time from when the primary instance makes an update to when the failover replica catches up with that update from its log. Replication lag should be acceptable to initiate the failover.

Once the failover replica catches up, it is promoted to the primary instance role i.e. the primary instance name and IP addresses are moved to the failover replica as shown in Figure 4-51. Doing this ensures that the client application can reconnect to the new primary instance without any change in the connection string.

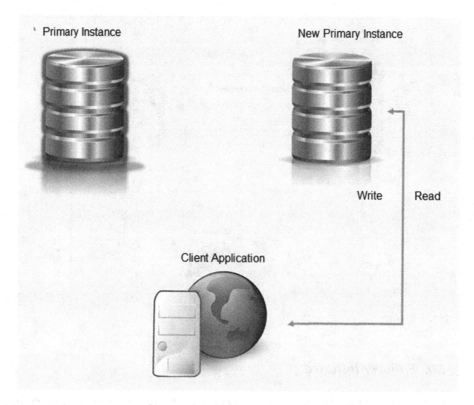

Figure 4-51. *Failover promoted as Primary*

In effect, from an application perspective there's no update required after failover. Only for some time during the failover the application won't be able to connect to the database. As the last step, CloudSQL recreates a failover replica in a healthy zone as shown in Figure 4-52.

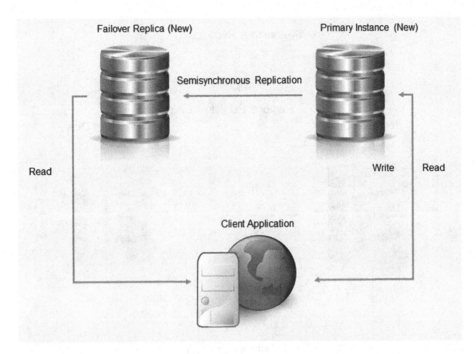

Figure 4-52. *New Failover replica created in the healthy zone*

Let's next look at the failover process of PostgreSQL database engine.

PostgreSQL

In PostgreSQL the HA enabled instance is referred to as regional instance and the replica for fault tolerance is called standby instance. The HA configuration is backed by Google's new Regional disks. Figure 4-53 shows the basic setup.

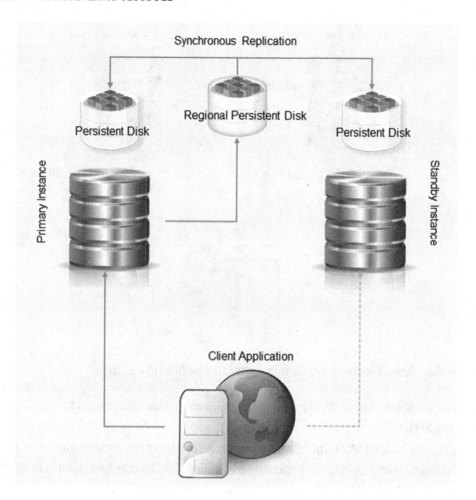

Figure 4-53. *HA enabled PostgreSQL instance*

As with MySQL, the failover process will be initiated as the primary instance becomes unresponsive. During failover the IP address and name of the primary instance is transferred to the standby instance and the instance is restarted. After failover, connected application resumes connection to the new primary instance without noticing any change as the connection details remains the same. Let's now enable high availability.

Enable High Availability

Navigate to instances page. Figure 4-54 shows the instances page. We can see *Add* in the High Availability column.

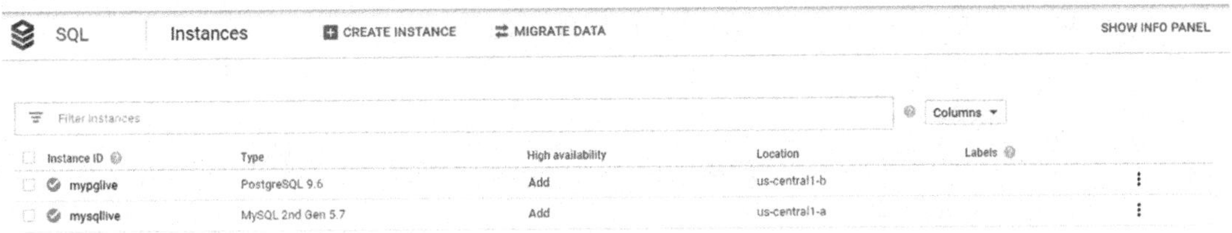

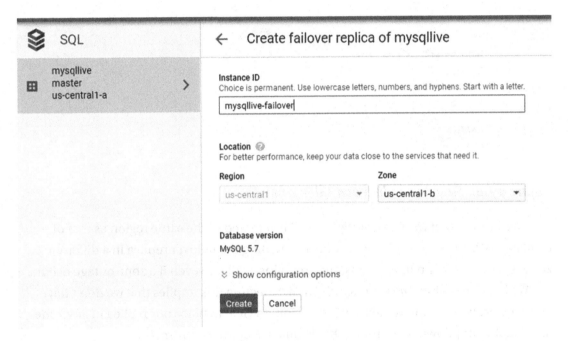

Figure 4-54. *Instances page*

Click on *Add* next to *mysqllive*. This takes us to the form shown in Figure 4-55 where we create the failover replica.

Figure 4-55. *Create Failover Replica*

As with Instance provisioning, we need to provide the instance id. For this example, we retain the default which comes auto populated. Next we need to specify where the instance is to be located. Notice that though it enables us to choose a zone, but the region is disabled. Figure 4-56 shows the available zones. Note that the zones listed omits the primary instance zone.

Figure 4-56. *Failover replica available zones*

This implies that the failover replica will be created in the same region as that of primary instance but in a different zone. By creating the failover replica in a different zone we can be certain that our instance remains available even if a zone outage occurs.

We have an option *Any* in zone selection. Selecting this implies that we don't have any zone preference and we leave the decision on GCP to place our replica in any zone listed in the dropdown. Let's retain the default selection *us-central1-b*.

The remaining parameters come configured as that of the primary instance. Since the prime responsibility of this instance is to act as a standby for the primary instance, we retain all the configurations as is and click on Create.

Within few minutes the instance is provisioned. The failover replica will be configured with the same configuration as the primary instance. Once provisioned it appear under the primary instance as shown in Figure 4-57.

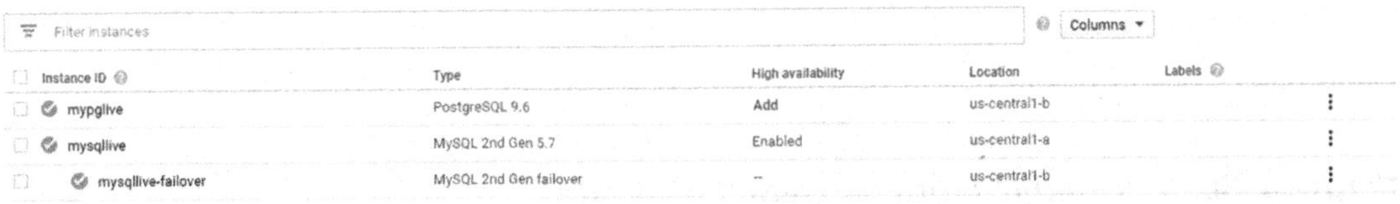

Instance ID	Type	High availability	Location	Labels
mypgllive	PostgreSQL 9.6	Add	us-central1-b	
mysqllive	MySQL 2nd Gen 5.7	Enabled	us-central1-a	
mysqllive-failover	MySQL 2nd Gen failover	--	us-central1-b	

Figure 4-57. *Failover replica listed*

It will be displayed in the left panel of the instance detail page as well as shown in Figure 4-58.

Figure 4-58. *Left Panel of the Instance detail page listing the failover replica*

Let's also look at enabling HA for a PostgreSQL instance. Like with MySQL instance, click on Add in the High Availability column next to the PostgreSQL instance in the instances page. It just prompts like Figure 4-59 to enable high availability.

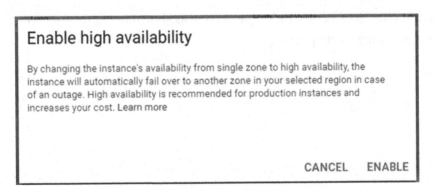

Figure 4-59. *PostgreSQL Enable HA Prompt*

Click *Enable* and High Availability is enabled as shown in Figure 4-60.

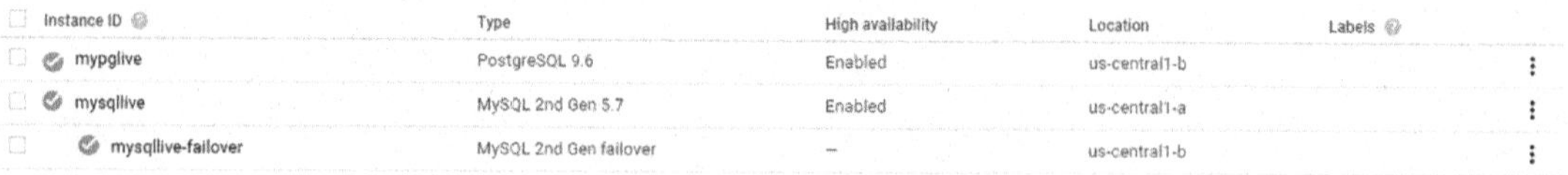

Instance ID	Type	High availability	Location	Labels
☐ ✅ mypglive	PostgreSQL 9.6	Enabled	us-central1-b	⋮
☐ ✅ mysqllive	MySQL 2nd Gen 5.7	Enabled	us-central1-a	⋮
☐ ✅ mysqllive-failover	MySQL 2nd Gen failover	–	us-central1-b	⋮

Figure 4-60. *HA enabled for PostgreSQL instance*

As is seen, unlike MySQL there's no separate instance provisioning being done. Let's next create Read replicas.

Read Replicas

Navigate to the instances page. Click on the Contextual menu next to *mysqllive* instance. Figure 4-61 shows the available options. Let's choose Create Read Replica.

Figure 4-61. *Contextual Menu for Read Replica creation*

This takes us to the Create Read Replica page as shown in Figure 4-62. This is similar to the failover replica create page.

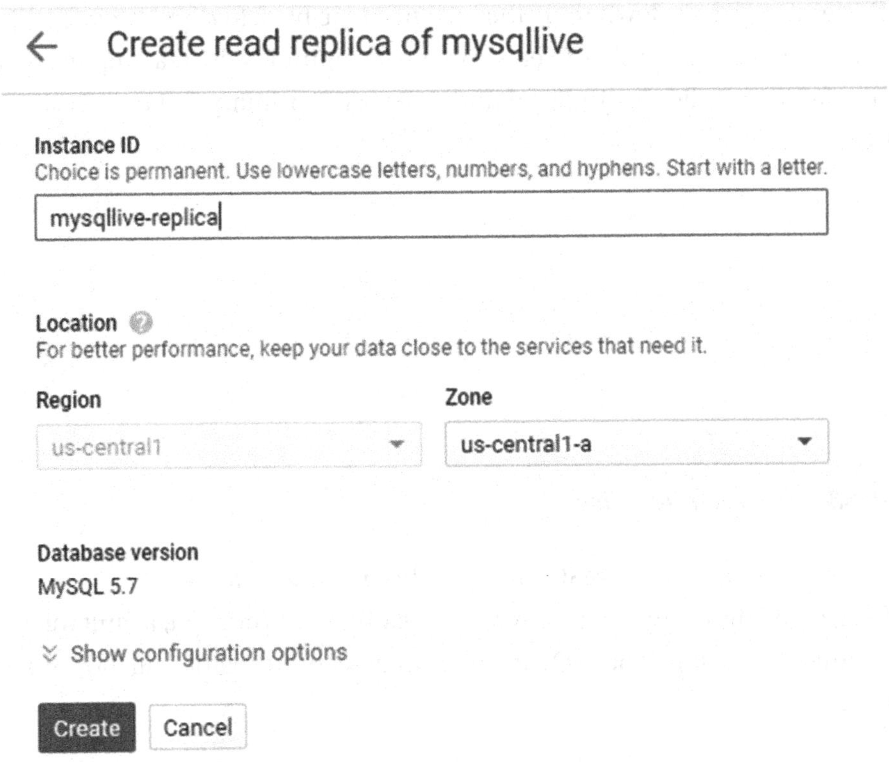

← **Create read replica of mysqllive**

Instance ID
Choice is permanent. Use lowercase letters, numbers, and hyphens. Start with a letter.

mysqllive-replica

Location ⓘ
For better performance, keep your data close to the services that need it.

Region

us-central1 ▾

Zone

us-central1-a ▾

Database version
MySQL 5.7

⌄ Show configuration options

Create   Cancel

Figure 4-62.   *Create Read Replica Page*

First we have to specify the Instance Id. As with Failover replica form, the read replica instance id also comes pre-populated. Let's retain the default ID. Next we specify the location for the replica. Like Failover Replica, region remains disabled, however note, unlike the failover replica the primary instance zone is listed in the Zone drop down. This implies we can create the read replica in any zone in the region including the primary instance zone as well. We retain the primary instance zone.

Like Failover replica, the read replica form also comes prepopulated with the primary instance configuration. However, since the read replicas are not standby for primary instance and will be primarily used to scale read requests, we can customize the read replica.

The primary configuration which we may change is the instance type, this choice depends on whether we require a more powerful (upgrade) or less powerful (downgrade) read replica. This is determined by our application workload, if its read heavy we can opt for a powerful read replica.

For this example, let's downgrade the instance type back to *db-n1-standard-1*. With all configuration in place we click Create. Within few minutes the read replica is enabled and like the failover replica is displayed underneath the primary instance as shown in Figure 4-63.

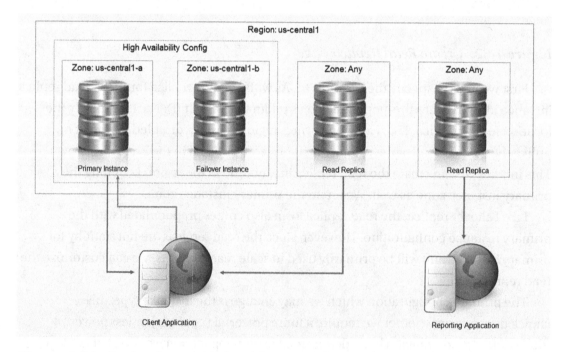

	SQL	Instances	➕ CREATE INSTANCE	⇄ MIGRATE DATA			SHOW INFO PANEL

	Instance ID	Type	High availability	Location	Labels	
✅	mypglive	PostgreSQL 9.6	Enabled	us-central1-b		⋮
✅	mysqllive	MySQL 2nd Gen 5.7	Enabled	us-central1-a		⋮
✅	mysqllive-failover	MySQL 2nd Gen failover	--	us-central1-b		⋮
⟳	mysqllive-replica	MySQL 2nd Gen read replica	--	us-central1-a		⋮

Figure 4-63. *Read Replica Listed*

The steps for creating PostgreSQL Read replica is same as above.

In effect, with failover replica and multiple read replicas created, a fault tolerant, high performing, scale out CloudSQL instance in us-cental1 region will look as shown in Figure 4-64.

Figure 4-64. *Fault tolerant, High Performing CloudSQL instance*

With the HA enabled system setup, let's next look at the way we can diagnose issues.

Logging

Logs are critical for identifying and diagnosing issues with the instance. Being managed logs capturing is built-in. Navigate to *Operations* tab in the Instance detail page. We will be redirected to screen as shown in Figure 4-65 which lists logs of all recent operations being performed on the instance.

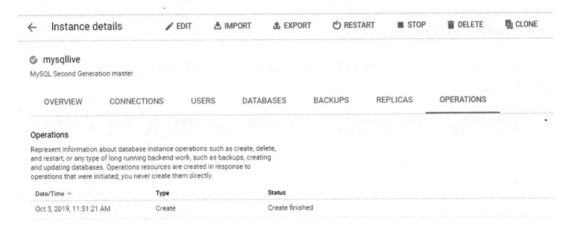

Figure 4-65. *Operations Tab*

However, we need to note that this logs are of operations being performed using Console, gcloud utility or CloudSQL API only.

In order to view error and logs from clients e.g. MySQL Client we can use *GCP Stackdriver logging Logs viewer*. Stackdriver logging enables us to log and analyze our log data. This also enables us to create a metric wherein we can create notifications as an event occurs for proactive resolutions.

Let's next look at the log viewer. Navigate to *Operations and Logs* card underneath *Overview* tab in the instance detail page. Click on *MySQL error logs* as shown in Figure 4-66.

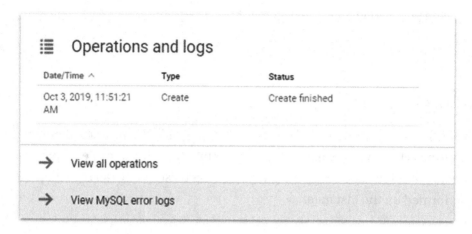

Figure 4-66. *MySQL Error Logs*

This takes us to the Stackdriver Logging Log Viewer as shown in Figure 4-67 with selections in place.

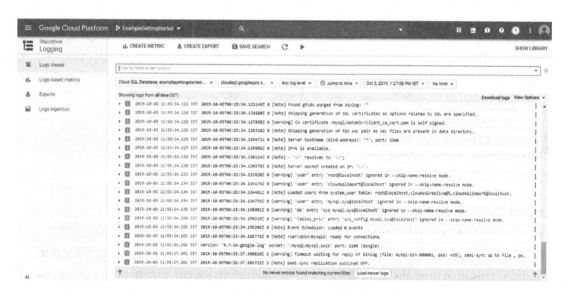

Figure 4-67. *Log Viewer*

As we can see it enables us to run analysis using Filter. We can also Create a Metric which can be monitored for notification purposes. To learn more on working with Log Viewer and Monitoring, refer Stackdriver Logging.[4]

---

[4]https://cloud.google.com/logging/

Stackdriver logging default logs for the ones shown in Figure 4-68.

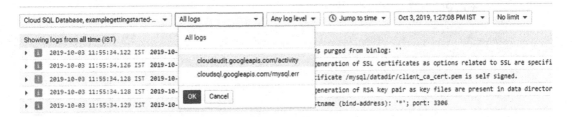

Figure 4-68. *CloudSQL Default Logging*

We can enable the log collection for our instance using the database flags options.

Note   Stackdriver logging charges will be applicable.

For this example, let's enable SLOW Queries Logging for our instance, this is important for individuals responsible for managing the MySQL database. This will enable us to identify inefficient or time-consuming which needs optimizations.

Navigate to instance detail page, click on *Edit Instance*. This opens the Edit Instance page as shown in Figure 4-69.

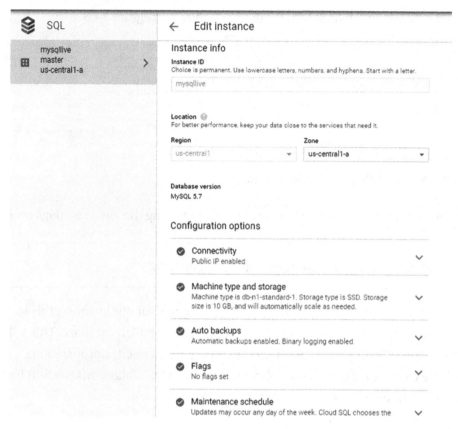

Figure 4-69. *Instance Edit*

Expand the *Flags* section. Click on *Add Item* and Add the following database flags
and their values

- log_output='FILE'

- slow_query_log=on

- long_query_time=2 (value is in seconds)

Figure 4-70 shows the sections with the inputs in place.

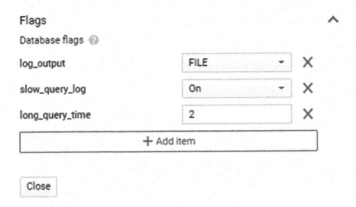

Figure 4-70. *Database Flags for Slow Query Logging*

Click on *Close* and *Save* buttons respectively for the instance to be updated. Navigate to the Log viewer, we will see the Slow Query Log enabled as shown in Figure 4-71.

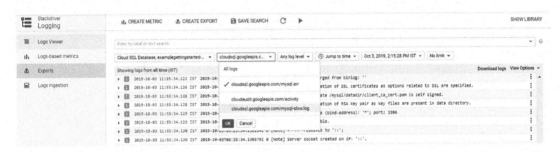

Figure 4-71. *Slow Query Logging enables in Log Viewer*

With this we covered important activities for setting up and managing CloudSQL in a live (production) environment.

Summary

In this chapter we configured CloudSQL to work in a high availability architecture. We also saw how to configure CloudSQL to work in a scale out architecture for high volume read applications using read replicas and also looked at ways of diagnosing the instance. With this we conclude usage of CloudSQL instance. Let's next begin with CloudSpanner.

CHAPTER 5

Cloud Spanner

Cloud Spanner is Google's cloud-native, enterprise-grade, always-on, fully managed NewSQL database service. It offers high availability with an industry-leading 99.999% availability SLA and horizontal scalability with consistent global ACID transactions.

Prior to getting started with Cloud Spanner, you need to get familiar with NewSQL. This chapter first takes a look at NewSQL. With digital transformation, many companies are building cloud applications. However, when building their applications, they have been forced to choose between traditional SQL databases (which guarantee ACID based transactional consistency) or the new NoSQL databases (which provide horizontal scaling capabilities). *NewSQL* brings SQL-ization to the NoSQL world.

> *NewSQL is a class of relational database management systems that seek to provide the scalability of NoSQL systems for online transaction processing (OLTP) workloads while maintaining the ACID guarantees of a traditional database system.*
>
> —Wikipedia

This chapter covers:

- Evolution of NewSQL

- An introduction to Cloud Spanner

- Spanner's availability and fit into the CAP theorem (the theorem for distributed databases)

- Design decisions

- Best fits

The next section looks at the history of databases and discusses the evolution of NewSQL.

© Navin Sabharwal, Shakuntala Gupta Edward 2020
N. Sabharwal and S. G. Edward, *Hands On Google Cloud SQL and Cloud Spanner*,
https://doi.org/10.1007/978-1-4842-5537-7_5

New in NewSQL

In the mid-1960s, the traditional RDBMS databases were born out of a need to separate code from data. Correctness and consistency were the two important metrics. The number of users querying these databases was considerably low, but the requirement of querying was extensive—unlimited queries could be run on the databases. As the data grew, vertical scaling was a feasible solution. In addition, the downtime required for database migration as well as recovery was acceptable by the user.

A couple of decades ahead, the Internet, big data, and the cloud added new sets of requirements from the databases. The requirements from databases were primarily divided into two categories: OLAP and OLTP.

OLAP (online analytical processing), also commonly known as data warehouses, deals with historical data for analytical processing and reporting. The workload is primarily read-only and the user base is limited. This requirement still fits in the traditional RDBMSs. In contrast, OLTP (online transactional processing) corresponds to highly concurrent data processing, characterized by short-lived predefined queries being run by real-time users. The queries are not read-only but write intensive as well.

While users access a smaller dataset when compared to OLAP users, the user base is considerable. At any given time, hundreds or thousands of users may be effectively querying the database concurrently. The workload can be both read and write operations. With this scale of users and the nature of operations being performed, the need for high availability increases, as every minute of downtime can cost thousands or even millions of dollars.

In effect, the important requirements for an OLTP databases are scalability, high availability, concurrency, and performance. This gave birth to NoSQL databases. In contrast to the relational data model of the RDBMS systems, in NoSQL, varied data models are used (e.g., document, key-value, wide columns, graphs, etc.). Each was purpose-built to meet a unique set of requirements. These databases are inherently schema-less by design and are not normalized.

Although these databases bring in higher availability, easier scalability, and better performance, they compromise on the strong consistency offered by RDBMSs. They offer eventual consistency. In effect, this is best for applications such as social media sites, where eventual consistency is acceptable. Users do not notice if they see a non-consistent view of the database. But this will not work where, in addition to scalability and high availability, consistency is also expected and is critical as well (such as with e-commerce platforms).

The expectation to combine the scalability and high availability of NoSQL with a relational model, transactional support, and SQL of RDBMS gave birth to NewSQL databases. This type of database is a game changer for those who have a need for the consistency provided by RDBMS and also need scale. The next section looks at the origins of Cloud Spanner at Google.

Origins of Cloud Spanner

Developers have relied on the traditional relational databases for decades to build applications that meet their business needs. In 2007, the year Spanner was built, most of Google's main critical applications—such as AdWords, Google Play etc.—were being running on massive, manually sharded MySQL implementations.

Although the manual sharding option enabled Google with a scale out mechanism that MySQL didn't support natively, it was unwieldy, so much so that re-sharding the database was a multi-year process. Google needed a database that had native, flexible sharding capabilities, adhered to relational schema and storage, was ACID-compliant, and supported zero downtime.

Faced with its need and the two sub-optimal choices, a team of Google engineers and researchers set out to develop a globally distributed database that could bridge the gap between SQL and NoSQL.

In 2012, a paper was published about Cloud Spanner, a database that offers the best of both the worlds. Table 5-1 lists its features.

Table 5-1. *Feature-Wise Comparison of Cloud Spanner, RDBMS, and NoSQL*

	Cloud Spanner	RDBMS	NoSQL
Schema	Yes	Yes	No
SQL	Yes	Yes	No
Consistency	Strong	Strong	Eventual
Availability	High	Failover	High
Scalability	Horizontal	Vertical	Horizontal
Replication	Automatic	Configurable	Configurable

In the same year, it was initiated for internal Google use to handle workloads of its main critical applications, such as AdWords and Google Play. It supports tens of millions of queries per second.

Over the years, it has been battle-tested internally within Google with hundreds of different applications and petabytes of data across datacenters around the world. After internal use, Google announced Cloud Spanner for use by GCP users in February 2017.

The company saw its potential to handle the explosion of data coming from new information sources such as IoT, while providing the consistency and high availability needed when using this data. Now that you are familiar with its origination, the next section explains Cloud Spanner in more detail.

Google Cloud Spanner

Spanner was built from the ground up to be a widely distributed database, as it had to handle the demanding uptime and scaling requirements imposed by Google's critical business applications. It can span across multiple machines, datacenters, and regions. This distribution was leveraged to handle huge datasets and workloads while still maintaining very high availability.

Spanner was also aimed to provide the same strict consistency guarantees provided by other enterprise-grade databases. In effect, Cloud Spanner is *a* fully managed, globally distributed, highly consistent database service and is specifically built from a cloud/distributed design perspective.

Being a managed service, it enables the developers to focus on application logic, value-add innovations and let Google take care of the mundane yet important tasks of maintenance and administrations. In addition, it enables you to do the following:

- Scale out your RDBMS solutions without complex sharding or clustering

- Gain horizontal scaling without migrating to a NoSQL landscape

- Maintain high availability and protect against disasters without needing to engineer a complex replication and failover infrastructure

- Gain integrated security with data-layer encryption

- Identity and access management and audit logging

You also need to note that Cloud Spanner is not a

- Simple scale-up relational database

- Data warehouse

- NoSQL database

The next section quickly familiarizes you with the CAP theorem, an important concept when dealing with distributed databases. It explains where Spanner fits in the CAP theorem.

Spanner and CAP Theorem

The CAP theorem states that a database can have only two of the three following desirable properties:

- C: Consistency, which implies a single value for shared data

- A: 100% availability, for both read and updates

- P: Tolerance to network partition

This leads to three kinds of systems, as shown in Figure 5-1:

- CA: Systems that provide consistency and availability

- CP: Systems that provide consistency and partition tolerance

- PA: Systems that provide partition tolerance and availability

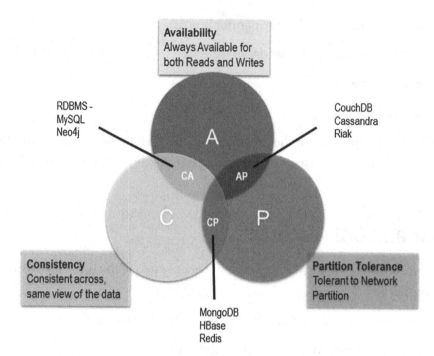

Figure 5-1. *CAP theorem Venn diagram*

The following sections cover insights from the Google whitepaper[1]. For distributed systems over a *wide area*, partitions are inevitable, although not necessarily common. If you believe that partitions are inevitable, any distributed system must be prepared to forfeit either consistency (AP) or availability (CP).

Despite being a globally distributed system, Spanner claims to be consistent and highly available. This implies that Spanner is a CA type of system, but the answer is no, as in the scenario of a network partition, Spanner chooses C and forfeits A, making it a CP system at heart. Google's strategy with Spanner is to improve availability as much as possible, claiming it to be an effectively CA system. Google has introduced many ways to improve availability to a very high level.

One way for claiming ***effective CA*** is to ensure a low number of outages due to partitions ensuring higher network availability. It's a major contribution to improve overall availability. This requirement of network availability for Google Spanner is helped enormously by Google's wide area network.

Google runs its own private global network that has been custom architected to limit partitions and is tuned for high availability and performance needs of systems

---

[1]https://storage.googleapis.com/pub-tools-public-publication-data/pdf/45855.pdf

like Spanner. Each datacenter is connected to the private global network using at least three independent fibers, ensuring path diversity for every pair of datacenters. There's significant redundancy of equipment and paths within each datacenter, ensuring that normally catastrophic events, such as cut fiber lines etc., do not lead to outages.

Another way that Spanner gets around CAP is via usage of *TrueTime*.

This is a service that enables the use of globally synchronized atomic clocks. This allows events to be ordered in real time, enabling Spanner to achieve consistency across regions and continents and even between continents with many nodes. TrueTime also enables taking snapshots across multiple independent systems, as long as they use (monotonically increasing) TrueTime timestamps for commit, agree on a snapshot time, and store multiple versions over time (typically in a log). This improves the recovery time and the overall availability.

The third way it gets around CAP is using the *Paxos* algorithm. This is used to reach consensus in a distributed environment. Paxos/consensus is the key in making everything work. One of the big reasons is the way transactions are committed and operations are handled during that. A two-phase commit protocol is used by geographically distributed traditional systems. This ensures that each site finishes its own work before finally marking the transaction as completed. Spanner makes each site a full replica of the others and uses a Paxos consensus algorithm to commit a transaction when a majority of sites have completed their work. Users of a particular site that hasn't finished updating can be rerouted to a site that has, until their own site is done. Although this eliminates the gridlock, it introduces slight latency during those specific intervals.

Along with these approaches, other software tricks help too. Spanner locks only a cell, which is a particular column in a particular row during write operations, rather than entire rows. In effect, it not only accelerates the commit, it also minimizes contention, ensuring full database consistency. In addition, for read-only operations that have tolerance for slightly stale data, an older version of the data can be made available. Another way Spanner speeds things up is by storing child data so that it is physically co-located with its parent data. This allows queries that include hierarchical data (like purchase orders and their line items) to be scanned in one sweep rather than requiring the database to traverse a join relationship between the two.

While the CAP theorem states that a distributed database can only achieve two out of the three properties, Spanner *cheats* in a good way through optimizations that side-step some of the normal constraints imposed by distributed databases and achieves greater than *five 9s (99.999%)* availability. Before you delve deeper into Cloud Spanner, the next section in this chapter looks at the best-fit workloads for Cloud Spanner.

Best Fit

The database industry now sees various database solutions. Each of them is a viable solution, each has its own solution space, and each is a fit for different workloads.

As an OLTP solution, Google Spanner is ideal for workloads supported by traditional relational databases, e.g. inventory management and financial transactions. Other examples of the solution space include applications providing probabilistic assessments, such as those based on AI and advanced analytics.

By probabilistic, I mean a methodology is chosen on the fly to compute and return the output quickly. You can call this methodology an algorithm. There can be various algorithms available for finding a solution, but it chooses on the fly the one that returns output quickly and the output is good enough. Examples include real-time price updates, or deciding the price to bid for delivering an advertisement in real-time to an end user. An example of this in Google is the challenge in Google AdWords applications to keep track of billions of clicks and rolling those up into advertisement placements and billing. Much of this is probabilistic, spanning large countries, and has low latency requirements.

Google's development of Spanner is a tribute to the technical inventiveness of Google's engineers, striving to solve the challenges of emerging probabilistic systems. Another potential use case for Spanner is large-scale public cloud email systems such as Gmail.

Development Support

Cloud Spanner keeps application development simple by supporting standard tools and languages. It supports schemas and DDL statements, SQL queries, distributed transactions, and JDBC drivers and offers client libraries for the most popular languages, including Java, Go, Python, PHP, Node.js, C#, and Ruby.

Summary

This chapter provided an overview of Cloud Spanner. To summarize

- Is it a distributed database? Yes

- Is it a relational database? Partially yes

- Is it an ACID compliant database? Yes

- Is it a SQL database? Mostly yes

- Is it CP or AP? CP, effectively CA, assumes 99.999% availability

The next chapter explains the way data is modeled, stored, and queried in Cloud Spanner.

CHAPTER 6

Cloud Spanner Explained

Now that you are familiar with Spanner, it's time to look more closely at its underlying concepts and features. As with any database, it is beneficial to do a deep dive before starting to work with it. This chapter explores the concepts that are important when working with Spanner, starting with instances. The chapter covers pointers for databases, tables, and keys. Along the way, it also covers the way operations are handled in Spanner.

This chapter covers:

- Data modeling concepts

- Design considerations to keep in mind when modeling with Spanner

- Data replication

- Transactions and understanding concurrent transactions, with an example

- Operations in the distributed environment

The next section begins with instances.

Instance

A Cloud Spanner instance is roughly analogous to an RDBMS server. The instance contains one or more databases and has allocated resources (compute and storage) that are used by all its databases. Figure 6-1 shows a hypothetical representation of an instance.

© Navin Sabharwal, Shakuntala Gupta Edward 2020
N. Sabharwal and S. G. Edward, *Hands On Google Cloud SQL and Cloud Spanner*,
https://doi.org/10.1007/978-1-4842-5537-7_6

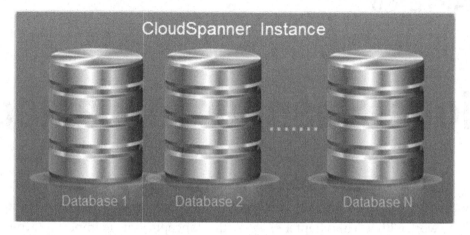

Figure 6-1. *Cloud Spanner instance*

The resources are allocated during instance creation and are controlled by two main configurations. These configurations decide the compute and the way data is replicated, stored, and computed.

Spanner replicates data automatically. The number of replicas (or copies) to be created and their placement is controlled by the first configuration (instance configuration). There are two options available: Regional and Multi-Regional. In a Regional configuration, data is replicated across three zones within a single region selected by the user. Whereas in a Multi-Regional configuration, data is replicated across four zones in different regions, which are determined by the continent selected by the user. In effect, Regional provides safety against failure of an entire zone, whereas Multi-Region provides higher availability guarantees by providing safety against failure of an entire region itself. Figure 6-2 shows a hypothetical representation of an instance with a Regional configuration.

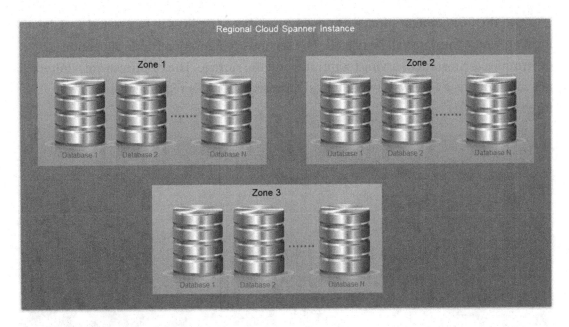

Figure 6-2. *Regional Cloud Spanner instance*

Figure 6-3 shows a hypothetical representation of an instance with a Multi-Regional configuration.

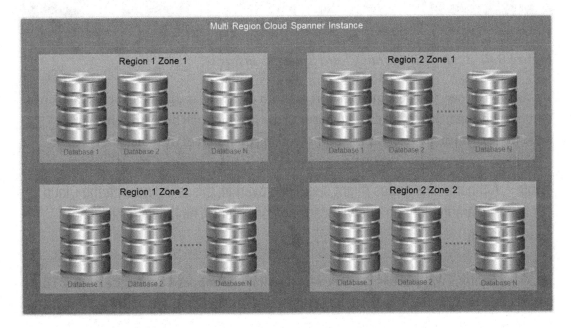

Figure 6-3. *Multi-Regional Cloud Spanner instance*

With the first configuration, we know the number of replicas to be created and the location where the data will be placed. The second configuration (node allocation) determines the instance serving (compute) and the storage. The resources are allotted per zone. Figure 6-4 shows a hypothetical representation of a regional instance with three nodes.

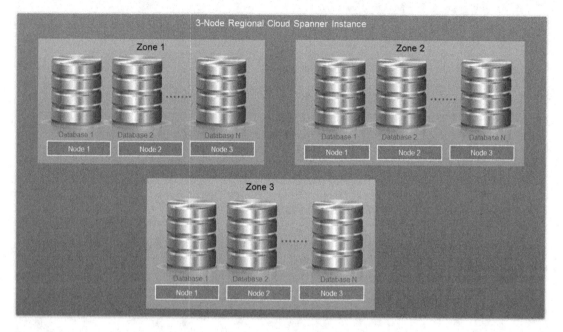

Figure 6-4. *3- Node Regional Cloud Spanner instance*

As you can see, you get equal resources (both compute and storage) across all zones. Within each zone, data of all the databases of the instance will be distributed across these nodes, which are responsible for processing their part of the data.

Note   Although nine nodes might seem like overkill, this is in line with the Cloud Spanner guarantee of rich querying, strong consistency, high availability, and performance.

Later sections will discuss the way data distribution happens across the nodes. The next section looks at the data modeling concepts found in Spanner.

Data Modeling

Cloud Spanner behaves like an RDBMS in many ways but with a few differences. This section explains Spanner's data modeling concepts, covering the differences wherever applicable. It begins with databases and tables.

Databases and Tables

Like in RDBMS, in Spanner as well:

- Databases are created to hold related data together in the form of tables.

- Tables store data in a structured format using rows and columns.

- Schemas are predefined with a number of columns, column names, and data types and size (if applicable).

However, in Spanner, you define only one constraint, the NULLABILITY constraint. This enables you to control whether the column can have NULL values or not. In addition, Spanner tables support limited data types, as listed in Table 6-1.

Table 6-1. *Spanner Supported Data Types*

Category	Data Type
Number	INT64, FLOAT64
Text	STRING
Date Time	TIMESTAMP, DATE
Boolean	BOOL
Bytes	Bytes
Complex	ARRAY

Primary Keys

While defining the schema in Spanner, it's mandatory to specify a primary key. Like RDBMS, Spanner's primary key uniquely identifies each row and can be made of a single column (single key) or a group of columns (composite key). But the primary key in Spanner also has a few differences.

- Primary key creation in RDBMS is not mandatory but in Spanner it's mandatory.

- The primary key of RDBMS contains one or more columns. The Cloud Spanner primary key can have zero columns as well. In this case, the table will contain only one row.

- The primary key of RDBMS can never be NULL; however, Spanner's primary key column can be NULLABLE. Since it's a unique identifier, only one row can have the NULL value.

In addition, the Spanner primary key controls data locality, as data is stored in sorted order (this defaults to Ascending) by the primary key values in key-value format. The value includes all of the respective non-key columns. Let's look at an example and create a table called Artists. The table schema looks like Table 6-2.

Table 6-2. *Artists Table Schema*

Column Name	Data Type	
Artist ID	INT64	Primary Key
FirstName	STRING [10]	
LastName	STRING [20]	
EMailId	STRING [50]	

The Artists table contains the data shown in Table 6-3.

Table 6-3. *Artists Data*

Artist ID	First Name	Last Name	EMailId
1	Mike	Jonas	mike.j@gmail.com
2	Steffi	Graph	steffig@gmail.com
3	Stephan	Chart	steph@gmail.com
4	Leslie	John	ljohn@gmail.com
5	Kate	Charlie	katec@gmail.com

Figure 6-5 shows a hypothetical representation of the physical layout of the Artists table, where with the Artist ID as the key, the remaining column data is stored as the value.

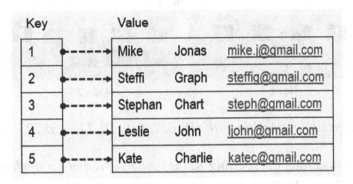

Figure 6-5. *Physical layout of the Artists table*

Being distributed, Spanner partitions the data automatically and distributes across its allotted node. The partitioning is done by Spanner along the primary key dimension. So, it's important to choose the primary key carefully.

Choose a Key to Avoid Hotspots

Keys should be chosen so that they enable even distribution of the data and do not create a *hotspot*. So what is hot spotting? Assume that the database hosting the Artists table is on a two-node instance. This implies that the table's data will be distributed across the two nodes along the primary key dimension, ArtistId. Figure 6-6 shows a hypothetical distribution of data across the two nodes.

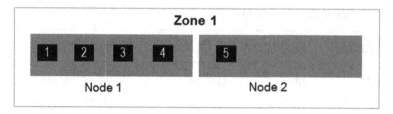

Figure 6-6. *Primary key ArtistId distribution across two nodes in Zone 1*

Since the primary key called ArtistId is a monotonically increasing integer ID, as you start inserting new data, being incremental in nature, all the new additions will start to happen at the end of the key space. In effect, all inserts will start to happen only on Node 2. Figure 6-7 shows inserts of new the Artist IDs 6, 7, 8, 9, 10, 11, and 12.

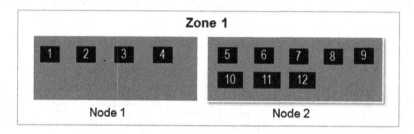

Figure 6-7. *Inserted new Artists with IDs 6, 7, 8, 9, 10, 11, and 12*

This scenario illustrates hot spotting, as the load weighs down a single node only. This effectively kills parallelization in Spanner, therefore affecting performance. In order to handle such scenarios, you should avoid keys that are sequentially ordered or monotonically increasing, like the ArtistId column. Instead, you should choose a key that evenly distributes data and enables even distribution of workload (reads and writes) and does not create a hotspot.

However, if it is unavoidable and you have to use a sequentially ordered key, you should see if you can *hash* it. Hashing has the effect of distributing across different servers quite evenly. In the previous example, if you hash Artist IDs, even distribution can be achieved as the hash values of the ArtistId columns will contain random alphanumeric data, which is highly unlikely to be monotonically increasing or decreasing. As a result, the representation will be free of hot spotting.

Note   There are various other techniques defined on the product site that you should take into consideration for efficient selection of the key.

The next section looks at the way related tables should be created for efficient querying.

Interleaving

Spanner enables you to choose the physical representation of your table data based on your querying pattern. In order to handle relationships where tables are related and are frequently queried together, Spanner enables you to define hierarchical (parent-child) relationship between the tables, which enables efficient retrieval as the data of the hierarchically related tables will be co-located and stored together on the disk.

Note   The parent/child relationship can be specified between the tables in up to seven levels of nesting.

The relationship is defined by creating the child table (table containing related information) as an interleaved table of the parent (main) table.

In order to understand this, the example introduces another table called Albums, which stores Artist-wise album details with schema and its data, as shown in Table 6-4 and Table 6-5 respectively.

Table 6-4. *Albums Table Schema*

Column Name	Data Type	
AlbumId	INT64	Primary Key
ArtistId	INT64	
Album Title	STRING [50]	

Table 6-5. *Albums Data*

Album ID	Artist ID	Album Title
1	1	Junk yard
2	1	Go On
3	2	Girls like you
4	2	Color Green
5	2	Purple

As of now, the Albums table is created like any other normal table. With the key IDs of both tables (Artists and Albums), the physical layout of the data now looks like Figure 6-8.

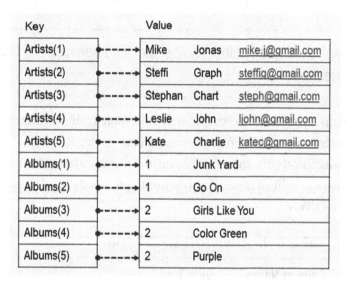

Figure 6-8. *Physical layout of the Artists and Albums tables*

As you can see, the data is stored in a contiguous space. In this case, it's quite possible that, while distributing the data across nodes, rows of the Albums table end up on one node and the Artists table on the other node. This will be apt if you don't have to query the tables together, but since in this case, you will be always querying Albums with reference to Artists, this representation will have a negative impact on performance. So in this case it's apt to create Albums as an interleaved table of Artists. While you do so, you need to note that Spanner uses the primary key of the parent table to store the child data with the corresponding parent record. So as you interleave the table, primary key column(s) of the parent table are mandatorily prefixed to the primary key of the child table (in the same order starting with the same column as in the parent table). So, now the primary key of the Albums table will be composed of ArtistId and AlbumId. With the interleaving defined, the table schema is as shown in Table 6-6 and the physical layout of both the tables is as shown in Figure 6-9.

Table 6-6. *Albums Table Schema*

Column Name	Data Type	
ArtistId	INT64	Primary Key (Column 1)
AlbumId	INT64	Primary Key (Column 2)
Album Title	STRING [50]	

Key	Value		
Artists(1)	Mike	Jonas	mike.j@gmail.com
Albums(1,1)	Junk Yard		
Albums(1,2)	Go On		
Artists(2)	Steffi	Graph	steffig@gmail.com
Albums(2,3)	Girls Like You		
Albums(2,4)	Colour Green		
Albums(2,5)	Purple		
Artists(3)	Stephan	Chart	steph@gmail.com
Artists(4)	Leslie	John	ljohn@gmail.com
Artists(5)	Kate	Charlie	katec@gmail.com

Figure 6-9. *Interleaved Artists and Albums tables*

As you can see, the data is interleaved. Every row from the Artists table is followed by all its rows from the child Albums table, which is determined by the ArtistId column value. This entire representation looks like a big flat table.

In effect, this process of inserting the child rows between the parent rows along the primary key dimension is called **interleaving**. The child tables are called **interleaved** tables and the parent tables are called the **root table** or **top-level tables**. As can be seen, this will enable fast querying, as data that's queried together is stored together.

So while designing your schema, it is important to identify the querying pattern to identify the tables that need to be co-located. That way, when you're actually creating the tables, proper interleaving can be defined.

You are now familiar with two important design decisions—choosing the proper primary key to avoid hot spotting and identifying the querying pattern to interleave the related tables. The next step is to understand another interesting concept, *splits*.

Splits

As you know by now, Cloud Spanner uses the primary key dimension to partition the data. Splits determine the point within the dimension where the partitions should happen. In effect, splits are used by Cloud Spanner to logically group the rows so that they are independent of each other and can be moved around independently without impacting the other group of data and performance.

Cloud Spanner automatically splits when it deems necessary due to size or load. Splits are done at the root row boundaries, where root row is the row in the root table, so that the root row plus all its descendants (row tree) are always in a single split. Figure 6-10 shows a row tree, i.e., root row plus all its descendants.

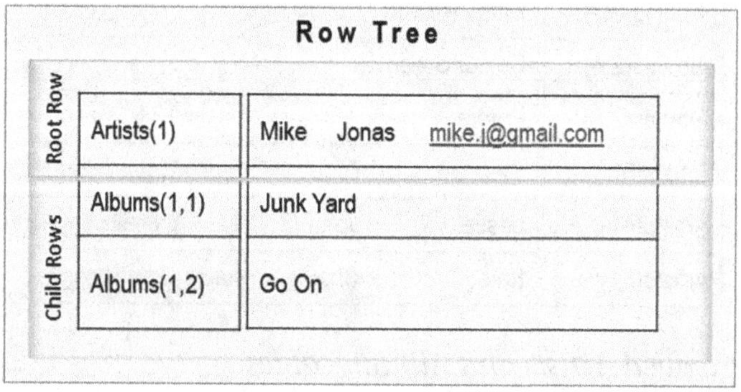

Figure 6-10. Row tree

Although you don't control when or how to split, you can control the way you define the root table and the row tree. In effect, it's important to choose the correct root table while designing the database to enable proper scaling.

Returning to the example, you can see that there are a bunch of possible splits (as you are querying details of albums for a particular artist), each corresponding to a distinct value of the Artist ID, as shown in Figure 6-11.

Split 1	Artists(1)	Mike	Jonas	mike.j@gmail.com
	Albums(1,1)	Junk Yard		
	Albums(1,2)	Go On		
Split 2	Artists(2)	Steffi	Graph	steffig@gmail.com
	Albums(2,3)	Girls Like You		
	Albums(2,4)	Colour Green		
	Albums(2,5)	Purple		

Figure 6-11. *Splits*

These are groups of rows that can be moved around without affecting any of the other rows. Splits complement the data distribution in Spanner. Having looked at important concepts of choosing a proper primary key, interleaving, and splits, it's time to look at the indexes.

Secondary Indexes

As you know by now, data is stored in sorted order by the primary key, so any query involving the primary key field will always result in faster querying. However, querying on other non-key fields will lead to full table scan, leading to slower query performances. In order to cater to this scenario, like other databases, Spanner enables you to create secondary indexes on the non-key fields.

Creating a secondary index on a field stores the indexed field in sorted order (specified while creation, defaults to Ascending otherwise) with the associated key field value. Let's say you want to index Artists by LastName (Ascending Order). Table 6-7 shows the data of Index on LastName.

Table 6-7. *ArtistsByLastName (Ascending)*

Last Name	Artist ID
Charlie	5
Chart	3
Graph	2
John	4
Jonas	1

So, if you query `Fetch Artist ID's with LastName values in the Range specified`, this index will be able to return results faster without any table scan as all the data is available within the index itself.

Storing Clause

Now you can rephrase the query to `Fetch Artists Id and FirstName where the LastName value is in the range specified`. Since in this case FirstName is not there in the index, this query will require a `JOIN` with the Artists table to fetch the FirstName, leading to a negative impact on query performance.

In order to cater to such a scenario, Spanner enables you to use the `STORING` clause, which copies the column's data in the index. Table 6-8 shows the index ArtistsByLastName `STORING` FirstName field as well.

Table 6-8. *ArtistsByLastName (Ascending) with FirstName Field Within the STORING Clause*

Last Name	Artist ID	First Name
Charlie	5	Kate
Chart	3	Stephan
Graph	2	Steffi
John	4	Leslie
Jonas	1	Mike

Interleaved Indexes

As with interleaved tables, Spanner enables you to create indexes based on your usage. Say you want to index the albums by name, but instead of indexing all the albums together, you want to index them for each Artist ID separately. To cater to this, Spanner enables you to create interleaved indexes. These will be interleaved within the parent (root) table and are analogous to having a local index per root row. Table 6-9 shows the interleaved index, AlbumsByNameForEachArtist.

Table 6-9. *AlbumsByNameForEachArtist*

Artist ID	Album Name	Album ID
1	Go On	2
1	Junk Yard	1
2	Color Green	4
2	Girls Like You	3
2	Purple	5

As with interleaved tables, this enables co-location of related rows near each other, in effect improving performance, as the data to be referred together is always placed together.

So, indexes can be really powerful as they make the querying faster by saving data in the format you need. However, the implications of secondary indexes are that you end up paying a storage penalty, as some data is going to be stored multiple times, like with interleaved indexes and the STORING clause. This has a further impact on the write performance.

With all the concepts in place, it's time to look at the way data will be distributed and replicated, with an example.

Replication

You know by now that Cloud Spanner instances automatically

- Replicate the data based on the instance configuration chosen

- Distribute the data based on the nodes allocated

- Split the data along the primary key dimension

With these details, you can consider an example of a five-node Cloud Spanner Regional configuration instance and look at the way data is distributed and replicated. As mentioned, the Regional configuration implies that the data will be replicated across three zones within a region. A five-node instance means within each zone, the data will be distributed across five nodes. A hypothetical representation of the instance looks like Figure 6-12.

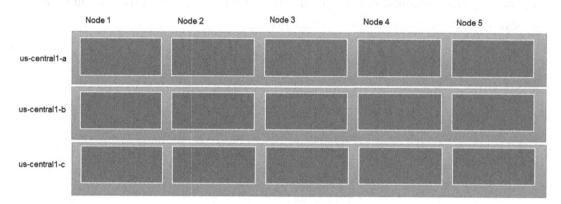

Figure 6-12. *Five-node instance with Regional configuration in us-central1 region*

Assume the instance hosts a database named TestDB, which contains a table called TableA with schema, as shown in Table 6-10.

Table 6-10. *TableA Schema*

Column Name	Data Type	
ID	INT64	Primary Key
Value	STRING	

Let's further assume the table has the splits outlined in Table 6-11.

Table 6-11. *TableA Split Details*

Split	Key Range
0	<100
1	>=100 and <500
2	>=500 and <1000
3	>=1000 and <2000
4	>=2000 and <2500
5	>=2500 and <4000
6	>=4000 and <7000
7	>=7000

Note   This split distribution is transparent to the user and is handled automatically by Cloud Spanner. The section is for understanding purposes only.

The distribution implies that if you have to look for a row with an ID 2500, you will have to check Split 5, as this is the split that holds data with a key range >=2500 and <4000. With all the assumptions, the hypothetical split distribution will look like Figure 6-13.

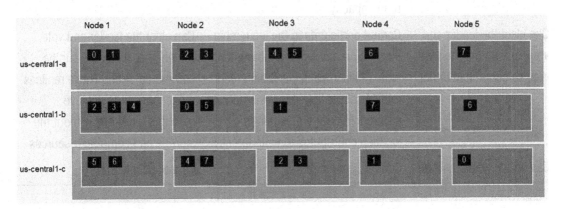

Figure 6-13. *Hypothetical representation of the data distribution*

Here's what you can learn from this distribution:

- Data is stored in the form of splits.

- A node hosts one or many splits. This will be the case when the number of splits is more than the number of nodes allotted to the instance.

- Replication is at the split level.

- The split copies (or replicas), which are replicated across independent failure zones, are determined by the instance configuration. In this example, you have three replicas for each split.

Each replica can serve different purposes based on its type. Table 6-12 lists the different types of Spanner replicas.

Table 6-12. *Replica Types*

Read/Write	Read Only	Witness
Replica holds full copy of the split	Replica holds full copy of the split	Do not maintain a full copy of data
Data is always up-to-date	Data can be stale	Not applicable
Serves both read and write traffic	Server read traffic only These nodes enable us to scale our read capacity	Serves neither read nor writes
Can elect the leader and vote for whether the write is to be committed or not	Cannot participate in the leadership election nor can vote for committing writes; this implies increasing read replicas doesn't increase the quorum size required for writes nor its location contributes to write latency	Can elect the leader and vote for whether the write is to be committed or not. These replicas make it easier to achieve quorums for writes without the storage and compute resources
Can be the leader as well	Cannot be a leader	Cannot be a leader

Each split replica forms a replica set. Within each set, one replica is elected as the leader and is responsible for all the writes to the split. All the other replicas (except the witness) can serve read requests. Figure 6-14 shows the leaders highlighted in orange for each replica set.

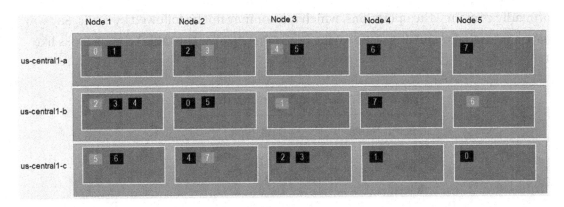

Figure 6-14. *Hypothetical representation of the data distribution with leaders highlighted*

Spanner uses synchronous, Paxos (consensus protocol) based replication schemes where, whenever a write is issued, every voting replica votes before the writes can be committed. The major concern Cloud Spanner addresses is database replication on a global scale and provisioning of data consistency, even when multiple users conduct transactions that require the system to connect to datacenters across the globe. Cloud Spanner eliminates the bottleneck by using Paxos, which relies on an algorithm to create consensus among globally distributed nodes to conduct the commit. Later in the chapter, you will delve deeper into the way this works while carrying out the read/write operations in Spanner. Prior to that, it's important that you understand the way operations happen.

Transactions

In Spanner, all operations—whether they are read, write, or read and write both—happen within a transaction. Spanner supports two modes of transaction: read/write and read only. These transaction modes differ in the way they handle access to the data. Let's begin with the read/write transaction mode.

Read/Write

Read/write mode enables modifications (inserts, deletes, and updates) to the data. For this, they acquire locks to ensure that the data remains consistent. These transactions primarily contain write operations, which may or may not be followed by reads. Say you have a table that maintains some savings accounts details. The table schema looks like Table 6-13.

Table 6-13. *Savings Account Table Schema*

Column Name	Data Type
Account ID	STRING
Amount	INT64
Last Operation	STRING
Last Modified Date	DATE

Figure 6-15 shows a read/write transaction and the operations that occur within it.

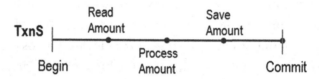

Figure 6-15. *Read/write transaction*

It first reads the amount from the table. Then it processes the data. Say, for example, that you check the amount. If it is greater than $100, you add $100's to it. Finally, you save the updated data. Figure 6-16 shows the locking mechanism; the locks are acquired at each step.

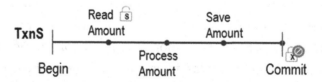

Figure 6-16. *Locks acquired*

As you can see, the read acquires a *shared* lock. Within the database at any point in time, you can have multiple concurrent transactions running. This lock enables the other transactions to continue reading. In effect, it does not block the other reads. When *commit* is initiated, it implies that the transaction is ready with the data to be applied back to the database. At this point it tries to acquire an *exclusive* lock on the data point. This will block all the new read requests for the data and will wait for the existing locks to be cleared. Once all the locks are cleared, it places the exclusive lock and applies all the writes. Once this is done, the lock is released. The Amount field will show the updated data.

Note that the updates in Cloud Spanner is not in-place updates, instead Spanner uses the MVCC (Multi Version Concurrent Control) method to modify the data. This implies that the writes do not overwrite the data. Instead, an immutable copy is created, which is timestamped with the write's transaction commit time. In effect, Cloud Spanner maintains multiple immutable versions of data. The next section looks at the read only transaction mode.

Read Only

This is the preferred transaction mode when the operations are just read operations and do not involve an update. This mode does not acquire locks and is also not blocked by any read/write transaction. Whenever it starts, it takes a *snapshot* of the data as valid at that point in time and all reads within the transaction will return the same value. In effect, all reads within the transaction will have a consistent view of the values. Let's further assume that the Account table contains data, as shown in Table 6-14.

Table 6-14. *Accounts Data*

Account ID	Amount	Last Operation	Last Modified Date
1	$1000	Credit	23rd August 2019
2	$90	Debit	18th August 2019

Figure 6-17 shows a read only transaction called *TxnR*.

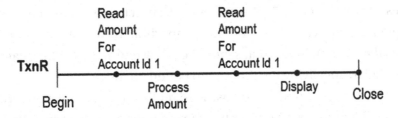

Figure 6-17. *Read only transaction*

215

As seen, you can have reads only with no updates. In general, you can use the reads to process and display the output to the end users. When you have multiple reads happening together, it's best to use the read only transaction mode. In TxnR all reads will return the result as $1000, as the Begin transaction has captured a snapshot of the data, and all reads refer to that snapshot.

There might be cases where you need to do single read calls or need to read data in parallel. Cloud Spanner enables you to do this with single reads options, which are reads outside the context of a transaction. The single reads are the simplest and fastest operations in Spanner.

By default, the reads within a read only transaction and single reads pick the most recent timestamp; however, Cloud Spanner enables you to control the freshness of the data. At any point in time, Cloud Spanner can perform reads up to one hour in the past.

Note   As you saw earlier, write leads to a creation of an immutable copy. In effect, at any given time, you will have multiple copies maintained. Cloud Spanner continuously garbage collects the old copy in the background to reclaim the storage space. This process is known as "version GC". By default, version GC reclaims the versions after they are one hour old. Because of this, Cloud Spanner cannot perform reads at read timestamps more than one hour in the past.

In effect, Cloud Spanner enables you to do two types of reads: strong reads and stale reads. *Strong reads* are the default reads that get the freshest data, wherein reads get to see the effect of all transactions that were committed prior to when the read started. *Stale reads* enable you to read past data and are further categorized into two types: *exact* staleness or *bounded* staleness. *Exact* staleness reads data at a user-specified timestamp, e.g., 2019-09-16T15:01:23. In *bounded* staleness, instead of specifying a timestamp, the user specifies a bound, such as 7s. Whenever the transaction is run based on the bound specified, Spanner chooses the newest timestamp within the bound. Bounded staleness is slower than the exact staleness reads; however, they return the freshest data. The read type is controlled by specifying the timestamp bound on the reads.

The read types are useful when you use read replicas to scale out reads. The read replicas can be a bit outdated. If the application is willing to tolerate staleness, then it can get faster responses, as they will be able to read from any nearest read replica and will not have to communicate with the leader replica, which may be geographically distant.

Now that you are familiar with the transaction modes available, let's next look at the way Spanner handles concurrent transactions across its distributed environment.

Handling Multiple Transactions

Cloud Spanner provides the strictest concurrency control, which is external consistency. This implies that multiple transactions can run side-by-side on different servers (which are possibly spread out across different datacenters in different time zones) without causing any inconsistencies. Proper timestamping is mandatory for achieving external consistency. For this, Spanner uses *TrueTime*, a Google developed technology. This is a highly available, distributed clock enabling applications running on Google Servers to generate monotonically increasing timestamps without any need for global communication.

You can understand this further with an example of an employee payroll system. It contains three tables. The table schemas are shown in Tables 6-15 through 6-17.

Table 6-15. *Salary Table Schema*

Column Name	Data Type
Employee ID	INT64
Month	STRING
Salary	INT64
Processed On	DATE

Table 6-16. *Advance Taken Table Schema*

Column Name	Data Type
Employee ID	INT64
Month	STRING
Advance Taken	INT64
Is Adjusted	BOOLEAN
Processed On	DATE

Table 6-17. *Reimbursement Table Schema*

Column Name	Data Type
Employee ID	INT64
Month	STRING
Reimbursement Amount	INT64
Is Processed	BOOLEAN
Processed On	DATE

Read/Write Transactions

Let's further assume you have two transactions running. The first transaction, called Tx1, is responsible for adjusting the advances taken and the second transaction, Tx2, adjusts the reimbursement amount. Figure 6-18 shows operations in transaction Tx1.

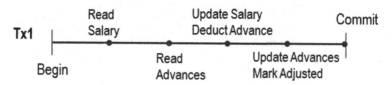

Figure 6-18. *Transaction for adjusting advances*

Figure 6-19 shows the operations in transaction Tx2.

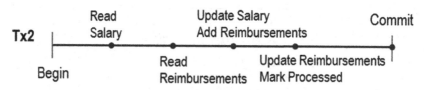

Figure 6-19. *Transaction for adjusting reimbursements*

Sequential Occurrence

Now you can see the concurrent occurrence of the two. Figure 6-20 shows the two transactions occurring one after another.

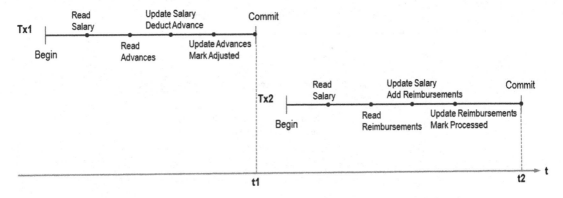

Figure 6-20. *Execution of read/write transactions one after the other*

As TrueTime is used to ensure proper timestamping, TrueTime guarantees that because Tx2 starts to commit after Tx1 finishes, all readers of the database will observe that Tx1 occurred before Tx2. This guarantees no update is ever lost.

Simultaneous Occurrence

Let's next look at the transactions starting side-by-side, as shown in Figure 6-21.

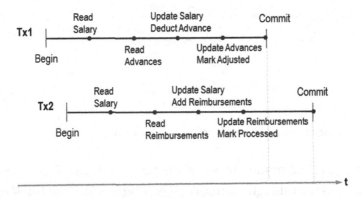

Figure 6-21. *Transactions occurring side-by-side*

The read's acquire shared lock is in both transactions. As the write of Tx1 starts to commit prior to Tx2, Tx1 tries to acquire an exclusive lock. It will wait for the Tx2 acquired read lock to be released. In this scenario, Spanner uses the *wound-and-wait* algorithm and aborts transaction Tx2 so that Tx1 can acquire and continue with its update. Figure 6-22 shows the read locks acquired.

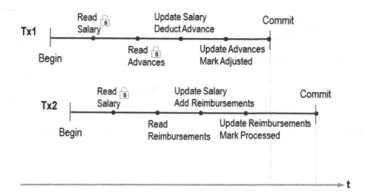

Figure 6-22. *Read locks acquired*

Figure 6-23 shows transaction Tx2 being aborted so that Tx1 can continue with its updates.

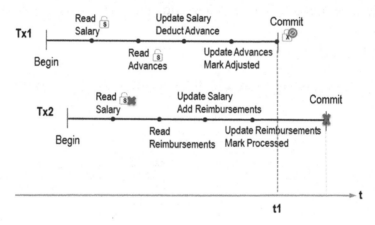

Figure 6-23. *Transaction aborted (wound-and-wait)*

In this process, the Tx2 commit fails and will be retried later. This is done to avoid deadlock. In addition, this also guarantees that no updates are ever lost if multiple concurrent transactions start, as at any point in time only one will be updating the data and the other will retry after some time. Under the hood, the age of each transaction is used to resolve the conflicting lock issue. The younger transaction will wait, but an older transaction will wound (abort) a younger transaction. By giving priority to the older transaction, Spanner ensures that eventually every transaction gets a chance to update.

Data Invalidated

Let's next look at the case shown in Figure 6-24, when Tx1 reads and changes Salary data and Tx2 reads the same data.

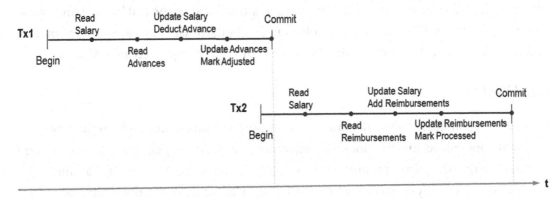

Figure 6-24. *Transactions (data invalidated)*

Since Tx2 started earlier than the Tx1 commit, it will read the Salary value, which is already invalidated due to changes made by Tx1. In this case as well, Tx2 will be terminated so that the update of Tx1 is not overwritten. In effect, prior to making the update, the transaction waits for the read locks to be released and also validates that all the read locks it acquired within the transaction are still valid. This implies no change is made to it after it has read the data.

Different Fields Updates

Take a look at the transaction shown in Figure 6-25.

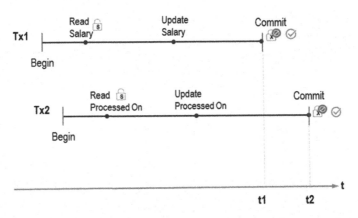

Figure 6-25. *Transactions updating different fields simultaneously*

Transaction Tx1 is working on the Salary field, whereas Tx2 works on the Processed On field. It is quite likely that both transactions will attempt to update the same row of data simultaneously. However, unlike the previous scenario, where transaction Tx2 was aborted to avoid the deadlock situation, here, both transactions will be executed successfully. This is due to the fact that Cloud Spanner locks at the cell level (a row and a column). The row is the same but the columns that both transactions are working on are different. So, there will be no conflict, as the cells that will be updated are different.

Blind Writes

Let's now look at the scenario of concurrent read/write transactions, where you have only write operations that are not followed by any reads. Such operations are called *blind writes*. Inserting the current month's salary details in the Salary table is an example. Write locks are usually exclusive, where only one writer updates the data. Although this prevents data corruption by preventing the race condition on the data, it does impact the throughput.

With blind writes in Spanner, the write locks are allowed to be shared. This is possible due to usage of TrueTime. TrueTime guarantees a unique timestamp to each transaction, so multiple blind writes can run in parallel, thereby updating the same data without worrying about data corruption or loss. This feature not only avoids race conditions but also brings in significant throughput for blind writes.

Read/Write with Read Only

Now you have a scenario of read/write and read only transactions running side-by-side, as shown in Figure 6-26.

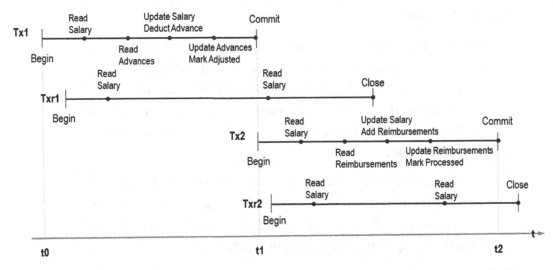

Figure 6-26. *Multiple read/write and read only transactions occurring side-by-side*

As you can see, the read only transactions Txr1 and Txr2 are interleaved in between the two read/write transactions, Tx1 and Tx2. You can further assume the Salary table data is as shown in Tables 6-18 through 6-20 at various timestamps.

Table 6-18. *Salary Data at t0*

Employee ID	Month	Salary	Processed On
1	Aug 2019	$1000	23rd Aug 2019

Table 6-19. *Salary Data at t1*

Employee ID	Month	Salary	Processed On
1	Aug 2019	$500	23rd Aug 2019

Table 6-20. *Salary Data at t2*

Employee ID	Month	Salary	Processed On
1	Aug 2019	$10000	23rd Aug 2019

Here are values read in each:

- In Txr1, all reads will show values, as on timestamp t0, which is $1000 only, as it started prior to the Tx1 commit and the snapshot taken was of timestamp t0. All reads within the transaction return the value from the snapshot, so even though the second read is after the Tx1 commit timestamp, the changes will not be reflected in this transaction read.

- The change of the Tx1 commit will be visible in the Txr2 read, as the snapshot for this transaction is after the Tx1 commit. Every read in this transaction will show $500. As with Txr1, reads in Txr2 will not show the changes made in transaction Tx2.

This guarantees safety against non-repeatable reads and dirty reads. *Non-repeatable reads* are reads within a transaction that see different values due to interleaved read/ write transactions. *Dirty reads* are reads that see a change that has not yet been committed.

Having looked at the way operations happen in Spanner, it's time to go back and look at the way Spanner carries out the read/write operations across its distributed dataset.

Distributed Transactions Explained

To understand distributed transactions, you need to return to the hypothetical data distribution, as shown in Figure 6-27.

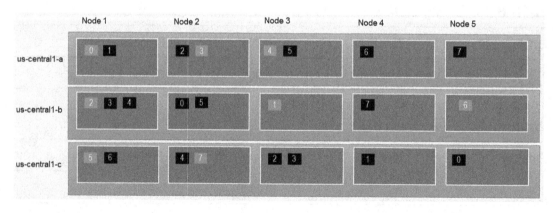

Figure 6-27. *Hypothetical representation of the data distribution with leaders highlighted*

The distributed data table schema and hypothetical split distribution are shown in Tables 6-21 and 6-22.

Table 6-21. *TableA Schema*

Column Name	Data Type	
ID	INT64	Primary Key
Value	STRING	

Table 6-22. *TableA Split Details*

Split	Key Range
0	<100
1	>=100 and <500
2	>=500 and <1000
3	>=1000 and <2000
4	>=2000 and <2500
5	>=2500 and <4000
6	>=4000 and <7000
7	>=7000

Let's begin with writes.

Writes

With data being distributed across splits, writes can have two main use cases:

- Involving a single split. An update statement is issued for row ID 7.

- Involving multiple splits. An update value of row IDs 410, 500, 1300, and 2300.

Let's begin with the first use case. The transaction issues the COMMIT statement to begin writing in the database. The following happens:

- Step1: Identifies the leader replica for the split. In this example, the split is 0 and the leader replica resides on node 1.

- Step2: The leader replica tries to acquire an exclusive lock on its local copy of the data. In addition, it forwards requests for agreement on committing to voting replicas.

- Step 3: If the lock is acquired and a majority of votes are received, it tries to assign a timestamp for commit and wait for its certainty. In parallel, it sends the writes to the other replicas hosting the data copy. Replicas store the writes to stable storage and communicate back to the leader. Once the majority of replicas have responded and the commit wait is over, the leader is sure the commit will begin.

- Step 4: Communicates the timestamp back to the client and leader. The other replicas start applying the changes.

- Step 5: After completion, the locks are released.

Since this write involves only a single split, it is the cheapest and fastest write. Let's now look at the second use case, which involves multiple splits. This kind of update uses an extra layer of coordination via the standard two-phase commit algorithm. Like in a single node operation, the transaction issues the COMMIT statement to begin writing in the database. The following happens:

- Step 1: Identify the leader replica for the splits. The splits are 1, 2, 3, and 4. The leader replicas reside across nodes 1, 2, and 3.

- Step 2: Since multiple splits are involved, one split leader picks up the role of the coordinator and the remaining leaders become the participants. For this example, assume that split 1 becomes the coordinator. As coordinator, its job is to ensure the atomicity of the transaction—the changes are applied on all the splits or no splits at all.

- Step 3: The first phase of the two phase commit.

  Like the single split reads, all the respective split leaders (irrespective of the role) try to acquire an exclusive lock on the local data copy. In this example, the following splits tries to acquire a write lock on the row IDs Split 1 => Row Id 410, Split 2 => Row Id 500, Split 3 => Row Id 1300, and Split 4 =>Row Id 2300.

  Each split leader records its set of locks by replicating them to at least a majority of its split replicas. Once they are able to hold the locks, they notify the coordinator.

  If all the split leaders are able to successfully acquire the lock, the coordinator moves to the next step.

  Like in a single split read, the coordinator then tries to assign a timestamp to the commit and wait for its certainty. In parallel, it sends the writes to all the replicas. Replicas store the writes to its stable storage and communicate back to the leader. Once the majority has responded and the commit wait is over, the second phase of the commit begins.

- Step 4: The second phase of the two phase commit.

  The coordinator communicates the outcome to all the participant's leaders. The participant's leaders communicate the same to all its replicas.

  The coordinator and all its participants apply the changes to their respective data. The coordinator leader communicates to the client that the transaction has been committed.

- Step 5: After the completion, the locks are released

Irrespective of whether the write involves a single node or is multi-node, a write is marked to be committed only when write-quorum is achieved or, in other words, the majority of voting replicas (replicas who are eligible to vote for a write commit) agree to commit the write. Writes always happen on the leader replica and the non-witness replicas of the replica set. The next section covers read operations.

Reads

As you already know by now, reads can be part of read/write transactions as well as read only transactions. Reads that are part of the read/write transactions will always be served by the leader replica, as it requires locking. Reads that are part of read only transactions (or single reads) can be served from any replica. The need to communicate with the leader replica depends on the read type method: strong or stale.

Strong reads can go to any replica, but *stale* reads always go to the closest available replica. Here's a strong read operation that reads rows with IDs >=0 and < 700.

1. Splits are identified. In this case, the splits are 0, 1, and 2. Being a strong read, the current TrueTime timestamp is picked and the request is sent to any replica of the splits 0, 1, and 2, along with the read timestamp.

2. This step depends on the replica type. In this case, you have only two possibilities—the replica is a leader or is not a leader.

    a) If the replica turns out to be the leader, reads can proceed directly, as data is always up to date on the leader.

    b) If it's not a leader replica, there are two new possibilities. The data is updated or is not updated.

        i. If the data is updated, reads are served as is.

        ii. If it's not up to date, it interacts with the leader to get the latest update. Once the updates are applied, the data state becomes the latest and the reads are served.

3. Results received from the replicas are combined and returned to the client.

If you do stale reads, then you can proceed without Step 2.b.(ii).

Summary

This chapter covered the way data is stored and looked at important modeling concepts, including a brief understanding of the way transactions are handled in Spanner. The next chapter starts on developing with Spanner.

CHAPTER 7

Getting Started with Spanner

Now that we understand the underlying concepts of CloudSpanner, its various features and the way it handles data, let's get started working with it.

In this chapter we will cover:

- Working with Spanner using Cloud Console

- Create a python program with Spanner as its database

Let's begin with provisioning our instance. As we know by now, an instance is allocation of resources that are used by the databases created within the instance.

Provisioning CloudSpanner Instance

Navigate to the URL `https://console.cloud.google.com/`. Login using your google account if not already logged in and ensure that your project is selected in the projects drop down. In order to run all exercises for CloudSpanner we have created project named *DemoSpanner*. Figure 7-1 shows the project selected.

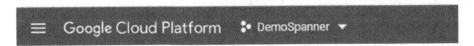

Figure 7-1. *Project selection*

Next we open the left Navigation menu and choose Spanner underneath the storage section as shown in Figure 7-2.

© Navin Sabharwal, Shakuntala Gupta Edward 2020
N. Sabharwal and S. G. Edward, *Hands On Google Cloud SQL and Cloud Spanner*,
https://doi.org/10.1007/978-1-4842-5537-7_7

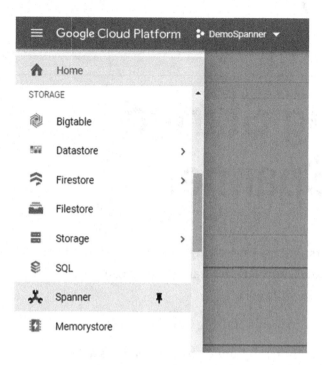

Figure 7-2. *Spanner underneath Storage Section*

Alternatively, we can key in spanner in the search bar and select Spanner from the dropdown menu as shown in Figure 7-3.

Figure 7-3. *Spanner in Search Bar (Top Panel)*

This takes us to the cloud spanner API page as shown in Figure 7-4. Click on **Enable**.

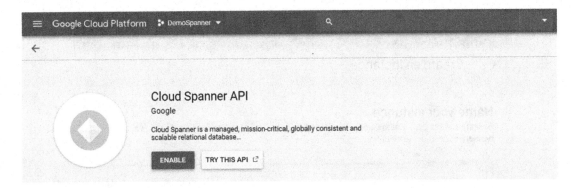

Figure 7-4. *Cloud Spanner API Page*

It takes few seconds for the API to be enabled and then we are redirected to the Cloud Spanner Page. Figure 7-5 shows the page.

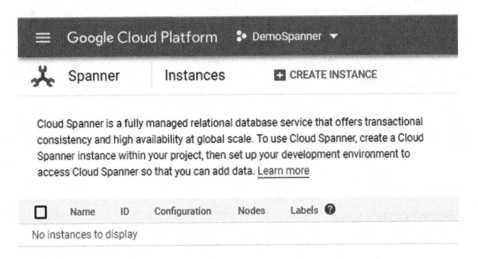

Figure 7-5. *Cloud Spanner Page*

You will see *Create Instance* button. Click on *Create Instance*. This takes us to the form as shown in Figure 7-6 wherein everything which is required to set up our instance is available.

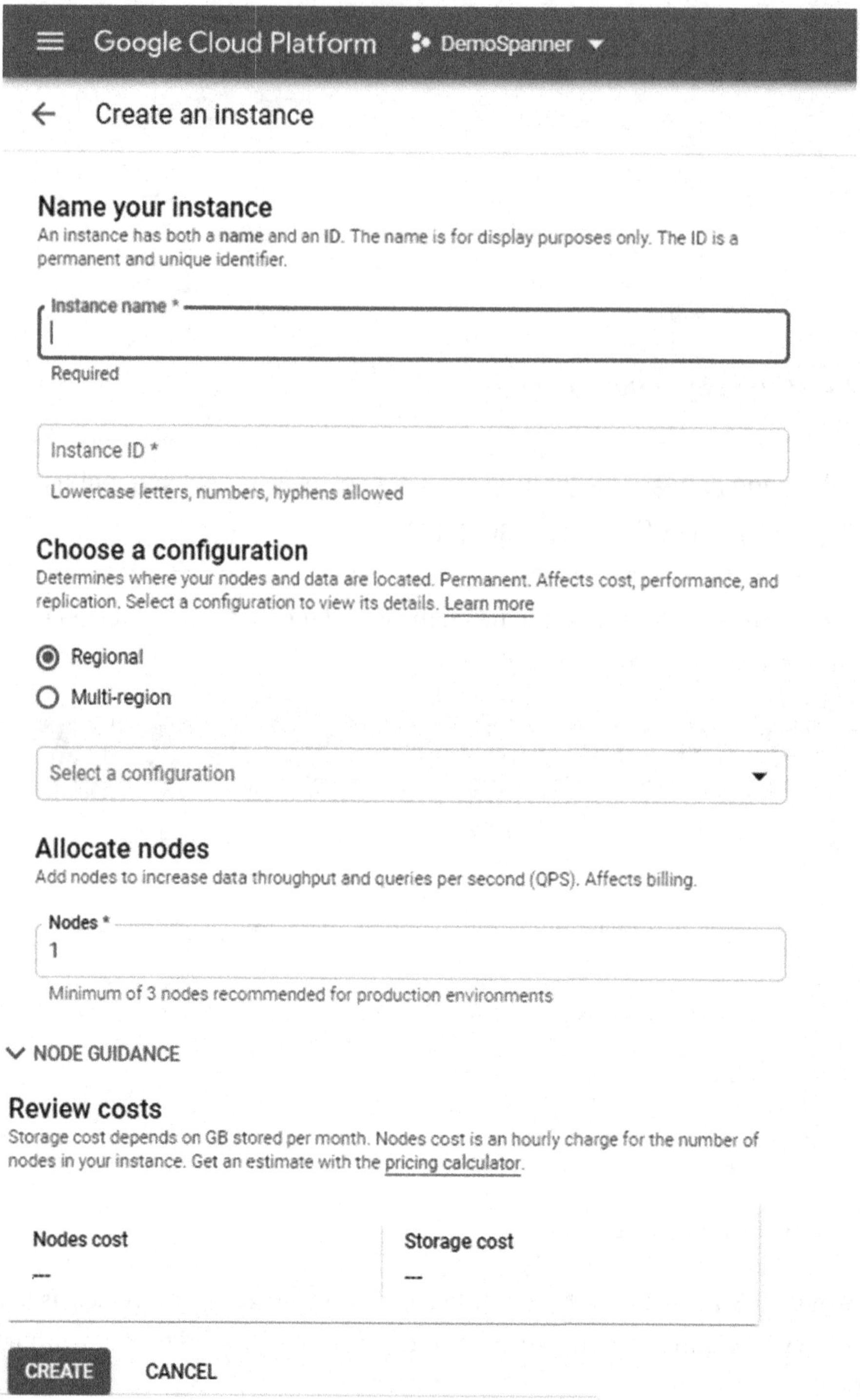

Figure 7-6. *Cloud Spanner Create Instance Page*

Let's begin with instance identification. The first section enables us to provide a Name and ID for our instance. We first specify a user-friendly name, this is used for display purposes only. Let's name the instance as *DemoCloudSpanner*. Next, we specify the Instance Id which is the identifier used to not only uniquely identify the instance but will also be used for any communication with the instance. We name it as *democloudspanner*.

Let's next choose the configuration. This provides us with two options: Regional and Multi-Region. Selecting the Regional option displays the Regions configured as shown in Figure 7-7 enabling us to choose the one which best co-locates with our reads/writes workload.

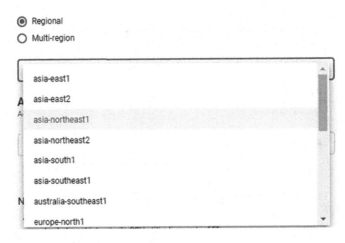

Figure 7-7. *Regional configuration*

Multi-Region choice displays the continents configured enabling us to choose the one which best covers the regions of our workload. Figure 7-8 shows the list of available continents.

Figure 7-8. *Multi-Region Configuration*

For this example, we choose Regional with asia-east1 region. As we make our selections, we can review the configuration details in the right-hand side panel as shown in Figure 7-9.

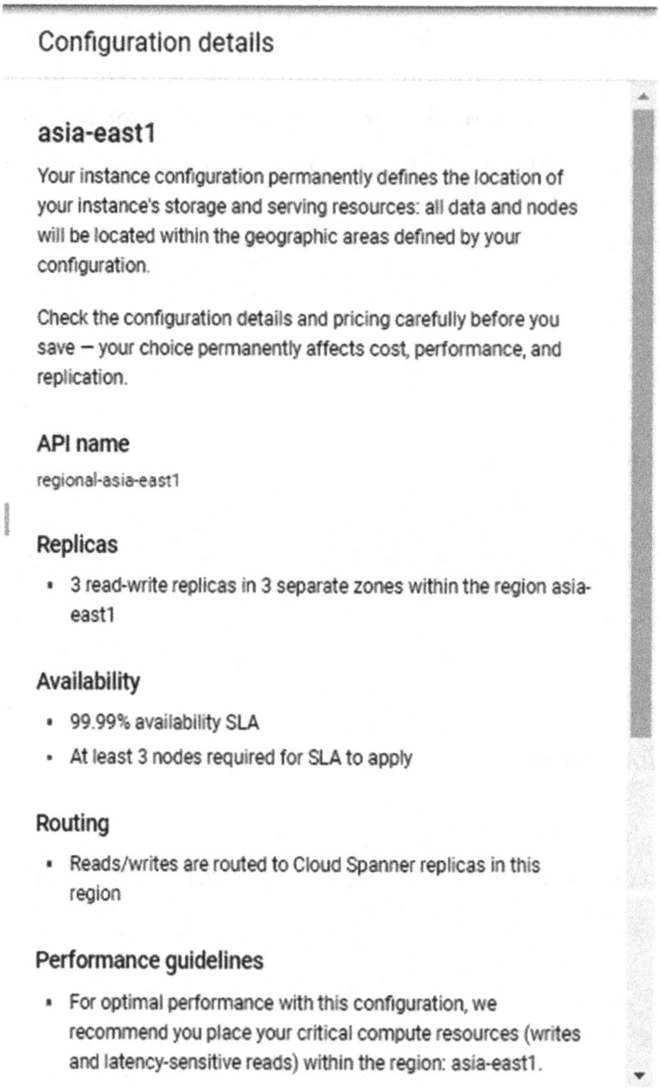

Configuration details

asia-east1

Your instance configuration permanently defines the location of your instance's storage and serving resources: all data and nodes will be located within the geographic areas defined by your configuration.

Check the configuration details and pricing carefully before you save — your choice permanently affects cost, performance, and replication.

API name

regional-asia-east1

Replicas

- 3 read-write replicas in 3 separate zones within the region asia-east1

Availability

- 99.99% availability SLA
- At least 3 nodes required for SLA to apply

Routing

- Reads/writes are routed to Cloud Spanner replicas in this region

Performance guidelines

- For optimal performance with this configuration, we recommend you place your critical compute resources (writes and latency-sensitive reads) within the region: asia-east1.

Figure 7-9. *Configuration Details*

Next, we allocate nodes to our instance. As we know nodes determine the serving and storage resources available to the instance in all its zones. While choosing we can take into consideration the Node Guidance provided by GCP as shown in Figure 7-10.

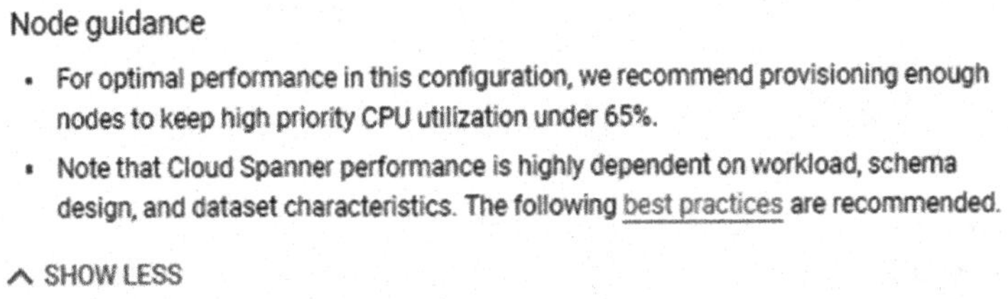

Node guidance

- For optimal performance in this configuration, we recommend provisioning enough nodes to keep high priority CPU utilization under 65%.
- Note that Cloud Spanner performance is highly dependent on workload, schema design, and dataset characteristics. The following best practices are recommended.

∧ SHOW LESS

Figure 7-10. *Node Guidance*

For this example, we retain the default allocation of one Node. With all the inputs in place the create instance page looks as shown in Figure 7-11.

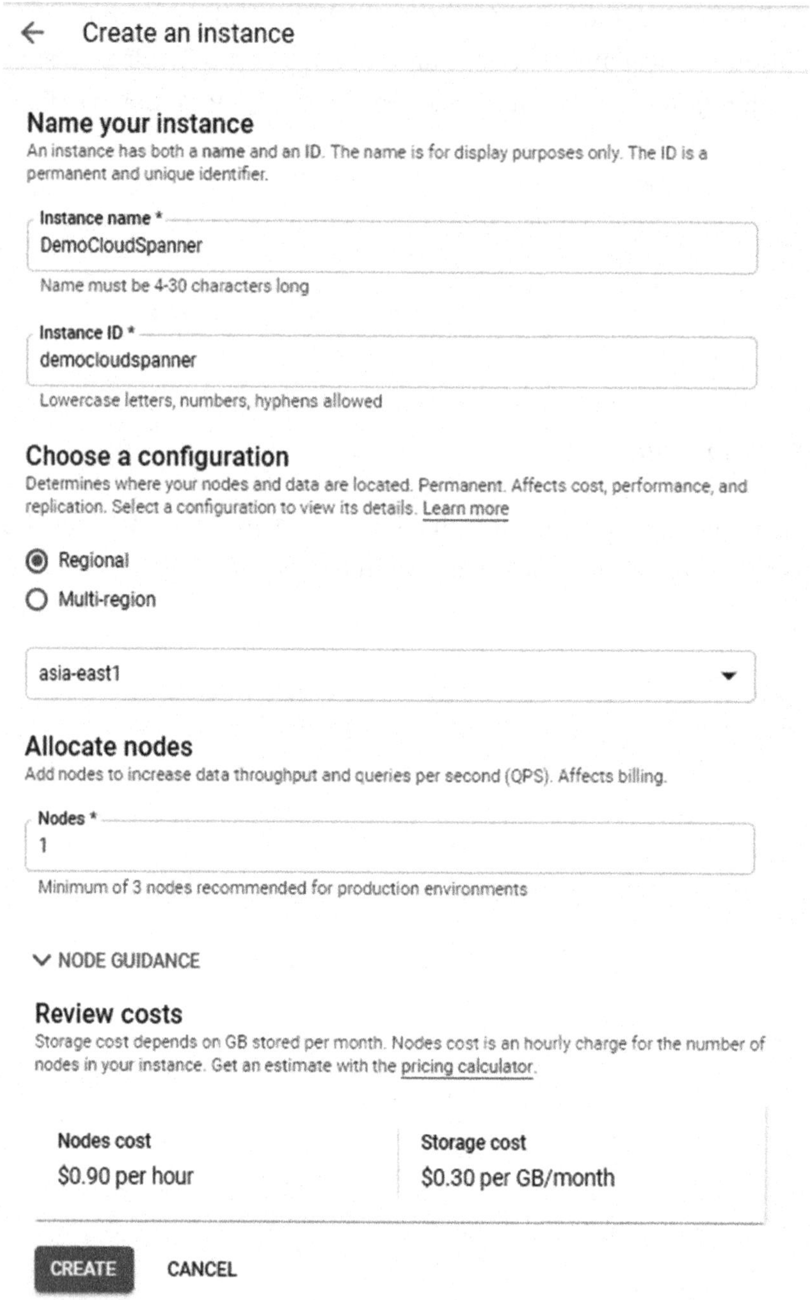

←   Create an instance

Name your instance

An instance has both a name and an ID. The name is for display purposes only. The ID is a permanent and unique identifier.

Instance name *

DemoCloudSpanner

Name must be 4-30 characters long

Instance ID *

democloudspanner

Lowercase letters, numbers, hyphens allowed

Choose a configuration

Determines where your nodes and data are located. Permanent. Affects cost, performance, and replication. Select a configuration to view its details. Learn more

⦿ Regional

◯ Multi-region

asia-east1   ▼

Allocate nodes

Add nodes to increase data throughput and queries per second (QPS). Affects billing.

Nodes *

1

Minimum of 3 nodes recommended for production environments

⌄ NODE GUIDANCE

Review costs

Storage cost depends on GB stored per month. Nodes cost is an hourly charge for the number of nodes in your instance. Get an estimate with the pricing calculator.

Nodes cost	Storage cost
$0.90 per hour	$0.30 per GB/month

CREATE   CANCEL

Figure 7-11. *Create instance page with all inputs filled in*

Review costs and adjust if required. Click on Create and wait for few seconds while Google provisions the instance for us. On successful creation of the instance we will be redirected to the Instance details page as shown in Figure 7-12.

Figure 7-12. *Spanner Instance Detail Page*

Let's take a moment here and familiarize ourselves with the options available on the page. All possible actions with the instance are displayed in the Top panel itself.

Edit Instance option enables us to adjust the nodes allocated. In effect, there's no need of planning and forecasting the resources required to provision upfront instead using the edit option we can change the nodes any time. Figure 7-13 shows the Edit Instance page.

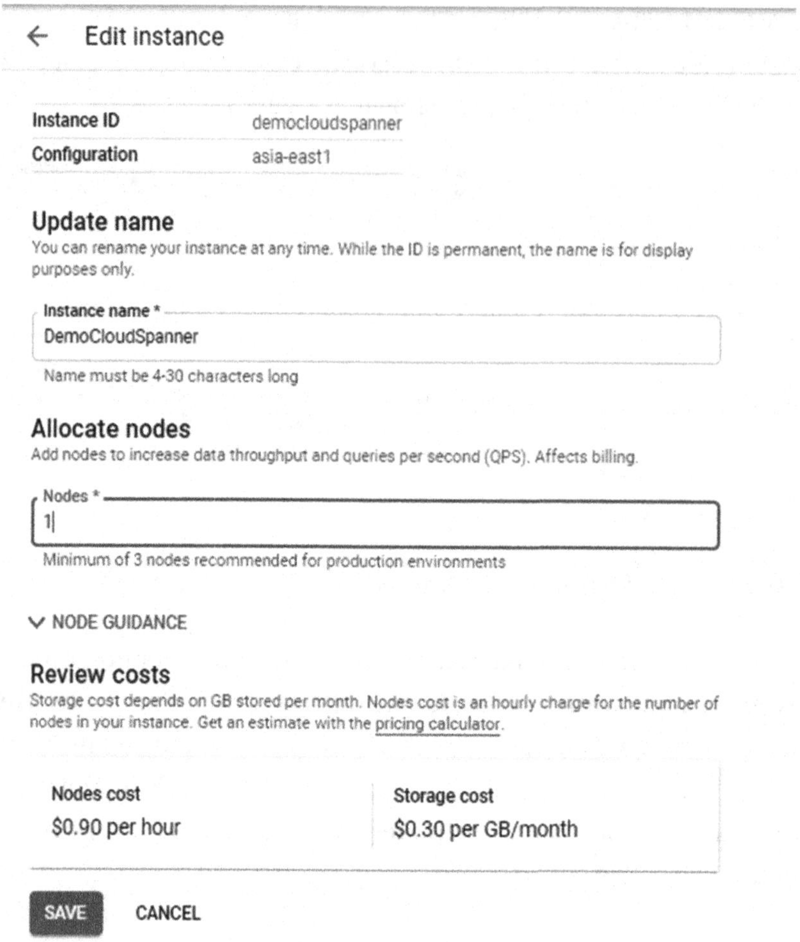

Figure 7-13. *Edit Instance Page*

In addition, this option also enables us to change the instance name anytime. Next to the Edit Instance option we have option to import/export data to/from a database within the instance.

Note   While Google's high availability claims may guarantee you will not lose any data, due to hardware or database failures, however we should have the ability to backup, to guard against human error such as dropping a table by accident or sabotage/espionage, application defects, and so on. As high availability guarantees don't replace a sound backup strategy. Cloud Spanner offers the import/export option which allows us to take the backups of the database into Avro format.

Click Export, populate the requested information such as a destination Google Cloud Storage bucket, the database to be exported. The database will be backed-up in Avro format to Google Cloud Storage. Figure 7-14 shows the Export page.

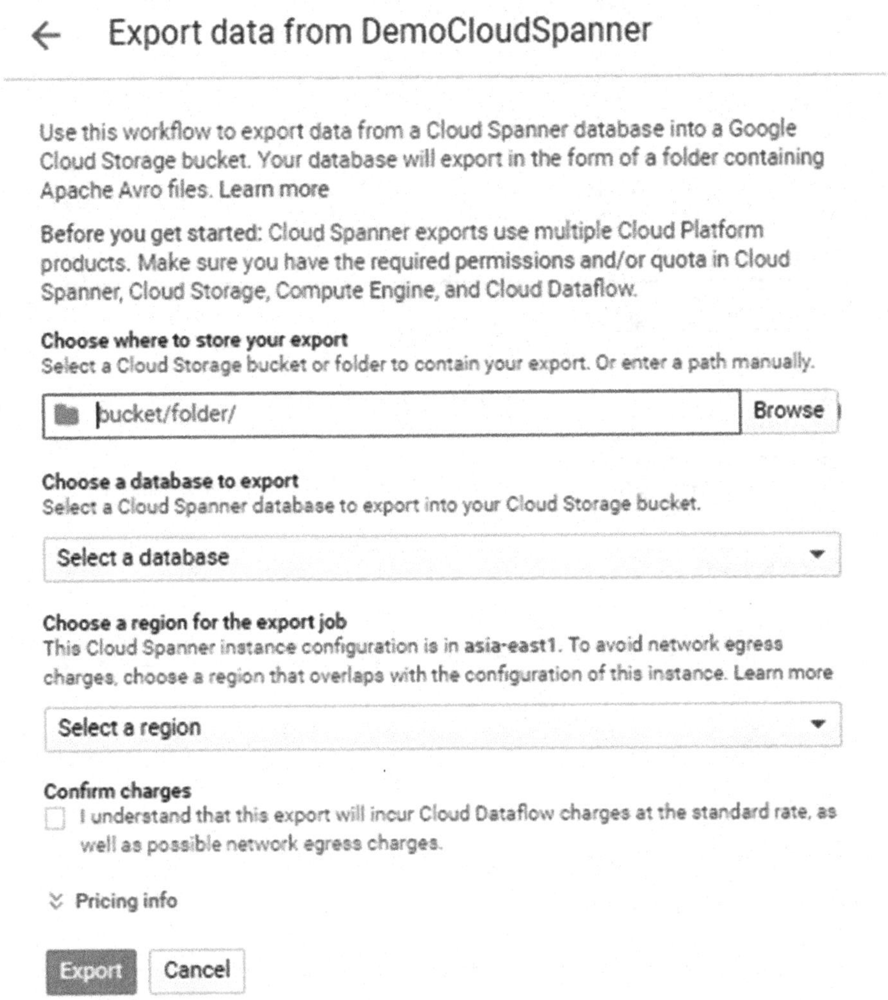

←   Export data from DemoCloudSpanner

Use this workflow to export data from a Cloud Spanner database into a Google Cloud Storage bucket. Your database will export in the form of a folder containing Apache Avro files. Learn more

Before you get started: Cloud Spanner exports use multiple Cloud Platform products. Make sure you have the required permissions and/or quota in Cloud Spanner, Cloud Storage, Compute Engine, and Cloud Dataflow.

Choose where to store your export
Select a Cloud Storage bucket or folder to contain your export. Or enter a path manually.

| 📁 bucket/folder/ | Browse |

Choose a database to export
Select a Cloud Spanner database to export into your Cloud Storage bucket.

| Select a database ▼ |

Choose a region for the export job
This Cloud Spanner instance configuration is in asia-east1. To avoid network egress charges, choose a region that overlaps with the configuration of this instance. Learn more

| Select a region ▼ |

Confirm charges
☐ I understand that this export will incur Cloud Dataflow charges at the standard rate, as well as possible network egress charges.

≫ Pricing info

[Export] [Cancel]

Figure 7-14.   *Export data page*

To restore a database, use the Import option, populate the inputs such as the Google Cloud Storage folder from where the data is to be restored, database name where the data will be restored. Figure 7-15 shows the Import data page.

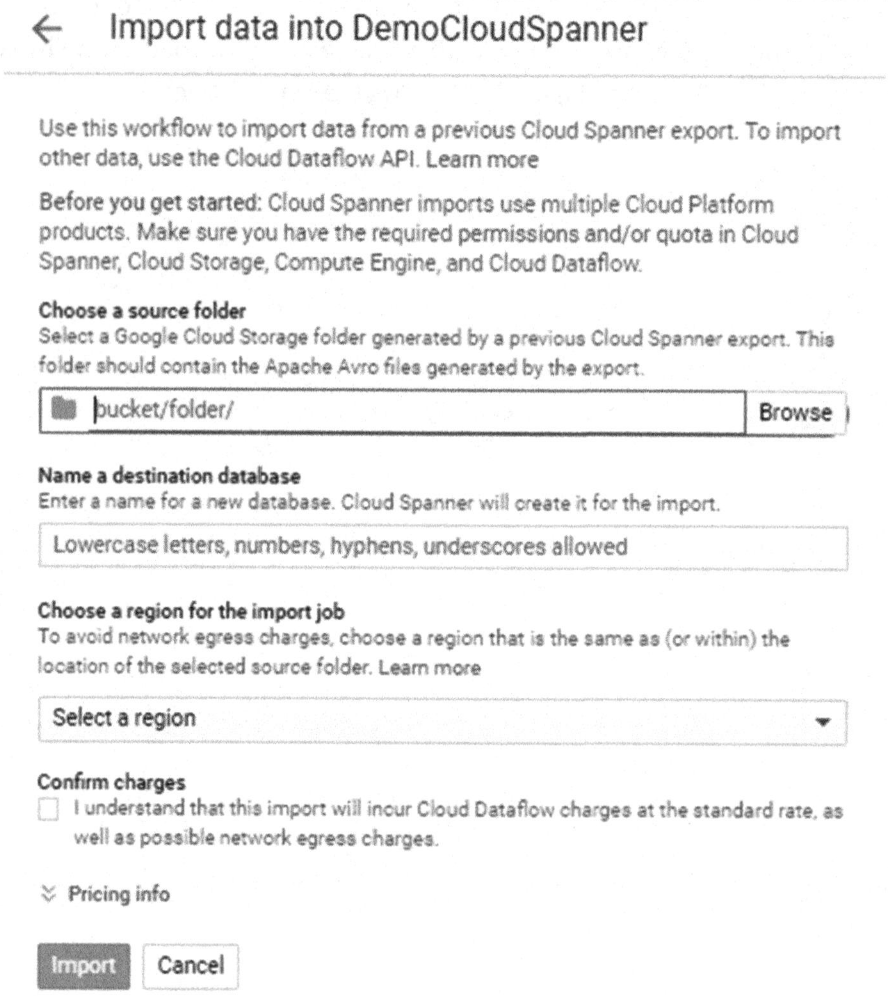

Figure 7-15. *Import Data page*

Note   The actual export and import is done using Google cloud DataFlow and we will be charged for the dataflow operation.

For the export option to work we should have databases created in the instance

Import option restores the data to a new database.

Along with the above options we have option to Create database and delete the instance itself. In addition, we have an overview tab and monitoring tab. The overview tab provides a summarized view of the instance whereas the Monitoring tab enables us to monitor the instance performance and usage as shown in Figure 7-16.

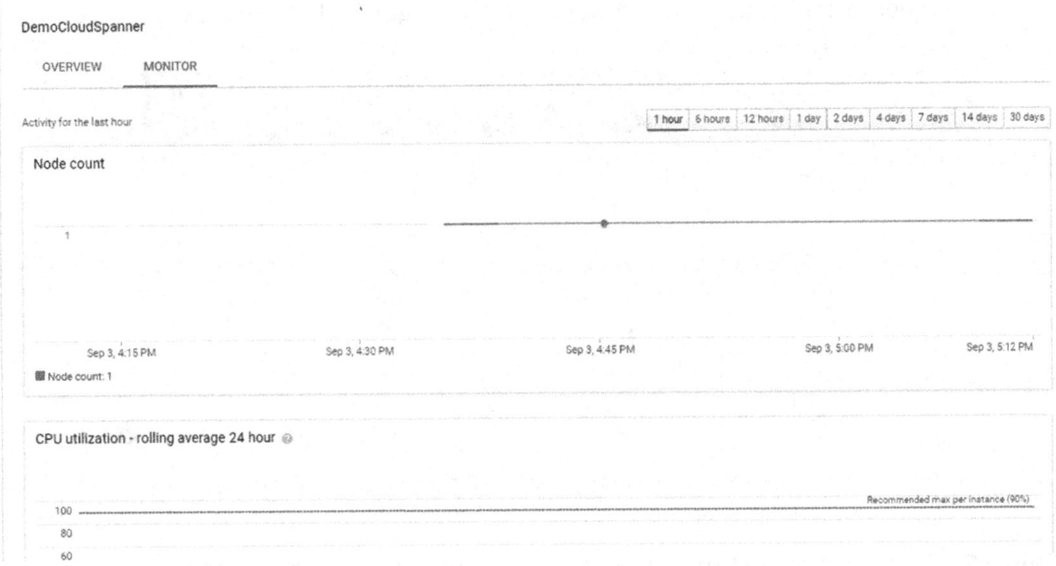

Figure 7-16. *Monitor Tab*

As seen the current hour is selected, however it enables us to change the time filter and review the data till last 30 days.

Feel free to explore the instance details page to familiarize yourself with it. Now that we have provisioned our Spanner instance, let's get started working with it. We will start with accessing the instance and working with it using Cloud Console Let's get started with the Cloud Console.

Getting Started in Cloud Console

This walkthrough will connect to the Spanner instance democloudspanner, create database and tables, load data in the table created and run few example queries.

Connect to the Spanner Instance

Once logged in to the Google Web Console, like with other activities first ensure our spanner project DemoSpanner is selected. Next navigate to Spanner instance page by selecting Spanner underneath Storage section. This takes us to the Spanner page which lists the Spanner instances created within the project. Figure 7-17 shows the instance page.

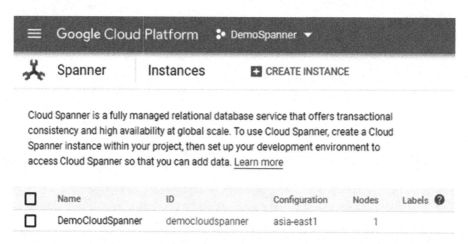

Figure 7-17. *Spanner Instance page with DemoCloudSpanner listed*

Click on the instance to open the instance detail page.

Create Database

In the instance detail page, click on Create database in the Top panel. This takes us to the Create Database Page as shown in Figure 7-18.

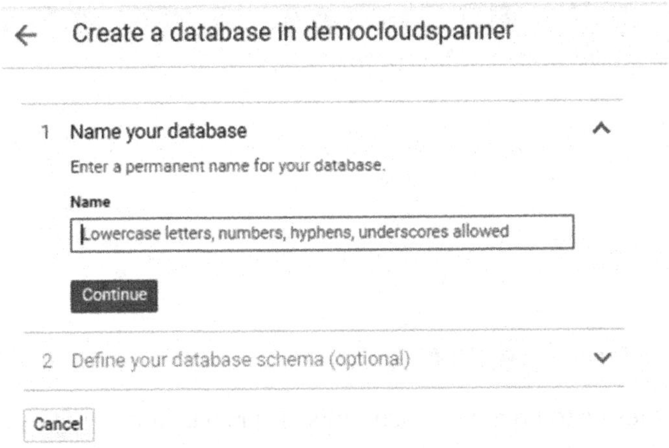

← Create a database in democloudspanner

1 Name your database   ⌃
   Enter a permanent name for your database.

   Name
   | Lowercase letters, numbers, hyphens, underscores allowed |

   Continue

2 Define your database schema (optional)   ⌄

Cancel

Figure 7-18. *Create database in Spanner (First Step)*

This is a two-step process. In the first step we name our database. For this example, let's name it as songs. Click on Continue. Figure 7-19 shows the second step.

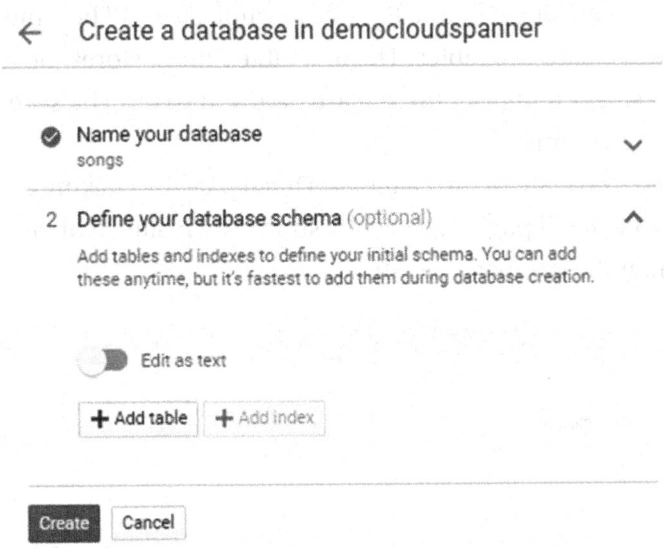

← Create a database in democloudspanner

✓ Name your database   ⌄
   songs

2 **Define your database schema** (optional)   ⌃
   Add tables and indexes to define your initial schema. You can add
   these anytime, but it's fastest to add them during database creation.

   ◯ Edit as text

   ➕ Add table   ➕ Add index

Create Cancel

Figure 7-19. *Create database in Spanner (Second Step)*

The second step which is also an optional step prompts us to specify the schema i.e. create tables and indexes for the database. For now, we create an empty database, leave the step as is and click on Create. Within few seconds the database will be created, and we will be redirected to the database detail page as shown in Figure 7-20.

Figure 7-20. *Database detail page*

This page enables us to create our schemas and run other activities against the database. Feel free to explore the page to familiarize yourself with it. We will explore few of the options as we move forward. Since the database is created with no schema defined, we can see that under the Tables section no table exists right now.

Create Schema

Let's go ahead and create our schema. For this example, we will be simulating a Music App wherein we will create two tables. The first table Album stores the Album details with fields such as singer name, album release date and so on. The second table stores Rating details for the albums.

Let's get started. Navigate to the Database Detail page by clicking on the Database Name in the instance detail page. Figure 7-21 shows the instance detail page listing the database song under the database section.

Figure 7-21. *Instance detail page listing Songs database*

Clicking the database, we will be redirected to the database detail page which is shown above in Figure 7-20. Click on Create table underneath the Tables section. We will be redirected to the Create Table form as shown in Figure 7-22.

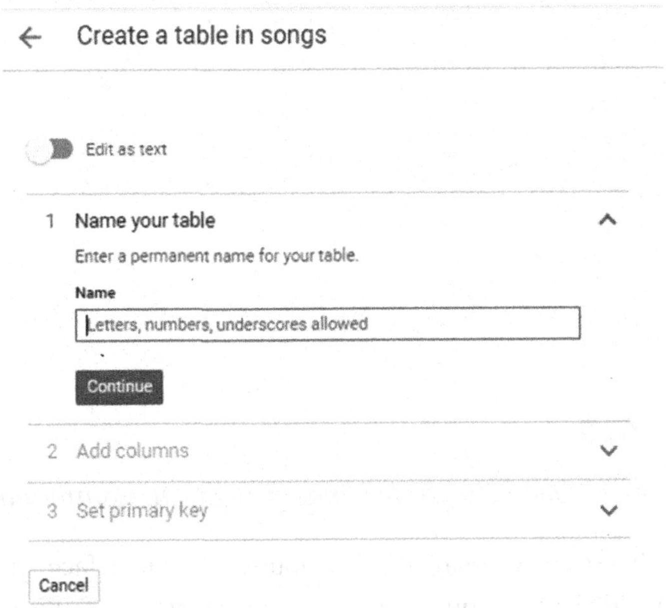

Figure 7-22. *Create Table in Songs database*

As we can see we have two options for specifying the Schema. First is using a GUI as shown in Figure 7-22. The other option is using DDL Commands. To enable the other option, we simply have to Toggle Edit as Text. This enables an interface as shown in Figure 7-23 enabling us to enter our DDL commands.

Figure 7-23. *Create Table in Songs database using DDL Commands*

For this example, we will be using the first option – GUI Interface for defining our schema. Toggle the Edit as Text option again and we will be back to the GUI interface.

We begin with our first table. The table creation using GUI is a three-step process. The first step prompts us to specify the name, in this case we name it as album. Click on Continue. Figure 7-24 shows the second step, which enables us to add the column details.

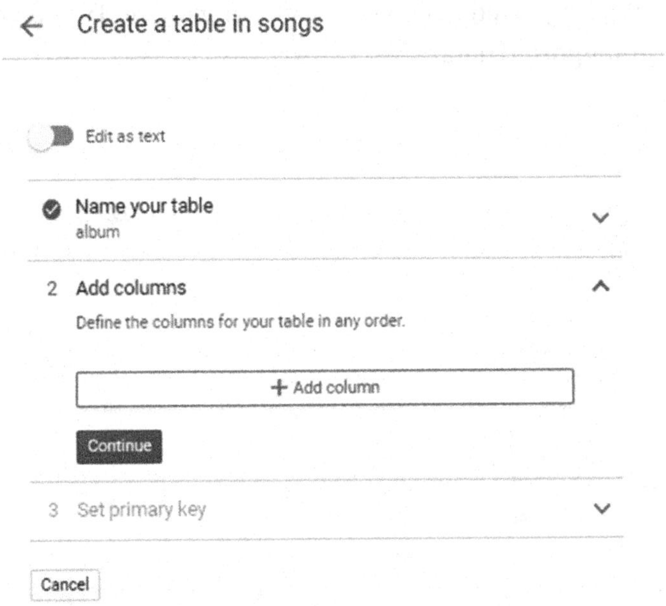

Figure 7-24. *Create Table (Step 2) Add Columns*

Click on Add Column. It prompts us to specify the Name, Data Type and whether the column is Nullable or Not as shown in Figure 7-25.

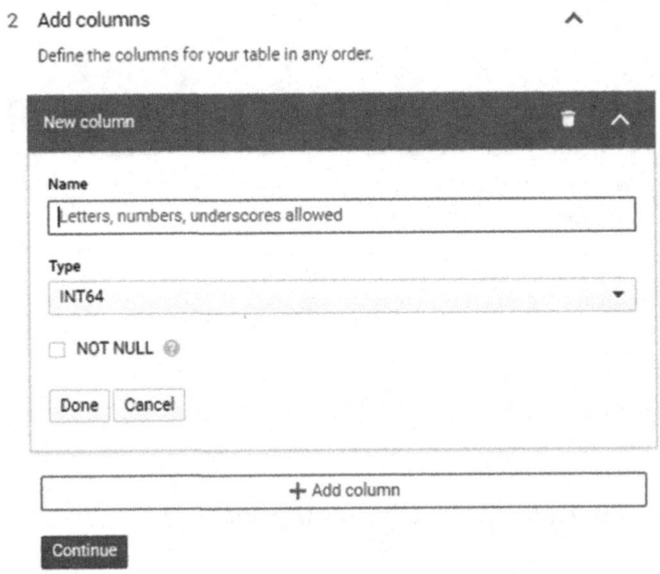

Figure 7-25. *Add New Column*

We can review the supported data types by clicking on the Type dropdown. Figure 7-26 lists the supported data types.

Figure 7-26. *Supported Data Types*

Let's create our first Column, albumId. Figure 7-27 shows all details filled in for AlbumId.

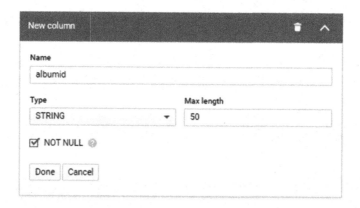

Figure 7-27. *Filled in Details for Column AlbumId*

Click on Done. Figure 7-28 shows the new column added.

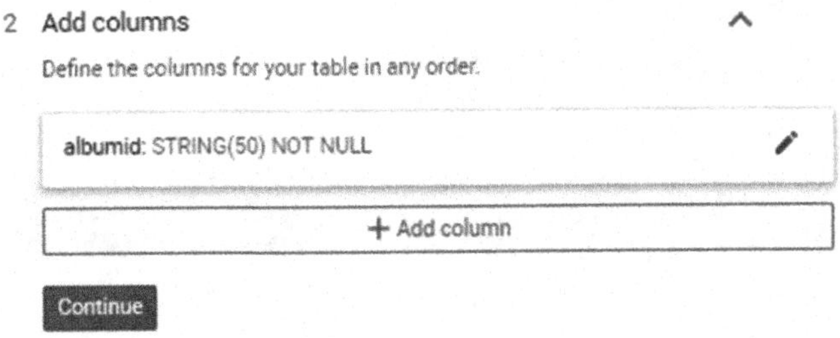

Figure 7-28. *New column added*

Similarly, we will add all other columns using Add Column option. With all columns added the screen will look as shown in Figure 7-29.

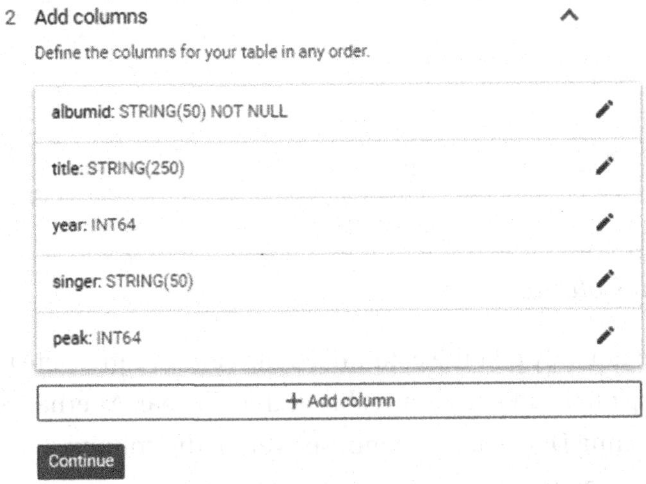

Figure 7-29. *Album Columns*

If required, we can edit the column details anytime by clicking on the edit option next to the column. Figure 7-30 shows the edit screen for column title.

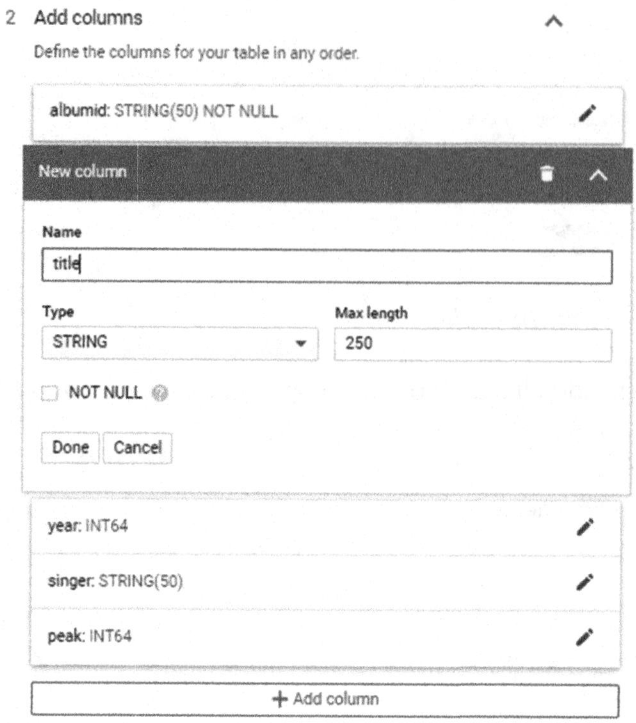

2   Add columns   ∧

Define the columns for your table in any order.

albumid: STRING(50) NOT NULL   ✏

New column   🗑   ∧

Name

title|

Type   Max length

STRING   ▾   250

☐ NOT NULL ⓘ

[Done] [Cancel]

year: INT64   ✏

singer: STRING(50)   ✏

peak: INT64   ✏

＋ Add column

Figure 7-30. *Edit Column*

It enables us to not only edit the column details, but we can delete the column also if required by clicking on the delete icon visible in the blue bar. Alternatively, we can delete the column by selecting Delete icon on mouse over on the column name. Figure 7-31 shows the delete icon on mouse over on the column Year.

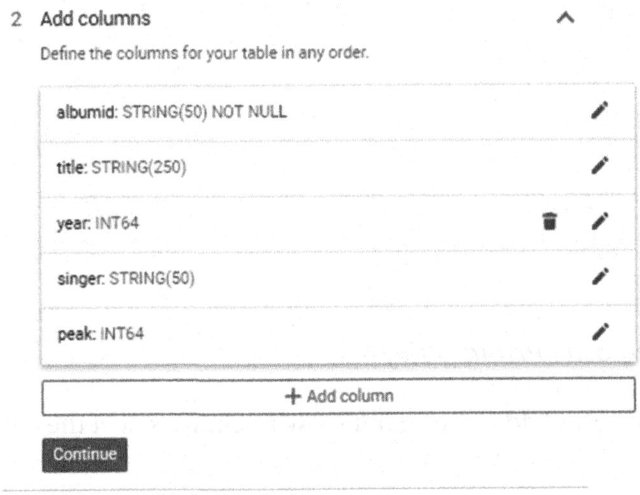

Figure 7-31. *Delete on Mouse Over*

Once we have specified the column details, click on continue. This takes us to the final Step as shown in Figure 7-32 for setting the primary key.

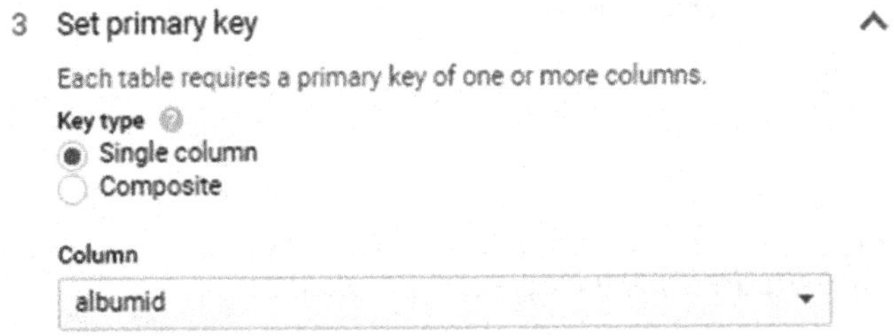

Figure 7-32. *Set Primary Key*

Default Single Column Key is selected with the first column of the table selected in the Column dropdown as shown in Figure 7-32. To specify key with multiple columns, select Composite option under Key type. Figure 7-33 shows the Composite Column option selected with the first column of the table added by default as one of the key columns. Add Column option can be used to add more columns.

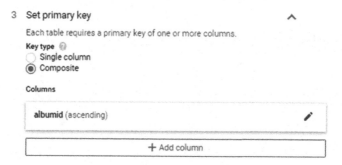

Figure 7-33. *Composite Primary Key*

Figure 7-34 shows the Add Column option wherein we select the column and specify the sort direction.

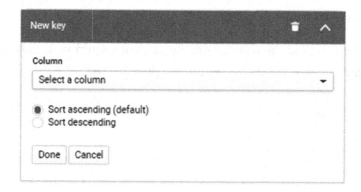

Figure 7-34. *Composite Primary Key – Add Column*

The columns added can be edited as well wherein either we can remove the column altogether or change the column detail and its sort direction as shown in Figure 7-35.

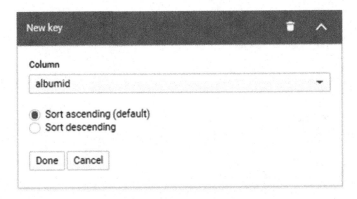

Figure 7-35. *Composite Primary Key – Edit Column*

Like column details, we can delete the columns directly as well on mouse over as shown in Figure 7-36.

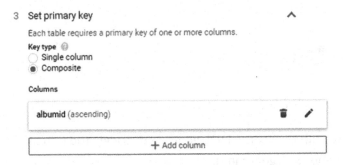

Figure 7-36. *Composite Primary Key – Delete hover Mouse Over*

For this example, we retain the default Single Column Key Type option with AlbumId selected in Column dropdown. Figure 7-37 shows all the details filled in for table Album.

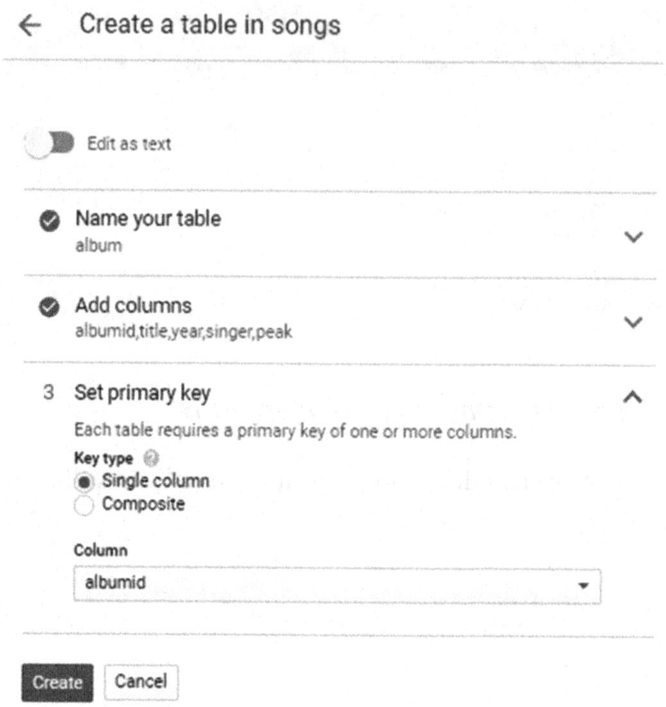

Figure 7-37. *Album Table Details*

At this point we can review the DDL generated. Toggle the Edit as Text option. Figure 7-38 shows the DDL generated.

← Create a table in songs

Edit as text

DDL statements
Add Spanner Database Definition Language SQL statements below. Separate statements with a semicolon. Learn more

```
1  CREATE TABLE album (
2      albumid STRING(50) NOT NULL,
3      title STRING(250),
4      year INT64,
5      singer STRING(50),
6      peak INT64,
7  ) PRIMARY KEY (albumid)
```

Create Cancel

Figure 7-38. *Albums Create DDL Statement*

If any change is required, we can edit in the DDL text itself or switch back to the GUI interface and make the necessary amendments. With the details verified, we Click on Create. Within few seconds the table is created, and the control is redirected to the Table Details page as shown in Figure 7-39.

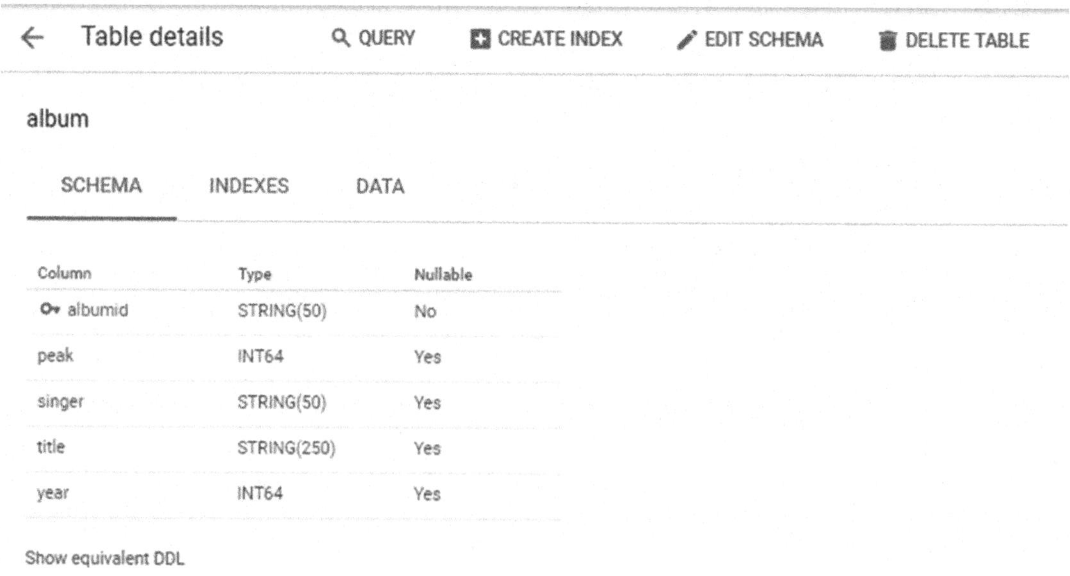

← Table details	Q QUERY	⊞ CREATE INDEX	✎ EDIT SCHEMA	🗑 DELETE TABLE

album

SCHEMA	INDEXES	DATA

Column	Type	Nullable
Oᵥ albumid	STRING(50)	No
peak	INT64	Yes
singer	STRING(50)	Yes
title	STRING(250)	Yes
year	INT64	Yes

Show equivalent DDL

Figure 7-39. *Album Table Details Page*

This enables us to perform operations on the table created e.g. create secondary indexes, execute queries, edit schema, insert data and so on. Feel free to explore the options available. For the time being we leave the table as is and move to create our next table Rating.

Navigate back to the song database detail page and click on Create table again. This time in addition to the other options we have an option to *Interleave in another table*. Figure 7-40 shows the Create table form with the interleaving option.

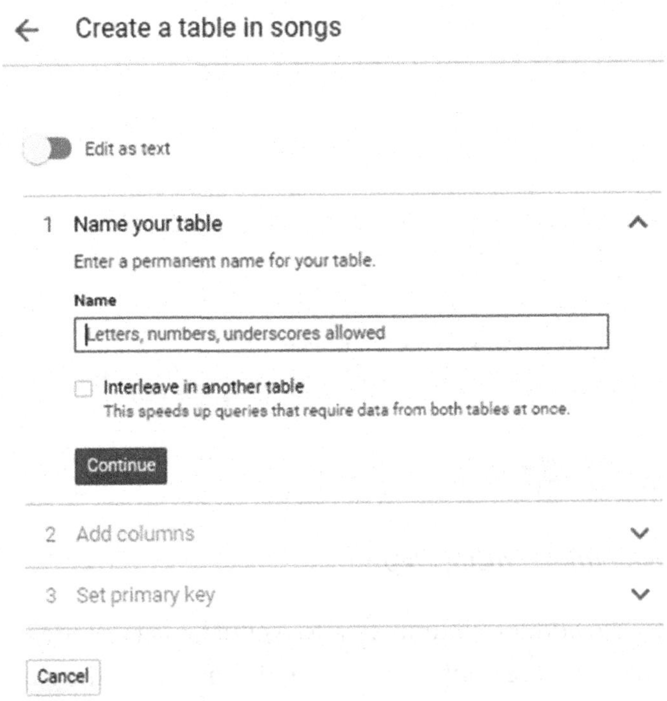

← Create a table in songs

Edit as text

1 Name your table   ∧
   Enter a permanent name for your table.
   Name
   | Letters, numbers, underscores allowed |

   ☐ Interleave in another table
      This speeds up queries that require data from both tables at once.

   Continue

2 Add columns   ∨

3 Set primary key   ∨

Cancel

Figure 7-40. Create table with Interleaving option

Since the Rating table holds the ratings for the albums which exists in the Album table, it's likely that the two tables will be queried together so we will choose the option of interleaving here.

Let's create the table. We start with naming the table, in this case we name it as *rating*. Select *Interleave in another table* option. The moment we select the option; we will be prompted to select the table in which this table is to be interleaved. Album comes selected as default as it's the only table created. We retain the selection. Next, we select Delete parent-child rows together option as our requirement is to delete the associated ratings when an album is deleted. With all the inputs the screen will look as shown in Figure 7-41.

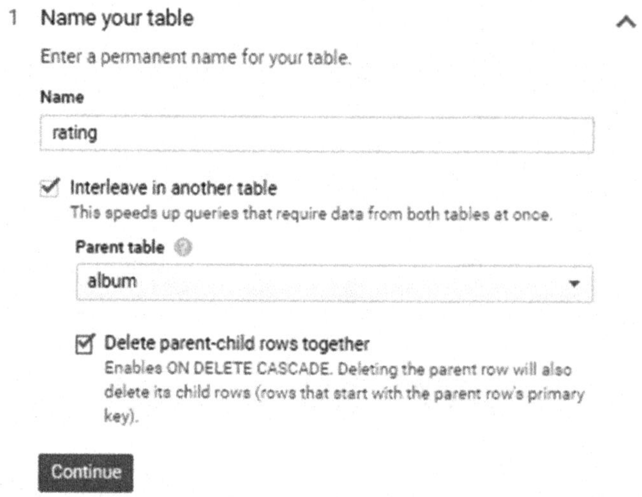

1   Name your table   ∧

Enter a permanent name for your table.

Name

| rating |

☑ Interleave in another table
This speeds up queries that require data from both tables at once.

Parent table ⓘ

| album ▾ |

☑ **Delete parent-child rows together**
Enables ON DELETE CASCADE. Deleting the parent row will also
delete its child rows (rows that start with the parent row's primary
key).

Continue

Figure 7-41. *Create table Rating Step 1*

Click on *continue* to add the column details. As the table is interleaved the primary
key column of the parent table is inherited and added as part of the child table (rating)
column list as shown in Figure 7-42. As we can see this column is non-editable, this
implies the parent primary key column cannot be removed or altered.

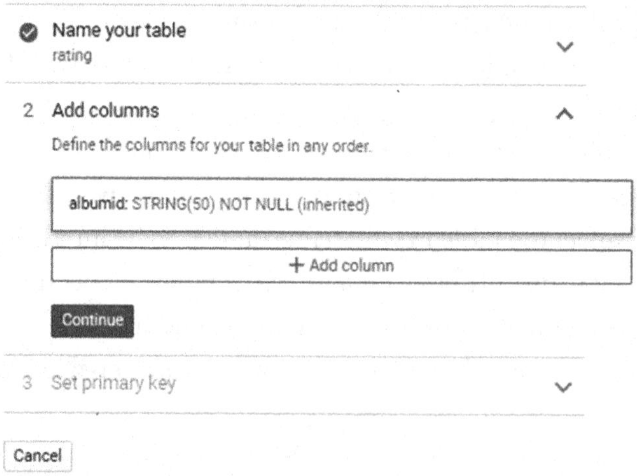

✓ Name your table   ∨
rating

2   Add columns   ∧

Define the columns for your table in any order.

| albumid: STRING(50) NOT NULL (inherited) |

| + Add column |

Continue

3   Set primary key   ∨

Cancel

Figure 7-42. *Interleaved tables – Primary Key Column of Parent Table*

Like we did above for table *albums*, click on *Add Columns* to add all the relevant
columns. Figure 7-43 shows all the columns added for table *rating*.

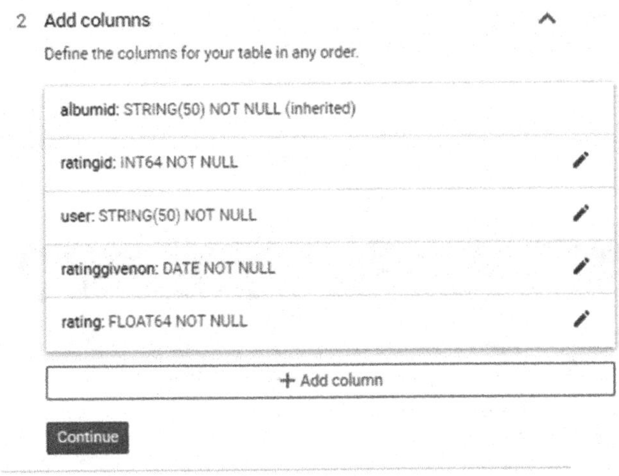

2   Add columns   ∧

Define the columns for your table in any order.

albumid: STRING(50) NOT NULL (inherited)

ratingid: INT64 NOT NULL   ✎

user: STRING(50) NOT NULL   ✎

ratinggivenon: DATE NOT NULL   ✎

rating: FLOAT64 NOT NULL   ✎

＋ Add column

Continue

Figure 7-43. *Ratings Column Details*

Click on *Continue* to specify the primary key next. Being interleaved the primary key of the parent table is inherited and added to the primary key column list as shown in Figure 7-44. The key type is set to *Composite* and is non-editable as the key will be combination of parent and child tables and will always comprise of multiple columns.

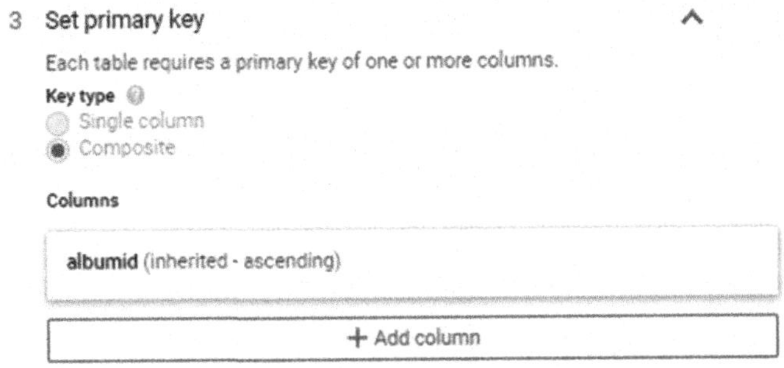

3   Set primary key   ∧

Each table requires a primary key of one or more columns.

Key type ⓘ
◌ Single column
◉ Composite

Columns

albumid (inherited - ascending)

＋ Add column

Figure 7-44. *Rating Primary Key – Inherited parent table key*

Click on *Add column* to add the child table column which will be part of the primary key. In here we select *RatingId* and retain the default ordering i.e. Ascending. Figure 7-45 shows the column selection for the key.

Figure 7-45. Rating Composite Primary Key

Click on *Done*. With all the inputs in place the form looks as shown in Figure 7-46.

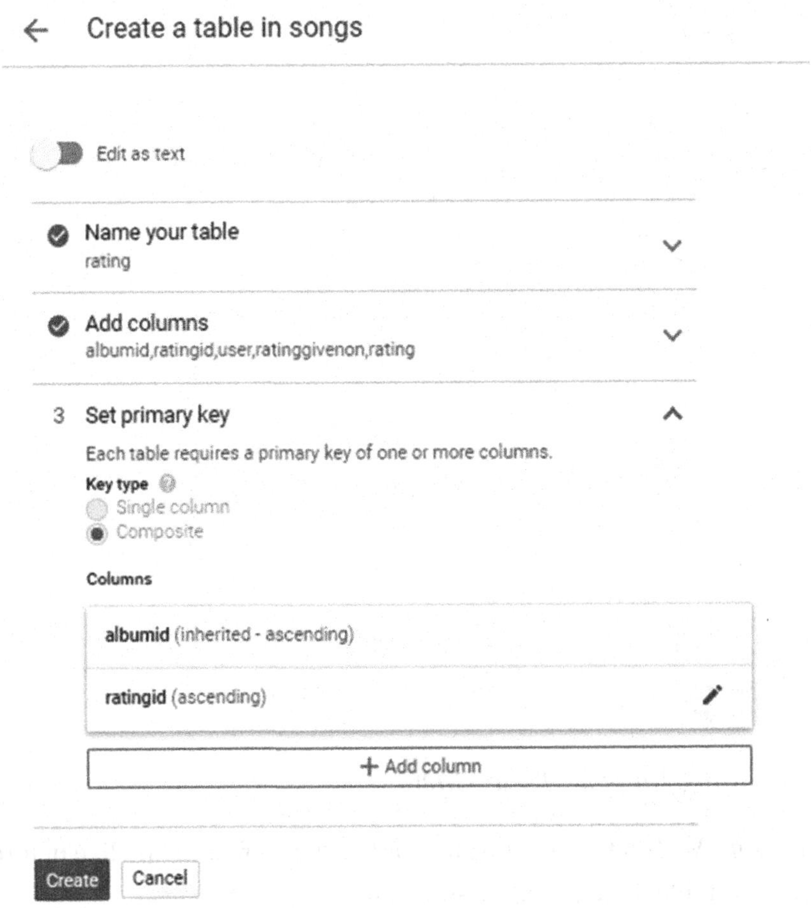

Figure 7-46. *Rating Table Details*

Click on *Edit as text* to review the equivalent command using the cloud spanner data definition language. Figure 7-47 shows the DDL statement generated.

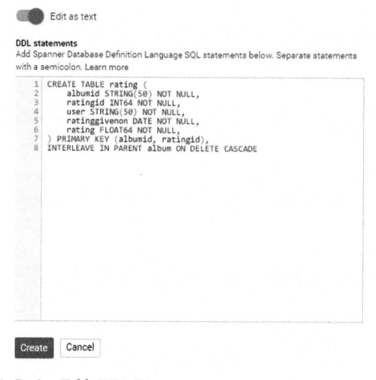

Figure 7-47. *Rating Table DDL Statement*

Click on *Create*. Within few seconds the table will be created and like before we will be redirected to its table details page as shown in Figure 7-48.

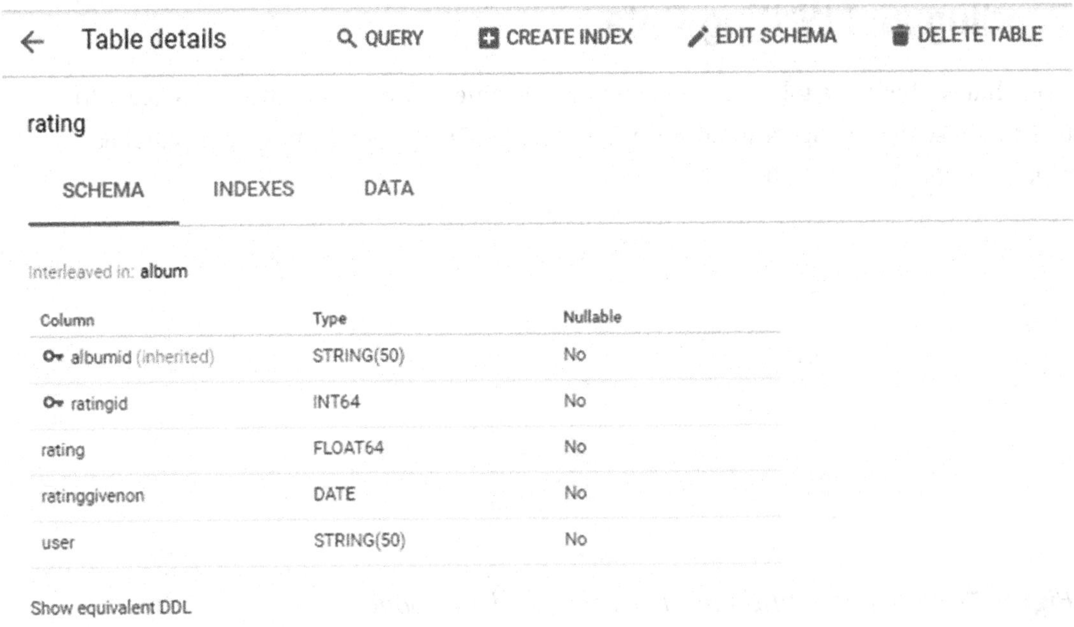

Table details
QUERY
CREATE INDEX
EDIT SCHEMA
DELETE TABLE
rating
SCHEMA
INDEXES
DATA
Interleaved in: album
Column
Type
Nullable
albumid (inherited)
STRING(50)
No
ratingid
INT64
No
rating
FLOAT64
No
ratinggivenon
DATE
No
user
STRING(50)
No
Show equivalent DDL

Figure 7-48. *Rating Table Details Page*

The left Panel displays the database hierarchy as shown in Figure 7-49. This lists the databases created on this instance and the table details underneath each database.

Spanner
DemoCloudSpanner
songs
Query
album
rating

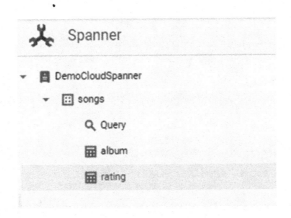

Figure 7-49. *Left Panel listing databases and its tables*

By the end of the above step we have an instance created with database *Songs* in it which comprises of two tables *Album* and *Ratings*.

Reading and Writing Data

Now that we have the tables in place let's load some sample data into it. Navigate to the database detail page and click on *Query* in the Top panel or in the left panel as highlighted in Figure 7-50.

Figure 7-50. *Query option in the Database detail page*

This opens the Query Console as shown in Figure 7-51.

Figure 7-51. *Query Console*

Let's load data into album *table* first using the below *insert* commands.

```
insert into album(albumid,title,year,singer)
values
('a1','something to remember',1981,'four tops'),
('a2','just cant get enough',1981,'Depeche mode'),
('a3','foolish beat',1987,'Debbie gibson'),
('a4','moments in love',1984,'ArtofNoise'),
('a5','HeadToToe',1987,'Lisa'),
('a6','eternal flame',1988,'The Bangles'),
('a7','money for nothing',1985,'dire Straits')
```

With the Command pasted in the Text area, click on *Run Query*. Within few seconds the data will be inserted in the table as shown in Figure 7-52.

Figure 7-52. *Rows inserted in Albums Table*

In order to verify, click on table *Album* in the left panel and in the Table details page click on the *Data tab*. We will be able to see the data inserted as shown in Figure 7-53.

Figure 7-53. *Album Table Data Tab*

In addition to using the above method, we can also use the *Insert* button in the *Data tab* to insert row in the table. Let's next insert data in the *rating* table using the below *insert* command.

```
insert into rating(albumid,ratingid,user,ratinggivenon,rating)
values
('a1',1,'demo1','2019-01-01',4.5),
('a1',2,'demo2','2019-02-11',4.0),
('a7',3,'demo3','2019-01-21',3.5),
('a1',4,'demo4','2019-06-01',1.5),
('a4',5,'demo5','2019-05-19',2.5),
('a5',6,'demo1','2019-01-03',4.0),
('a3',7,'demo4','2019-01-05',4.5),
('a2',8,'demo6','2019-01-08',3.5),
('a1',9,'demo7','2019-01-10',3.0),
('a6',10,'demo1','2019-04-13',4.5),
('a7',11,'demo1','2019-01-21',4.0),
('a1',12,'demo8','2018-12-31',2.5),
('a3',13,'demo0','2019-02-14',1.5),
('a2',14,'demo11','2019-01-12',4.5),
('a5',15,'demo1','2019-09-18',4.0),
('a4',16,'demo15','2019-01-01',3.0),
('a1',17,'demo19','2019-01-05',2.0),
('a2',18,'demo1','2019-08-10',1.0),
```

```
('a3',19,'demo9','2019-10-12',4.5),
('a4',20,'demo18','2019-06-30',4.0),
('a5',21,'demo19','2019-01-02',4.0),
('a6',22,'demo12','2019-01-05',3.5),
('a7',23,'demo14','2019-06-08',2.0)
```

Click on *Run Query* to insert data in the table. Figure 7-54 shows the records inserted in the table.

Query database: songs

```
 1  insert into rating(albumid,ratingid,user,ratinggivenon,rating)
 2  values
 3   ('a1',1,'demo1','2019-01-01',4.5),
 4   ('a1',2,'demo2','2019-02-11',4.0),
 5   ('a7',3,'demo3','2019-01-21',3.5),
 6   ('a1',4,'demo4','2019-06-01',1.5),
 7   ('a4',5,'demo5','2019-05-19',2.5),
 8   ('a5',6,'demo1','2019-01-03',4.0),
 9   ('a3',7,'demo4','2019-01-05',4.5),
10   ('a2',8,'demo6','2019-01-08',3.5),
11   ('a1',9,'demo7','2019-01-10',3.0),
12   ('a6',10,'demo1','2019-04-13',4.5),
13   ('a7',11,'demo1','2019-01-21',4.0),
14   ('a1',12,'demo8','2018-12-31',2.5),
15   ('a3',13,'demo0','2019-02-14',1.5),
16   ('a2',14,'demo11','2019-01-12',4.5),
17   ('a5',15,'demo1','2019-09-18',4.0),
18   ('a4',16,'demo15','2019-01-01',3.0),
19   ('a1',17,'demo19','2019-01-05',2.0),
20   ('a2',18,'demo1','2019-08-10',1.0),
21   ('a3',19,'demo9','2019-10-12',4.5),
22   ('a4',20,'demo18','2019-06-30',4.0),
23   ('a5',21,'demo19','2019-01-02',4.0),
24   ('a6',22,'demo12','2019-01-05',3.5),
25   ('a7',23,'demo14','2019-06-08',2.0)
26
```

Run query ▾   Clear query   SQL query help

Suggestions: Ctrl + Space Run query: Ctrl + Enter

Schema   Results table   Explanation

23 rows inserted

This statement inserted 23 rows and did not return any rows.

Query complete (509.16 ms elapsed)

Figure 7-54. *Rows inserted in Ratings table*

Like with *Album,* click on the *rating* table and select the *data tab* in the table details page to verify that the data is inserted as shown in Figure 7-55.

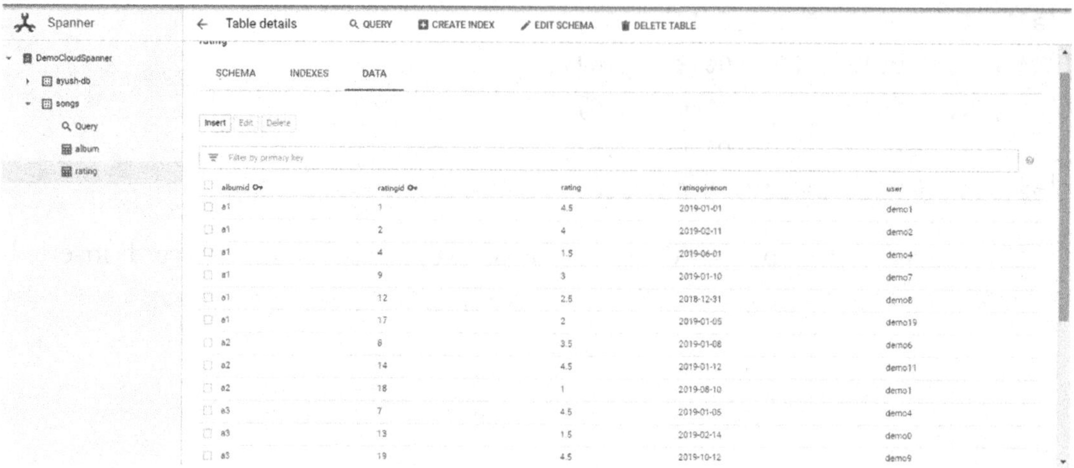

Figure 7-55. *Ratings table Data Tab*

With the data in place let's now start querying the tables. Navigate to the query console by clicking on *Query* underneath the database in the Left panel. This opens the query console.

Let's begin with a very simple query where we want to view album wise ratings details. Execute the following query.

```
SELECT *
FROM Album A, Rating R
WHERE A.AlbumId = R.AlbumId
```

This query will display album wise all ratings provided till date as shown in Figure 7-56.

Query database: songs

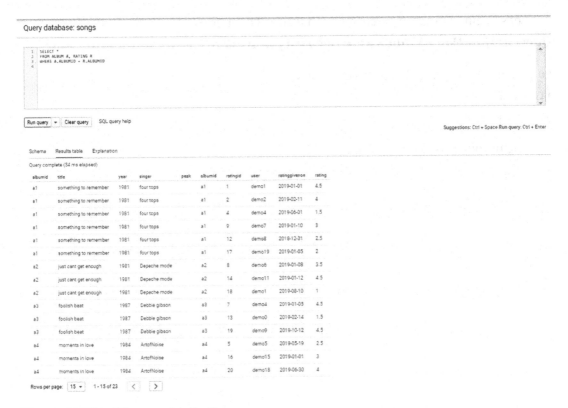

Figure 7-56. *Album wise Ratings*

Now let's say we want answers for the following questions from the data we have loaded.

- How many albums were released per Year?

- Give me two years with most number of releases

- How many users have rated for each album?

- Show me albums where rating received is above a number say more than 2.

- Show me albums ordered by average ratings received and that too the one with maximum rating on the top.

- Show me albums with average rating more than or equal to 4

- Show me what's the average rating for a particular singer say Lisa.

Let's begin with the answers for each using SQL queries.

Query 1: How Many Albums were released per Year?

```
select year, count(*) albumsreleased
from album
group by year;
```

The output is as shown in Figure 7-57.

Query database: songs

```
1  select year, count(*) albumsreleased from album group by year;
```

Run query   ▾   Clear query   SQL query help

Schema   Results table   Explanation

Query complete (28.69 ms elapsed)

year	albumsreleased
1988	1
1987	2
1985	1
1984	1
1981	2

Figure 7-57. *Year wise Albums Released*

Query 2: Give me two years with most number of releases?

In order to answer this, we will add ordering and limit clause to the above query. The query to be executed in the console is as below

```
select year, count(*) albumsreleased
from album
group by year
order by 2 desc limit 2;
```

The output is the two years with maximum number of releases as shown in Figure 7-58.

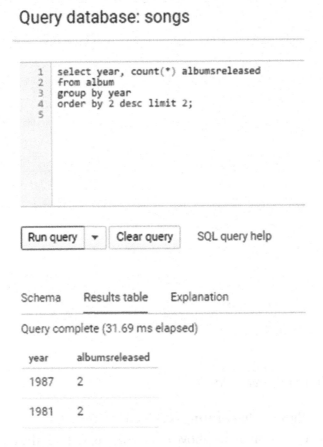

Figure 7-58. *Two years with maximum releases*

Query 3: How many users have rated for each album?

```
select a.title, count(r.user) RatingsRecieved
from album a inner join rating r
on a.albumid=r.albumid
group by a.title
```

The output is as shown below in Figure 7-59.

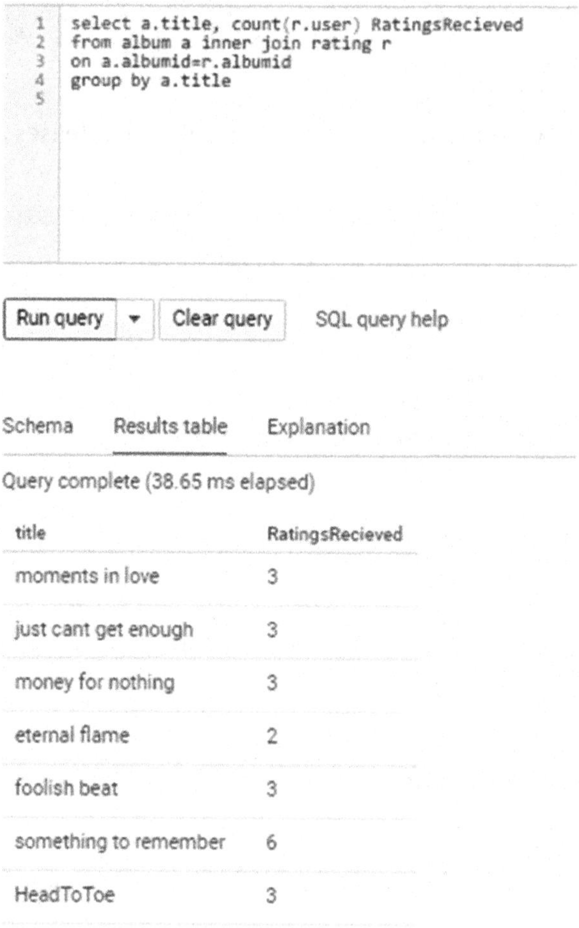

```
1    select a.title, count(r.user) RatingsRecieved
2    from album a inner join rating r
3    on a.albumid=r.albumid
4    group by a.title
5
```

Run query ▾   Clear query   SQL query help

Schema   Results table   Explanation

Query complete (38.65 ms elapsed)

title	RatingsRecieved
moments in love	3
just cant get enough	3
money for nothing	3
eternal flame	2
foolish beat	3
something to remember	6
HeadToToe	3

Figure 7-59. *Album wise Vote count*

Query 4: Show me albums where rating received is above 2.

This query is an extension of the above query where we filter the data by the vote count and exclude the ones where the vote count is less than 2. The query to be executed is as below.

```
select a.title, count(r.user) RatingsRecieved
from album a inner join rating r
on a.albumid=r.albumid
group by a.title
having count(r.user)>2
```

The output is as shown in Figure 7-60.

Figure 7-60. Album with Votes greater than 2

We can see that the album eternal flame is not displayed in the output as that was the only album with ratings received as 2.

Query 5: Show me list of albums ordered by descending order of average ratings received (Max-to-Min)

```
select a.title, avg(r.rating) avgrating
from album a inner join rating r
on a.albumid=r.albumid
group by a.title
order by 2 desc
```

Output is as shown in Figure 7-61.

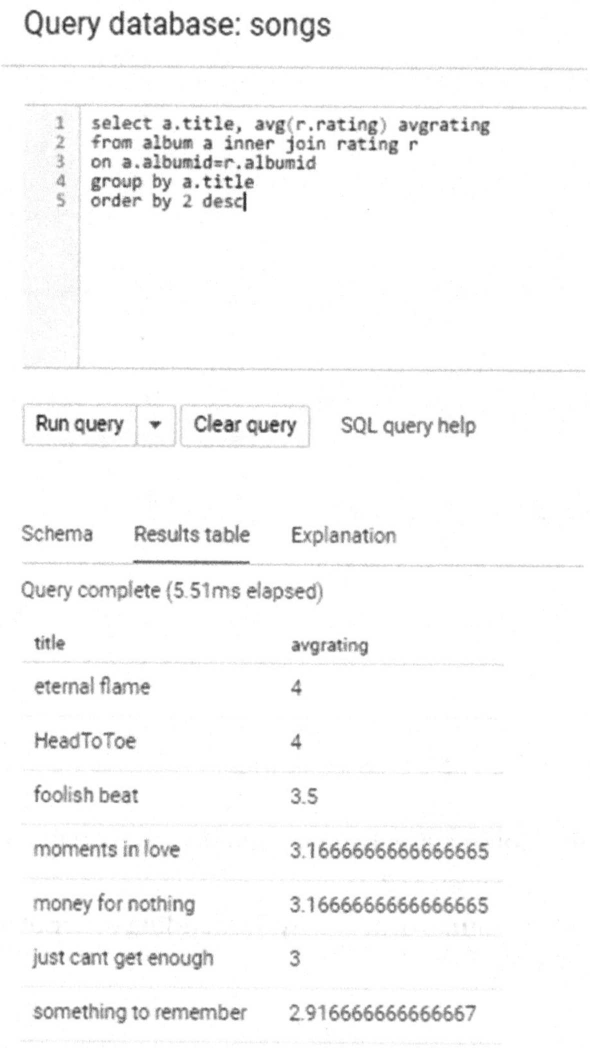

Query database: songs

```
1  select a.title, avg(r.rating) avgrating
2  from album a inner join rating r
3  on a.albumid=r.albumid
4  group by a.title
5  order by 2 desc
```

Run query ▾ Clear query   SQL query help

Schema   Results table   Explanation

Query complete (5.51ms elapsed)

title	avgrating
eternal flame	4
HeadToToe	4
foolish beat	3.5
moments in love	3.1666666666666665
money for nothing	3.1666666666666665
just cant get enough	3
something to remember	2.916666666666667

Figure 7-61. *Album wise Average Rating*

Query 6: Show me albums with average rating more than or equal to 4

```
select a.title, avg(r.rating) avgrating
from album a inner join rating r
on a.albumid=r.albumid
group by a.title
        having avg(r.rating)>=4
```

The output is as shown below in Figure 7-62.

Figure 7-62. *Album with Average Ratings greater than or equal to 4*

Query 7: Show me what's the average rating for a particular singer say Lisa

The final query is to show average rating for all albums of a given singer/artist. The artist in question is Lisa. In order to answer we execute the below query

```
select avg(r.rating) avgrating
from album a inner join rating r
on a.albumid=r.albumid
where a.singer='Lisa'
```

The output is as shown below in Figure 7-63.

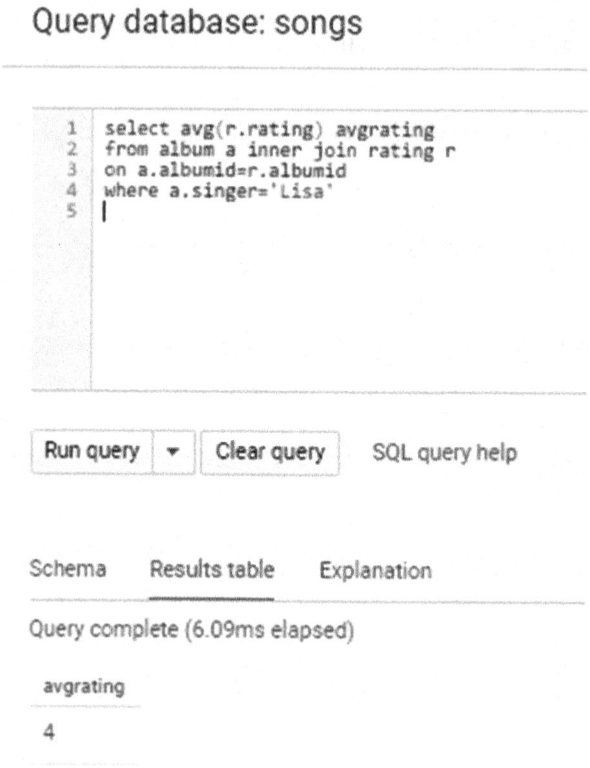

Query database: songs

```
1   select avg(r.rating) avgrating
2   from album a inner join rating r
3   on a.albumid=r.albumid
4   where a.singer='Lisa'
5   |
```

Run query ▾   Clear query   SQL query help

Schema   Results table   Explanation

Query complete (6.09ms elapsed)

avgrating
4

Figure 7-63. *Lisa's average rating*

Now that we have familiar in working with Spanner using Cloud Console, let's next get started with programming with Spanner.

Python Program – Feast Out

Feast Out program is our Python Program which we developed in Chapter 3 with CloudSQL as the database. The program maintains the list of registered restaurants and as users visit the feedback is captured along with the user details. Let's redevelop the program with Spanner as the database. To reiterate, the program lets the users perform the following actions:

- Register a new Restaurant

- Capture user's feedback for the visiting Restaurant

- Capture User details

- Update user details

- Unregister an existing Restaurant

- Find out best rated restaurant

- Find out top 2 restaurants basis on the specified parameter e.g. Food Quality

- Find out Users with Birth date within a week of the date specified

- Find out users with any of their special day falling in the month specified.

Before we get started with programming, the first thing which we have to do is to create the database in Spanner. For this we will be using our DemoSpanner project and democloudspanner instance which we created earlier.

Database Schema

Like we did earlier let's create an empty database *eatout*. Figure 7-64 shows the *eatout* database create form.

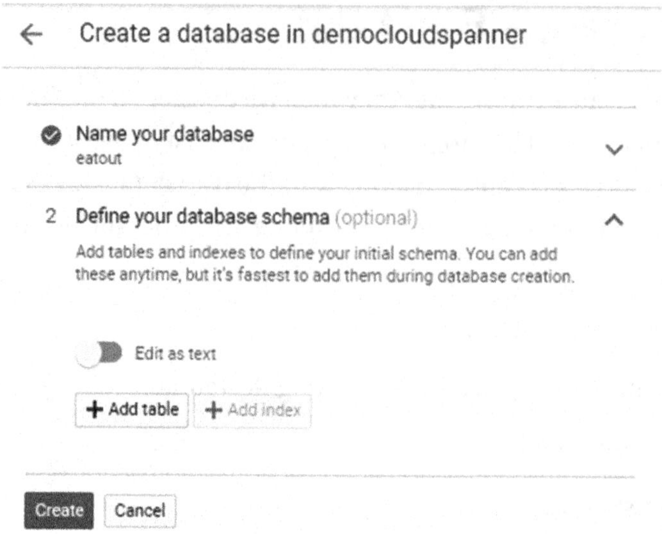

Figure 7-64. *Create Database eatout*

With the database created, let's now create the tables. As we did earlier open the Create table form, however this time instead of using the GUI option, we will use the DDL command. As we know by now, to enter the DDL statement, toggle *Edit as Text* option.

The Spanner Create DDL for table *restaurant* is as shown below.

```
CREATE TABLE restaurant (
        id STRING(10) NOT NULL,
        name STRING(50) NOT NULL,
        cuisine STRING(50) NOT NULL,
        region STRING(50) NOT NULL,
        location STRING(50) NOT NULL,
) PRIMARY KEY (id)
```

Figure 7-65 shows the Create Table form pasted with the DDL command for *restaurant*.

← Create a table in eatout

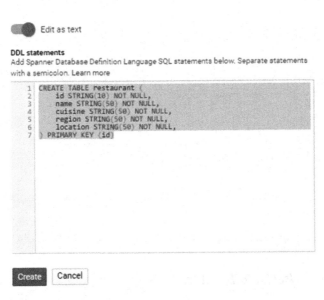

Figure 7-65. *Create restaurant Table*

DDL for table *userdetails* is as shown below.

```
CREATE TABLE userdetails (
        id STRING(10) NOT NULL,
        name STRING(50) NOT NULL,
        phonenumber STRING(50) NOT NULL,
        emailid STRING(50),
        birthday DATE,
        spousebirthday DATE,
        anniversary DATE,
) PRIMARY KEY (id);
CREATE UNIQUE INDEX phoneindex ON userdetails (phonenumber);
```

Figure 7-66 shows the Create Table form pasted with the DDL command for *userdetails*.

Figure 7-66. *Create UserDetails Table*

Finally, below is the DDL for *userfeedback* table

```
CREATE TABLE userfeedback (
        id STRING(10) NOT NULL,
        userid STRING(10) NOT NULL,
        visitdate DATE NOT NULL,
        foodquality INT64 NOT NULL,
        servicequality INT64 NOT NULL,
        ambience INT64 NOT NULL,
        livemusic INT64 NOT NULL,
        valueformoney INT64 NOT NULL,
        cleanliness INT64 NOT NULL,
        foodvariety INT64 NOT NULL,
        feedbackid STRING(10) NOT NULL,
) PRIMARY KEY (id, feedbackid), INTERLEAVE IN PARENT restaurant ON DELETE
CASCADE
```

Figure 7-67 shows the Create Table form pasted with the DDL command for *userfeedback*.

Figure 7-67. *Create userfeedback Table*

The Left panel with the database and schema looks as shown in Figure 7-68.

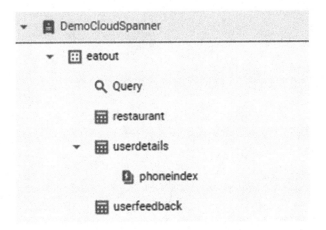

Figure 7-68. *eatout schema*

Now that we have the schema in place, we will begin with environment readiness. We first provision our VM instance from where we will execute our Python program.

Provision Compute Instance

Steps for provisioning is similar to the ones we executed in CloudSQL, the only difference is its provisioned in the DemoSpanner project. To reiterate the steps:

- Navigate to Cloud Console Left Navigation Menu

- Select VM Instances Option underneath the compute section

- Click on Create Instance.

- On the subsequent screen, select New VM Instance. Provide Name, in here we name it as feastingspanner. Change the Boot Disk to Ubuntu 18.04 LTS Minimal. Leave the remaining configuration as is. With all the inputs the form look like Figure 7-69.

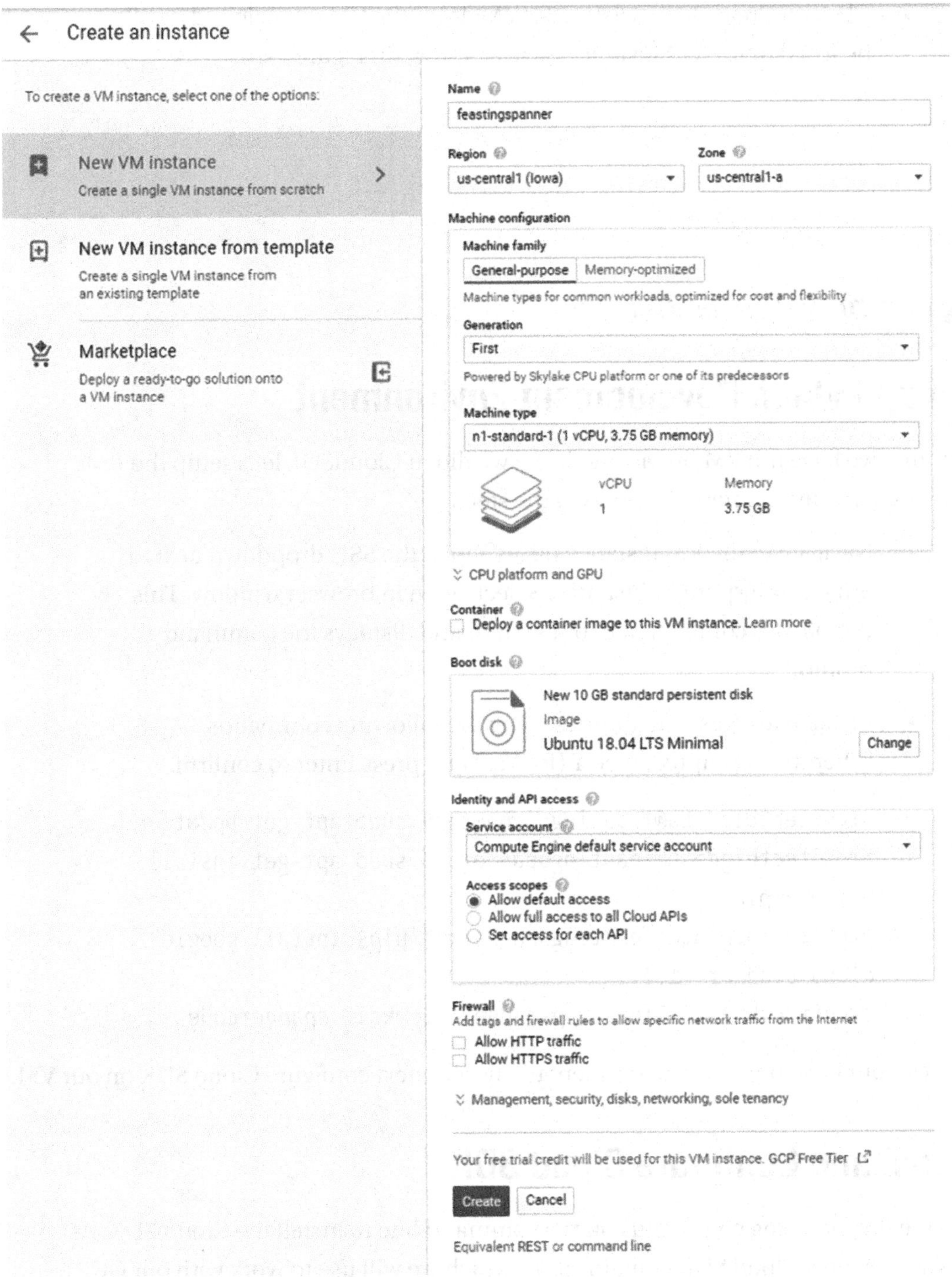

← Create an instance

To create a VM instance, select one of the options:

New VM instance
Create a single VM instance from scratch >

New VM instance from template
Create a single VM instance from
an existing template

Marketplace
Deploy a ready-to-go solution onto
a VM instance

Name ⓘ

feastingspanner

Region ⓘ   Zone ⓘ
us-central1 (Iowa)   ▼   us-central1-a   ▼

Machine configuration

Machine family

| General-purpose | Memory-optimized |

Machine types for common workloads, optimized for cost and flexibility

Generation
First   ▼

Powered by Skylake CPU platform or one of its predecessors

Machine type
n1-standard-1 (1 vCPU, 3.75 GB memory)   ▼

| | vCPU | Memory |
| | 1 | 3.75 GB |

⌄ CPU platform and GPU

Container ⓘ
☐ Deploy a container image to this VM instance. Learn more

Boot disk ⓘ

New 10 GB standard persistent disk
Image
Ubuntu 18.04 LTS Minimal   [Change]

Identity and API access ⓘ

Service account ⓘ
Compute Engine default service account   ▼

Access scopes ⓘ
● Allow default access
○ Allow full access to all Cloud APIs
○ Set access for each API

Firewall ⓘ
Add tags and firewall rules to allow specific network traffic from the Internet
☐ Allow HTTP traffic
☐ Allow HTTPS traffic

⌄ Management, security, disks, networking, sole tenancy

Your free trial credit will be used for this VM instance. GCP Free Tier ↗

[Create]   Cancel

Equivalent REST or command line

Figure 7-69. *Create VM feastingspanner*

- Click on Create to provision the VM. With the VM provisioned it will be listed in the VM instance page as shown in Figure 7-70.

Figure 7-70. *VM instance list*

Set up Python Development Environment

Now that we have the VM provisioned, like we did in CloudSQL let's setup the development environment. Reiterating the steps

- Navigate to the VM instance pages. Open the SSH dropdown next to our feastingspanner instance. Select Open in browser window. This establishes connection to our system and displays the command prompt.

- Install packages and libraries using the following commands. Wherever prompted, type Y (for Yes) and press Enter to confirm.

```
architectbigdata@feastingspanner:~$ sudo apt-get update
architectbigdata@feastingspanner:~$ sudo apt-get install
python3-pip
architectbigdata@feastingspanner:~$ pip3 install google-
cloud-spanner==1.7.1
architectbigdata@feastingspanner:~$ mkdir spannercode
```

With our development environment ready, let's next configure Cloud SDK on our VM.

Install and Configure Cloud SDK

Execute the following commands on the command line to install the Cloud SDK. As we know by now Cloud SDK contains tools which we will use to work with our GCP products and services from our command line.

```
architectbigdata@feastingspanner:~$ echo "deb [signed-by=/usr/share/
keyrings/cloud.google.gpg] https://packages.cloud.google.com/apt cloud-sdk
main" | sudo tee -a /etc/apt/sources.list.d/google-cloud-sdk.list
architectbigdata@feastingspanner:~$ curl https://packages.cloud.google.com/
apt/doc/apt-key.gpg | sudo apt-key --keyring /usr/share/keyrings/cloud.
google.gpg add -
architectbigdata@feastingspanner:~$ sudo apt-get update && sudo apt-get
install google-cloud-sdk
architectbigdata@feastingspanner:~$ sudo apt-get install google-cloud-sdk-
app-engine-python
architectbigdata@feastingspanner:~$ sudo apt-get install google-cloud-sdk-
app-engine-python-extras
```

When prompted, type Y (for Yes) and press Enter to confirm. With Cloud SDK installed, let's run through the commands for configuration of gcloud. Enter command

```
architectbigdata@feastingspanner:~$ gcloud init
```

This provides us with options to configure. It starts with network diagnostics. Post completion of the network diagnostic checks, it prompts to choose the Google Account as shown below.

```
architectbigdata@feastingspanner:~$ gcloud init
Welcome! This command will take you through the configuration of gcloud.

Your current configuration has been set to: [default]

You can skip diagnostics next time by using the following flag:
  gcloud init --skip-diagnostics

Network diagnostic detects and fixes local network connection issues.
Checking network connection...done.
Reachability Check passed.
Network diagnostic passed (1/1 checks passed).

Choose the account you would like to use to perform operations for
this configuration:
 [1] 426492330137-compute@developer.gserviceaccount.com
 [2] Log in with a new account
Please enter your numeric choice:  2
```

We choose to **_Log in with a new account_**. When prompted, type Y and press enter. It will generate a link for us to get the verification code, which need to be entered as the next step. Like with CloudSQL, Follow the link, get the verification code from there and paste it against _Enter Verification code_ prompt. Post verification it will confirm your login as shown below and prompt us to pick the cloud project to use.

```
You are running on a Google Compute Engine virtual machine.
It is recommended that you use service accounts for authentication.

You can run:

  $ gcloud config set account `ACCOUNT`

to switch accounts if necessary.

Your credentials may be visible to others with access to this
virtual machine. Are you sure you want to authenticate with
your personal account?

Do you want to continue (Y/n)?   Y

Go to the following link in your browser:

    https://accounts.google.com/o/oauth2/auth?code_challenge=uQ4WLga
    kxQhwxuAvkCKIdukreruoKhYJiAror8LMpP8&prompt=select_account&code_
    challenge_method=S256&access_type=offline&redirect_uri=urn%3Aietf%
    3Awg%3Aoauth%3A2.0%3Aoob&response_type=code&client_id=32555940559.
    apps.googleusercontent.com&scope=https%3A%2F%2Fwww.googleapis.
    com%2Fauth%2Fuserinfo.email+https%3A%2F%2Fwww.googleapis.
    com%2Fauth%2Fcloud-platform+https%3A%2F%2Fwww.googleapis.
    com%2Fauth%2Fappengine.admin+https%3A%2F%2Fwww.googleapis.com%2Fauth%2F
    compute+https%3A%2F%2Fwww.googleapis.com%2Fauth%2Faccounts.reauth

Enter verification code: 4/qwECVPrVzz7A1ffR9eXHKdFslzSMJDlUxj_
qwGGpmEJDRzkOshZKqzg

To take a quick anonymous survey, run:
  $ gcloud alpha survey
```

You are logged in as: [architectbigdata@gmail.com].

Pick cloud project to use:
 [1] demospanner-251710
 [2] demotsdb
 [3] mysql-ha-project
 [4] Create a new project
Please enter numeric choice or text value (must exactly match list item):   1

We choose our Spanner project *demospanner-251710*. This sets our project and prompts to configure a default compute region and zone, specify N, and we are done with the configuration of our cloud SDK as shown below

Your current project has been set to: [demospanner-251710].

Do you want to configure a default Compute Region and Zone? (Y/n)?   n

Created a default .boto configuration file at [/home/architectbigdata/.
boto]. See this file and
[https://cloud.google.com/storage/docs/gsutil/commands/config] for more
information about configuring Google Cloud Storage.
Your Google Cloud SDK is configured and ready to use!

* Commands that require authentication will use architectbigdata@gmail.com
by default
* Commands will reference project `demospanner-251710` by default
Run `gcloud help config` to learn how to change individual settings

This gcloud configuration is called [default]. You can create additional
configurations if you work with multiple accounts and/or projects.
Run `gcloud topic configurations` to learn more.

Some things to try next:

* Run `gcloud --help` to see the Cloud Platform services you can interact
with. And run `gcloud help COMMAND` to get help on any gcloud command.
* Run `gcloud topic --help` to learn about advanced features of the SDK
like arg files and output formatting

287

Now that we have the Cloud SDK configured, let's next generate the application default credentials. Enter the command:

```
architectbigdata@feastingspanner:~$ gcloud auth application-default login
```

Wherever prompted, type Y (Yes) and press enter. This will generate a link for us to fetch the verification code, follow the URL like we did in the above step, enter the verification code against the prompt and that's it. The credentials wills be saved to a file as shown below.

```
architectbigdata@feastingspanner:~$ gcloud auth application-default login
You are running on a Google Compute Engine virtual machine.
The service credentials associated with this virtual machine
will automatically be used by Application Default
Credentials, so it is not necessary to use this command.

If you decide to proceed anyway, your user credentials may be visible
to others with access to this virtual machine. Are you sure you want
to authenticate with your personal account?

Do you want to continue (Y/n)?   Y

Go to the following link in your browser:

    https://accounts.google.com/o/oauth2/auth?code_challenge=Eo-8KWxS7INx
    hpRdktwJS2Ic2HMA8KXEXB_8a2pe21c&prompt=select_account&code_challenge_
    method=S256&access_type=offline&redirect_uri=urn%3Aietf%3Awg%3Aoauth%
    3A2.0%3Aoob&response_type=code&client_id=764086051850-6qr4p6gpi6hn506
    pt8ejuq83di341hur.apps.googleusercontent.com&scope=https%3A%2F%2Fwww.
    googleapis.com%2Fauth%2Fuserinfo.email+https%3A%2F%2Fwww.
    googleapis.com%2Fauth%2Fcloud-platform+https%3A%2F%2Fwww.googleapis.
    com%2Fauth%2Faccounts.reauth
Enter verification code: 4/qwGt9I5qyVE7Rx5girQSl1bS_Jj1--
hmfjeCRhzJWX9649qAGOfsZjU

Credentials saved to file: [/home/architectbigdata/.config/gcloud/
application_default_credentials.json]
```

These credentials will be used by any library that requests Application Default Credentials.

To generate an access token for other uses, run:
```
gcloud auth application-default print-access-token
```

With the SDK configured, let's start with our python code next. For this we assume that you are familiar with Python programming.

Python Program

To start with we will first import the following libraries

```
import json
import random as r
from google.cloud import spanner
```

Next we establish connections with our Spanner database with the following line of code.

```
spanner_client = spanner.Client()
instance = spanner_client.instance("democloudspanner")
database = instance.database("eatout")
```

Following this we list all available options for the user to act with. Against each option we create a method.

```
            print("Select the operations to perform:")
            print("1. Register Restaurant")
            print("2. Load User Feedback")
            print("3. Fetch the top rated restaurant")
            print("4. Top 2 basis on my input")
            print("5. List users with birthdays in next 7 days from the
                    date specified")
            print("6. List users with any of there occasion in given month")
            print("7. Delete Restaurant")
            print("0. Exit")
            operation = input()
```

```
        if(operation=='1' or operation == 1):
            print("Selected: Register Restaurant")
            register_restaurant()
        if(operation == '2' or operation == 2):
            print("Selected: Load User Feedback")
            user_input()
        if(operation == '3' or operation== 3):
            print("Selected: Fetch top rated restaurant")
            query_1()
        if (operation == '4' or operation == 4):
            print("Selected: Top 2 on the basis of input")
            query_2()
        if (operation == '5' or operation == 5):
            print("Selected: List users with birthday")
            query_3()
        if (operation == '6' or operation == 6):
            print("Selected: List users with any occassion")
            query_4()
        if (operation == '7' or operation == 7):
            print("Selected: Delete Restaurant")
            delete_restaurant()
        if( operation == '0' or operation == 0):
            print("Thank You")
            break
```

With all this in place the main looks as below.

```
if __name__ == "__main__":
    try:
        # instance_id = input("Enter the Instance Id of Spanner:   ")
        # database_id = input("Enter the Database Id of Spanner
                            Instacne:   ")
        spanner_client = spanner.Client()
        instance = spanner_client.instance("democloudspanner")
        database = instance.database("eatout")
```

```python
while True:
    print("Select the operations to perform:")
    print("1. Register Restaurant")
    print("2. Load User Feedback")
    print("3. Fetch the top rated restaurant")
    print("4. Top 2 basis on my input")
    print("5. List users with birthdays in next 7 days from the
            date specified")
    print("6. List users with any of there occasion in given
            month")
    print("7. Delete Restaurant")
    print("0. Exit")
    operation = input()
    if(operation=='1' or operation == 1):
        print("Selected: Register Restaurant")
        register_restaurant()
    if(operation == '2' or operation == 2):
        print("Selected: Load User Feedback")
        user_input()
    if(operation == '3' or operation== 3):
        print("Selected: Fetch top rated restaurant")
        query_1()
    if (operation == '4' or operation == 4):
        print("Selected: Top 2 on the basis of input")
        query_2()
    if (operation == '5' or operation == 5):
        print("Selected: List users with birthday")
        query_3()
    if (operation == '6' or operation == 6):
        print("Selected: List users with any occassion")
        query_4()
    if (operation == '7' or operation == 7):
        print("Selected: Delete Restaurant")
        delete_restaurant()
```

```
            if( operation == '0' or operation == 0):
                print("Thank You")
                break

    except Exception as e:
        print(e)
```

Next, we will look at individual method. Let's start with register restaurant method. This takes a file input and loads the data in the restaurant table.

```
def register_restaurant():
    try:
        f_name = input("Enter File name to upload Restaurant Data        ")
        with open(f_name, 'r') as json_file:
            line = json_file.readline()
            count = 1
            while line:
                input_json1 = json.loads(line)
                uid = generate_uuid()
                r_rname = str(input_json1["name"])
                r_cuisine = str(input_json1["cuisine"])
                r_region = str(input_json1["region"])
                r_location = str(input_json1["location"])
                def insert_restaurant(transaction):
                    row_ct = transaction.execute_update("""INSERT
                    Restaurant (Id,Name,Cuisine,Region,Location) VALUES
                    ("%s", "%s", "%s", "%s", "%s") """ % (
                uid, r_rname, r_cuisine, r_region, r_location))
                database.run_in_transaction(insert_restaurant)
                print("Record No - " + str(count) + "  Insertion Successful
                        for Restaurant name -- " + r_rname)
                count = count + 1
                line = json_file.readline()

    except Exception as e:
        print(e)
```

We can see reference to a function to generate a unique identifier. This looks like below; we generate a 5-character random identifier.

```
def generate_uuid():
    "'Function generating random unique id of 5 digit"'
    random_string = "
    random_str_seq = "0123456789abcdefghijklmnopqrstuvwxyzABCDEFGHIJKLMNOPQ
                       RSTUVWXYZ"
    uuid_format = 5
    for n in range(uuid_format):
        random_string += str(random_str_seq[r.randint(0, len(random_str_
                         seq) - 1)])
    return random_string
```

We will be using the same function for generating UserId and FeedbackId as well while creating a new user and inputting feedback data, which we will see in a while.

We next look at methods for loading the user feedback data. As we have seen in CloudSQL as well, Phone Number is unique and is used to check if a user exists. If user exists, the data will be updated else a new user is created. With the UserId created the feedback data is loaded in the User Feedback table.

```
def user_input():
    try:
        f_name = input("Enter File name to upload User Detail and
                       Feedback Data     ")
        with open(f_name, 'r') as json_file:
            line = json_file.readline()
            count = 1
            while line:
                input_user = json.loads(line)
                pno = str(input_user["pno"])
                def read_then_write(transaction):
                    results = transaction.execute_sql("""SELECT Id FROM
                    UserDetails WHERE phonenumber='%s'""" % (pno))
                    ud_id = False
                    for result in results:
                        ud_id = result[0]
```

```
                if ud_id:
                    user_update(input_user,transaction)
                    user_feedback(input_user, ud_id,
                    transaction=transaction)
                else:
                    ud_id = generate_uuid()
                    fb_id = generate_uuid()
                    user_details(input_user, ud_id,
                    transaction=transaction)
                    user_feedback(input_user, ud_id,fb_id,
                    transaction=transaction)

            database.run_in_transaction(read_then_write)
            print(str(count) + " Record Successfully Inserted/Updated")
            count = count + 1
            line = json_file.readline()

    except Exception as e:
        print(e)

def user_update(input_json,transaction):
    try:
        pno = str(input_json["pno"])
        us_name = str(input_json["name"])
        us_eid = str(input_json["emailid"])
        us_selfdob = str(input_json["selfdob"])
        us_spdob = str(input_json["spousedob"])
        us_ma = str(input_json["anniversary"])
        row_ct = transaction.execute_update("""UPDATE UserDetails SET
        Name = '%s' , Emailid='%s', birthday='%s', SpouseBirthday='%s',
        Anniversary='%s' where phonenumber='%s'""" % (
                    us_name, us_eid, us_selfdob, us_spdob, us_ma, pno,))
        print("User Record Updated successfully ")
    except Exception as e:
        print(e)
```

```python
def user_details(input_json=None, ud_id=None,transaction=None):
    try:
        user_id = ud_id
        ud_rname = str(input_json["name"])
        ud_pn = str(input_json["pno"])
        ud_eid = str(input_json["emailid"])
        ud_selfdob = str(input_json["selfdob"])
        ud_spdob = str(input_json["spousedob"])
        ud_ma = str(input_json["anniversary"])
        row_ct = transaction.execute_update("""INSERT UserDetails (Id,Name,
        phonenumber,Emailid,birthday,Spousebirthday,Anniversary) VALUES
        ("%s", "%s", "%s", "%s", "%s","%s","%s")""" % (
            user_id, ud_rname, ud_pn, ud_eid, ud_selfdob, ud_spdob, ud_ma))
        print("User Detail Record Insertion Successful")

    except Exception as e:
        print(e)

def user_feedback(input_json=None, us_id=None,fb_id=None,transaction=None):
    try:
        fb_dov = str(input_json["dateofvisit"])
        fb_resid = str(input_json["restid"])
        fb_fq = int(input_json["foodquality"])
        fb_sq = int(input_json["servicequality"])
        fb_amb = int(input_json["ambience"])
        fb_music = int(input_json["music"])
        fb_vfm = int(input_json["valueformoney"])
        fb_clean = int(input_json["cleanliness"])
        fb_fv = int(input_json["foodvariety"])

        row_ct = transaction.execute_update("""INSERT userfeedback
        (feedbackid,UserId,VisitDate, id,FoodQuality,ServiceQuality,
        Ambience,LiveMusic,ValueForMoney,Cleanliness,FoodVariety) VALUES
        ("%s","%s", "%s", "%s", %s, %s,%s,%s,%s,%s,%s)""" % (fb_id,us_id,
        fb_dov, fb_resid, fb_fq, fb_sq, fb_amb, fb_music, fb_vfm, fb_
        clean, fb_fv))
```

```
        print("Feedback Record Insertion Successful")

    except Exception as e:
        print(e)
```

The next method deletes the restaurants; like with other options we take file with restaurant ids to be deleted.

```
def delete_restaurant():
    try:
        f_name = input("Enter File name to Delete Restaurant Data        ")
        with open(f_name, 'r') as json_file:
            line = json_file.readline()
            while line:
                input_json1 = json.loads(line)
                restid = str(input_json1["id"])
                data = (restid,)
                def delete_restaurant(transaction):
                    row_ct = transaction.execute_update("""DELETE
                    Restaurant WHERE Id = '%s'"""%(data))
                database.run_in_transaction(delete_restaurant)
                print(" Restaurant Successfully Deleted")
                line = json_file.readline()
    except Exception as e:
        print(e)
```

We will now look at the methods for querying. First query fetches the Top-Rated restaurant as shown below.

```
def query_1():
    try:
        def query1(transaction):
            results = transaction.execute_sql("select r1.name from (select
            id, avg((((foodquality+servicequality+ambience+livemusic+
            valueformoney+cleanliness+foodvariety)*1.0)/7) avgratingacrossall
            from userfeedback group by id order by 1 desc limit 1)tbla,
            Restaurant r1 where tbla.id=r1.id")
            for result in results:
```

```
        print(result,"\n")
      database.run_in_transaction(query1)
  except Exception as e:
      print(e)
```

Second method as shown below enables fetching restaurant basis on Food Quality and Quality of Service. This input choice will be provided by the user.

```
def query_2():
  try:
    print("Enter parameter on which restaurants has to be compared  :")
    parameter = input()
    if parameter == 'foodquality':
      def query2(transaction):
        results = transaction.execute_sql(
          "select r1.name from (select id, avg(foodquality)
          avgratingselected from userfeedback group by id order by 1 desc
          limit 2)tbla, Restaurant r1 where tbla.id=r1.id")
        for result in results:
          print(result, "\n")
      database.run_in_transaction(query2)

    if parameter == 'servicequality':
      def query2(transaction):
        results = transaction.execute_sql(
          "select r1.name from (select Id, avg(servicequality)
          avgratingselected from userfeedback group by id order by 1 desc
          limit 2)tbla, Restaurant r1 where tbla.id=r1.Id")

        for result in results:
          print(result, "\n")

      database.run_in_transaction(query2)
  except Exception as e:
    print(e)
```

Third and fourth query is from restaurant perspective, where the third query enables to find out users with date of birth in 7 days.

```python
def query_3():
  try:
    print("Enter the date for which the birthday has to be checked :")
    date_input = input()

    def query3(transaction):
      results = transaction.execute_sql(
        """select Name, phonenumber, Emailid from UserDetails where
        EXTRACT(MONTH FROM birthday) =EXTRACT(MONTH FROM DATE '%s') and
        EXTRACT(DAY FROM birthday) between EXTRACT(DAY FROM DATE '%s') and
        EXTRACT(DAY FROM DATE '%s')+7""" % (
        date_input, date_input, date_input))

      for result in results:
        print(result, "\n")

    database.run_in_transaction(query3)
  except Exception as e:
    print(e)
```

And the fourth query returns user with any occasion date in the month of the date specified.

```python
def query_4():
  try:
    print("Enter the date for which occassion has to checked :")
    date_input = input()
    def query4(transaction):
      results = transaction.execute_sql(
        """select Name, PhoneNumber, emailId from UserDetails where
        EXTRACT(MONTH FROM birthday) =EXTRACT(MONTH FROM DATE '%s') or
        EXTRACT(MONTH FROM SpouseBirthday) =EXTRACT(MONTH FROM DATE '%s')
        and EXTRACT(MONTH FROM Anniversary) =EXTRACT(MONTH FROM DATE
        '%s')""" % (
        date_input, date_input, date_input))

      for result in results:
       print(result, "\n")
```

```
    database.run_in_transaction(query4)
  except Exception as e:
    print(e)
```

The columns, database names and credentials are hardcoded for simplicity. With everything combined, the complete code is available for download at https://github.com/architectbigdata/cloudspanner.

Now that we have the code in place, lets execute and validate.

Run and Verify

Prior to executing let's connect to our database and check all the tables. Navigate to the Query tool underneath the eatout database and execute the following queries one by one.

```
select count(*) from restaurant;
select count(*) from userdetails;
select count(*) from userfeedback;
```

The database shows our tables with no data as shown in the below figures. Figure 7-71 shows table *restaurant*.

Figure 7-71. *Restaurant select*

Figure 7-72 shows table *userdetails*.

Figure 7-72. *userdetails select*

And Figure 7-73 shows table *userfeedback*.

Figure 7-73. *userfeedback select*

Let's begin the execution of our program. Login to the provisioned VM.

Note   The code is saved in spannercode directory on the VM by the name of spanner.py

---

Enter the following command in the Ubuntu prompt

```
architectbigdata@feastingspanner:~/spannercode$ python3 spanner.py
```

This displays the output as shown below

```
Select the operations to perform:
1. Register Restaurant
2. Load User Feedback
3. Fetch the top rated restaurant
4. Top 2 basis on my input
5. List users with birthdays in next 7 days from the date specified
6. List users with any of there occasion in given month
7. Delete Restaurant
0. Exit
```

We choose Option 1 to create the restaurant data first.

```
1
Selected: Register Restaurant
Enter File name to upload Restaurant Data
```

It prompts for the file name; we specify the name as restaurants.txt.

Note   All the data files are copied in the spannercode directory. Content is same as the one we used in CloudSQL

As the program executes, status message is displayed and post successful completion it displays again the choice of actions as shown below.

```
Enter File name to upload Restaurant Data       restaurants.txt
Record No - 1  Insertion Successful for Restaurant name -- Pirates of Grill
Record No - 2  Insertion Successful for Restaurant name -- Barbeque Nation
Record No - 3  Insertion Successful for Restaurant name -- Pizza Hut
Record No - 4  Insertion Successful for Restaurant name -- Dominos
Record No - 5  Insertion Successful for Restaurant name -- Haldiram
Record No - 6  Insertion Successful for Restaurant name -- Bikaner
Record No - 7  Insertion Successful for Restaurant name -- Bikaner
Record No - 8  Insertion Successful for Restaurant name -- Taj
```

Select the operations to perform:

1. Register Restaurant

2. Load User Feedback

3. Fetch the top rated restaurant

4. Top 2 basis on my input

5. List users with birthdays in next 7 days from the date specified

6. List users with any of there occasion in given month

7. Delete Restaurant

0. Exit

Let's validate the data. Run the select command on the restaurant table in the query console. It displays the data we inserted above. Figure 7-74 shows the output of the select query.

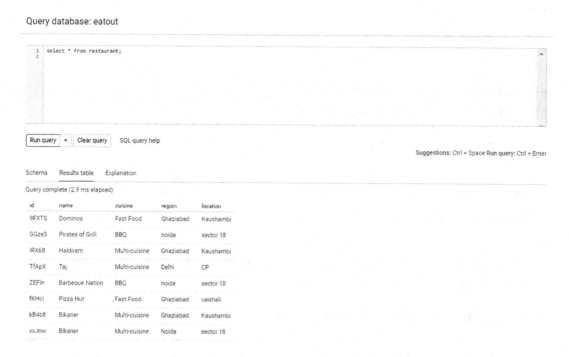

Figure 7-74. *Restaurant data inserted*

With the restaurant data loaded, let's next load the user feedback data. We select Option 2. Just like Option 1, we will be prompted for the filename. We specify the name as userfeedback1.txt. As the data is inserted the state is displayed as shown below.

```
2
Selected: Load User Feedback
Enter File name to upload User Detail and Feedback Data        userfeedback1.
txt
User Detail Record Insertion Successful
Feedback Record Insertion Successful
1 Record Successfully Inserted/Updated
User Detail Record Insertion Successful
Feedback Record Insertion Successful
2 Record Successfully Inserted/Updated
User Detail Record Insertion Successful
Feedback Record Insertion Successful
3 Record Successfully Inserted/Updated
User Detail Record Insertion Successful
Feedback Record Insertion Successful
4 Record Successfully Inserted/Updated
User Detail Record Insertion Successful
Feedback Record Insertion Successful
5 Record Successfully Inserted/Updated
Select the operations to perform:
1. Register Restaurant
2. Load User Feedback
3. Fetch the top rated restaurant
4. Top 2 basis on my input
5. List users with birthdays in next 7 days from the date specified
6. List users with any of there occasion in given month
7. Delete Restaurant
0. Exit
```

As shown above the operation is successful, let's validate the tables by running select on both userdetails and userfeedback tables. Figure 7-75 shows the data for *userdetails*.

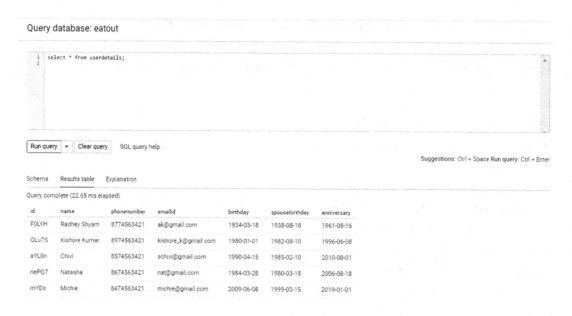

Figure 7-75. *userdetails data inserted*

Figure 7-76 shows the data for *userfeedback*.

Figure 7-76. *userfeedback data inserted*

Let's again choose option 2 with a different file name *userfeedback2.txt*.

```
2
Selected: Load User Feedback
Enter File name to upload User Detail and Feedback Data        userfeedback2.
txt
User Record Updated successfully
Feedback Record Insertion Successful
1 Record Successfully Inserted/Updated
User Detail Record Insertion Successful
Feedback Record Insertion Successful
2 Record Successfully Inserted/Updated
Select the operations to perform:
1. Register Restaurant
2. Load User Feedback
3. Fetch the top rated restaurant
4. Top 2 basis on my input
5. List users with birthdays in next 7 days from the date specified
6. List users with any of there occasion in given month
7. Delete Restaurant
0. Exit
```

In here we have a new as well as an existing user giving feedback. As shown above we can see update record executed successfully. Let's run the select on both the tables. Figure 7-77 shows output for *userdetails*.

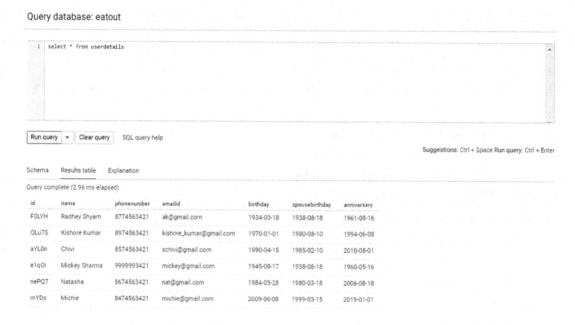

Figure 7-77. *userdetails data*

Figure 7-78 shows output of *userfeedback*.

Figure 7-78. *userfeedback data*

We can see *Kishore Kumar* was an existing user, data is updated for him and the new user Mickey Sharma data is created. Feedback of both users is also saved.

With the data in place, let's query the data. We choose Option 3 to display the top-rated restaurant, the output is as below.

```
Select the operations to perform:
1. Register Restaurant
2. Load User Feedback
3. Fetch the top rated restaurant
4. Top 2 basis on my input
5. List users with birthdays in next 7 days from the date specified
6. List users with any of there occasion in given month
7. Delete Restaurant
0. Exit
3
Selected: Fetch top rated restaurant
['Barbeque Nation']
```

Next we choose option 4. This prompts for the parameter. We enter Food Quality. The output is as below

```
Select the operations to perform:
1. Register Restaurant
2. Load User Feedback
3. Fetch the top rated restaurant
4. Top 2 basis on my input
5. List users with birthdays in next 7 days from the date specified
6. List users with any of there occasion in given month
7. Delete Restaurant
0. Exit
4
Selected: Top 2 on the basis of input
Enter parameter on which restaurants has to be compared  :
foodquality
['Barbeque Nation']
['Haldiram']
```

We next choose query to display users with their birthday within 7 days from the date 2019-08-12, the output is as below

```
Select the operations to perform:
1. Register Restaurant
2. Load User Feedback
3. Fetch the top rated restaurant
4. Top 2 basis on my input
5. List users with birthdays in next 7 days from the date specified
6. List users with any of there occasion in given month
7. Delete Restaurant
0. Exit
5
Selected: List users with birthday
Enter the date for which the birthday has to be checked :
2019-08-12
['Mickey Sharma', '9999993421', 'mickey@gmail.com']
```

Let's next list users whose any of the special days falls in the month of August. The output is as below:

```
Select the operations to perform:
1. Register Restaurant
2. Load User Feedback
3. Fetch the top rated restaurant
4. Top 2 basis on my input
5. List users with birthdays in next 7 days from the date specified
6. List users with any of there occasion in given month
7. Delete Restaurant
0. Exit
6
Selected: List users with any occassion
Enter the date for which occassion has to checked :
2019-08-01
['Radhey Shyam', '8774563421', 'ak@gmail.com']
['Mickey Sharma', '9999993421', 'mickey@gmail.com']
```

Finally let's unregister restaurants entry for Bikaner. We choose option 7 and specify file *delete.txt*.

```
Select the operations to perform:
1. Register Restaurant
2. Load User Feedback
3. Fetch the top rated restaurant
4. Top 2 basis on my input
5. List users with birthdays in next 7 days from the date specified
6. List users with any of there occasion in given month
7. Delete Restaurant
0. Exit
7
Selected: Delete Restaurant
Enter File name to Delete Restaurant Data      delete.txt
 Restaurant Successfully Deleted
 Restaurant Successfully Deleted
```

The output shows data is deleted. Let's validate by running select on restaurants. Figure 7-79 shows the output of the select.

Figure 7-79. *Restaurant data*

We can see the entries of Bikaner no longer exist. Finally, we exit our program by keying in 0.

```
Select the operations to perform:
1. Register Restaurant
2. Load User Feedback
3. Fetch the top rated restaurant
4. Top 2 basis on my input
```

5. List users with birthdays in next 7 days from the date specified

6. List users with any of there occasion in given month

7. Delete Restaurant

0. Exit

0

Thank You

architectbigdata@feastingspanner:~/spannercode$

With all the fun working with Spanner, it's time to wrap up now.

Wrap Up

We need to ensure to clean up for saving precious resources. This is a pretty easy step, just go to the respective instance details page by clicking on the instance name and click on delete instance.

Figure 7-80 shows the VM Instances page. Select *Delete* option next to the VM instance.

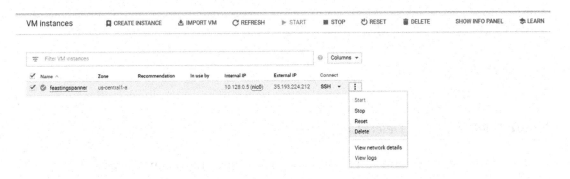

Figure 7-80. *VM Instance select Delete*

This prompts for confirmation as shown in Figure 7-81.

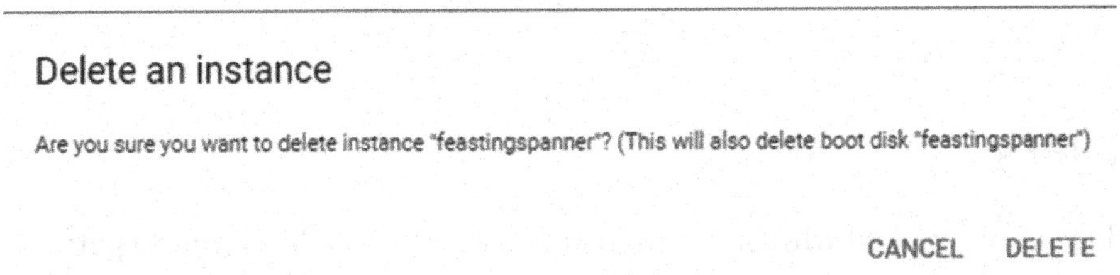

Delete an instance

Are you sure you want to delete instance "feastingspanner"? (This will also delete boot disk "feastingspanner")

CANCEL   DELETE

Figure 7-81. *VM Instance Delete Confirmation*

Click on *Delete*. Figure 7-82 shows the Spanner instance detail page. Click on *Delete Instance* button.

Figure 7-82. *Spanner Instance detail page, select Delete Instance*

This prompts us to confirm deletion by typing in the instance name as shown in Figure 7-83.

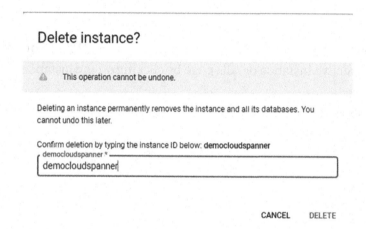

Figure 7-83. *Spanner Delete Confirm deletion*

Enter the instance name and click *delete*. Within seconds the instances will be deleted, and all associated resources will be freed and cleared.

Note   Not deleting these instances will result in per hour costs being charged to your account for the cloud resource usage.

Summary

In this chapter we worked with Spanner instance using console as well as python program. With this we conclude usage of Spanner instance. Let's finally look at the best practices for working with both CloudSQL as well as Spanner in the next chapter.

CHAPTER 8

Best Practices

Now that you are familiar with the relational database offerings of GCP—Cloud SQL and Cloud Spanner—it's time to look at some of the best practices that will enable you to plan the usage of these cloud databases efficiently. Let's begin with Cloud SQL.

Cloud SQL Best Practices

This section covers the best practices for efficient usage of the Cloud SQL instance.

Plan Resources Efficiently

Ensure sufficient resources are available as per the workload.

Storage

If an instance runs out of storage, there is a possibility that it might stop accepting requests or go offline. You should either ensure that you have selected Enable Automatic Storage Increase for the instance or manually monitor the usage and take necessary actions.

When automatic storage is enabled, storage is checked every 30 seconds and if it falls below the threshold size, additional storage is automatically added to the instance. However, while enabling this, you need to keep in mind that increasing storage is allowed, but once increased the storage cannot be decreased. You should enforce a limit as well because a sudden spike due a temporary increase in traffic can lead to a permanent increased in storage cost for the instance.

When manually monitoring the storage, keep check of the usage and employ techniques (such as purging activities) that routinely delete unused data and drop tables that are no longer required. If the storage is not freed up, you can employ techniques to

313

© Navin Sabharwal, Shakuntala Gupta Edward 2020
N. Sabharwal and S. G. Edward, *Hands On Google Cloud SQL and Cloud Spanner*,
https://doi.org/10.1007/978-1-4842-5537-7_8

check the threshold and run scripts to manually increase the storage incrementally. The status of the storage usage can be viewed on the Cloud Console.

Navigate to the Instance Detail page. In the Overview tab you have options to select the parameter. Select Storage Usage. By default, it shows the current hour's usage. However, you can change it up to the last 30 days and analyze the behavior. Figure 8-1 shows the Storage Usage option.

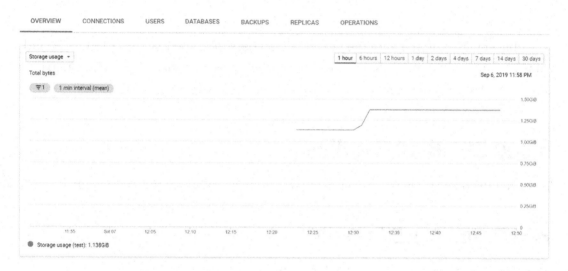

Figure 8-1. *Storage Usage option in the Overview tab of the Instance Detail page*

CPU

CPUs should be planned and assigned based on the workload. If the workload consists of CPU-intensive queries, such as sorting, regexes, and other complex functions, the instance might be throttled. As per the recommendation, CPU utilization of the instance should not be over 98% for six hours. This implies improperly sized instance for the workload it's dealing with. Like storage usage, CPU utilization can also be analyzed in the Overview tab of the Instance Details page. Figure 8-2 shows the CPU utilization. If you find that CPU is becoming a bottleneck, move to a higher tier machine or a machine with better CPU capacity.

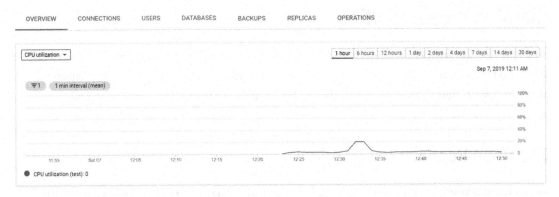

Figure 8-2. *CPU Utilization option in the Overview tab of Instance Detail page*

RAM

Caching is extremely important for read performance. You should compare the size of the dataset to the size of RAM of your instance. Ideally the entire dataset should fit in 70% of the instance's RAM. That way, the queries will not be constrained to IO performance. If this is not the case, consider increasing the size of your instance's tier. The RAM usage can also be analyzed using the first card in the Overview tab of the Instance Detail page. Figure 8-3 shows the Memory Usage option.

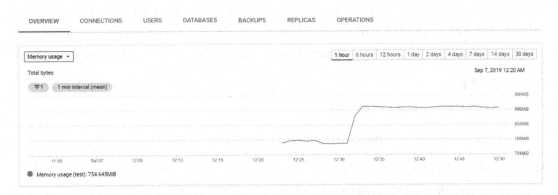

Figure 8-3. *Memory Usage option in the Overview tab of Instance Detail page*

Note   Stack driver monitoring can be used to monitor the usage and raise an alert if a specified threshold is breached. Accordingly, actions can be performed to either kill processes consuming the resources or increase the resource itself.

Maintenance Activities

Maintenance activities comprise disruptive updates that can lead to system restarts. If they are not specified, this can lead to disruptive updates any time of the day. Specify the window in which these updates have the least or no impact on your application/business/end users.

Use Read Replicas

If you have read-heavy workloads, create read replicas so as to offload the read traffic from the primary instance.

Instance Location

Ensure that the database is located near the writer/reader. Otherwise, sending data across datacenters introduces latency and leads to slower performance.

Keep Tables to a Reasonable Number

While designing your schema, keep a check on the number of tables being created across all databases in an instance. The count should be less than 10,000.

Avoid using too many tables, as more tables can lead to the instance being unresponsive and can have a negative performance impact. Keep tabs on the tables getting created. Use the following queries to determine the table count on your instance:

```
SELECT COUNT(*)
FROM information_schema.tables;
```

Run the following command to check database-wise tables:

```
SELECT TABLE_SCHEMA, COUNT(*)
FROM information_schema.tables
group by TABLE_SCHEMA;
```

You should try reducing the tables you created but if the data architecture requires a large number of tables, you should consider splitting them across multiple instances such that the split data is independent and does not lead to inter-instance querying.

Sharding at Designing

Instead of having one large instance, if possible you should consider using multiple small Cloud SQL instances, i.e., shard the instances wherever possible. Otherwise, you will be limited with everything happening on a single server and will have performance bottlenecks once the instance is at its maximum limit (due to no support for horizontal scaling for writes).

Connection Management

There's a limit to the number of concurrent connections that can be made to the instances. So, you need to keep in mind the following while managing them:

- Use connection management practices (such as connection pooling and exponential backoff) to help improve the application's use of resources, thus helping to stay within the connection limit.

- Avoid connection leakages. Ensure applications are closing the connections properly and not leading to leakages.

- Test application behaviors for outages to test for failovers and maintenance updates. During these events, there's a high possibility of the primary instance being unavailable. The application should be coded to handle such outages by employing connection management techniques such as exponential backoff.

- Keep transactions small and short.

Certificates

All the certificates used should be kept up-to-date. For example, if you are using Cloud Proxy, you should keep the cloud SQL proxy up-to-date.

Long-Running Operations

Long-running operations cannot be cancelled or stopped until they are complete. In addition, only one operation can run against an instance at a time. So long-running operations should be planned in a way so they don't overlap with any other operations on the instance.

Use Unique Instance Names

Instance names cannot be reused immediately after deletion, because Cloud SQL reserves the names for a few days. If you have to frequently create and delete instances, you should consider using a timestamp as part of the name to avoid conflicts.

MySQL-Instance Specific Pointers

This section includes a few pointers specific to the MySQL database engine.

Limit the Replication Lag (<1200 Seconds)

A higher replication lag can lead to downtime during failover. Failover is initiated when the primary instance is unresponsive and a higher value in the replication lag makes the failover instance unusable, leading to a failover downtime. In effect, you need to ensure that it's less than the limit, which is capped at 1200 seconds. Keep monitoring the lag using the Replication Delay metric from the Overview tab of the failover replica Instance Details page.

If it seems to be on the high side, take corrective action (find ways to throttle the incoming load on the master or design a data architecture by sharding the data at the design level itself).

Database Flags

As you know by now, database flags are used to configure and tune the instance by adjusting parameters and options. Various flags are available; however, you need to keep the following in mind when adjusting the values of the flags listed in Table 8-1.

Table 8-1. *Database Flags*

Flag	Description	Recommended Setting	Impact if Set Otherwise
general_log	Enables the MySQL general log	If On then set the log_output flag to FILE	Slow restarts
slow_query_log	Enables logging to identify the slow performing queries	If On then set the log_output flag to FILE	Slow restarts
max_heap_table_size	Determines size of the memory table	Retain the default	Instance outage due to out of memory error
temp_table_size	Determines size of the temp table	Retain the default or carefully plan the workload so as not to exceed the instance capacity	Instance outage due to out of memory error
query_cache_size and query_cache_type	Together they determine the size of the query cache	Retain the default or carefully plan the workload so as not to exceed the instance capacity	Instance outage due to out of memory error

Having covered the Cloud SQL pointers, the next section looks at some Cloud Spanner pointers.

Cloud Spanner Pointers

This section covers pointers that you need to keep in mind to efficiently design for a Cloud Spanner instance.

Slower Transactions with Scale Out

Spanner provides cross-node transactions with ACID guarantees and can scale out write transactions linearly. However, the scale is accomplished by accepting some trade-offs such as increasing latency with each node due to increase in network latency in votes for write. This means the transaction will become slow as you scale out more.

Migrating Workloads from Existing SQL Setups Is a Cumbersome Task

If you are migrating workloads from an existing SQL setup to Spanner, you need to note that Spanner is neither MySQL nor ANSI SQL compliant, so migrating the workload from MySQL or any ANSI SQL compliant RDBMS requires some level of re-architecture or re-platforming.

Specify Referential Integrity at Design Time

As you know, when designing a data model, Spanner enables you to define interleaved parent/child relationships at the table level, enabling you to co-locate data to be referred together for efficient retrieval. In addition, while defining the model, you check for referential integrity applicability. That is, any deletion in the parent table will cascade the deletion to the child table as well. It's important that while designing, you ensure the tables are accordingly defined. If you fail to do so, referential integrity won't be defined and it won't be automatically enforced, offloading the usual RDBMS-native activity to the application programmers, which is not an ideal scenario. In addition, if you later need to change a regular table to a child table, this will lead to recreating the table, leading to downtime.

Co-Located Joins Offer Performance Benefits

While designing, you need to ensure that tables that will be referred together are co-located using the interleaved options. Co-located joins offer performance benefits over joins that require indexes or back joins. Note that JOINs across non-interleaved tables suffer performance penalties.

Be Careful When Choosing Your Primary Key

The choice of columns for the primary key is very important, as changing the primary key (adding/removing columns) in later stages is not supported in Spanner. You will have to end up dropping and recreating the table, which means downtime.

In addition, when choosing a primary key, it is recommended not to choose a column with values that are monotonically increasing or decreasing (such as auto-increment IDs, timestamp columns, and so on), as this can accidentally lead to hotspots. If you are forced to use such IDs because of applications or other constraints, use hashing techniques to avoid the pitfalls of hotspots.

Being a primary-key oriented design permits Cloud Spanner to be very fast when accessing data using the primary key. However, you need to keep the following issues in mind when working with it:

- The primary key value cannot be updated easily. If you must update it, you must first delete the original primary key and then insert the updated value.

- Any UPDATE and DELETE operation must specify a primary key in the where clause. There can't be a DELETE ALL or UPDATE ALL statement.

Specify the FORCE_INDEX Directive

Cloud Spanner chooses an index automatically in rare circumstances. If the query requests a column that is not stored in the index, Spanner will not choose a secondary index automatically. In effect, you must use the FORCE_INDEX directive in the code wherever applicable to choose the secondary index.

Multitenancy Support Availability

For the multitenancy requirement, you should include a customer ID column in the table and make it the first key column, so that each customer has good locality.

Cloud Spanner will automatically split the data across the nodes based on the size and load patterns. For example, say you have a Tickets table that stores user tickets that are being created. Ticket ID is the primary key for that table. If you have to introduce multitenancy support, introduce a Customer ID column in the table. The primary key becomes a composite key of Customer ID as the first column followed by the Ticket ID. This way, you can have a single table for all your customers while the data is still uniquely identifiable for each customer.

Why not opt for separate databases for each customer? If you do this, you will be restricted to 100 customers per instance due to the spanner limit of 100 databases per instance. However, if your application requires you to store data in different databases, you should go for a separate database for each customer.

Avoid Existing Schema Changes

Although schema updates are allowed in Cloud Spanner, note that the time it takes to update the schema depends on whether the update requires validation of existing data or backfill of any data.

For example, if you want to change an existing column that allows NULL values to be NOT NULL, the Cloud Spanner will validate all the existing data in the columns before marking the change as successful or not. That means that the time it takes for the change to happen depends on the amount of data in the table, the number of nodes in the instance, and the load on the same. Similarly, if you add a new index to an existing table, the index will be refilled, which is a time consuming activity.

Some schema updates can also impact the behavior of requests to the database before the schema update completes. Continuing with the previous example, where you are adding NOT NULL to a column, Cloud Spanner almost immediately begins rejecting writes for new requests that use NULL for the column. If the new schema update ultimately fails for data validation, there will be a period of time when writes are blocked, even if the old schema would have accepted them.

If schema changes are unavoidable, the best practice is:

- Ensure that existing data meets the constraints imposed by the schema update. For example, if you're adding a NOT NULL annotation to an existing column, check that the column does not contain any existing NULL values.

- If you're writing to a column, table, or index that is undergoing a schema update, ensure that the values being written meet the new constraints.

- If you're dropping a column, table, or index, ensure that no write or read transactions are in process.

Note   Any schema change that does not require existing data validation or filling will be quick (such as adding a new column).

Random Batch Ordering

When you're issuing multiple batches for the schema change, the order in which the changes are applied is random. Thus, you have to ensure idempotent changes so that changes applied in any order lead to the same state.

Say, for example, you issue two batches where one batch contains `ALTER TABLE Students ALTER COLUMN Name STRING (100)` and the other batch contains the statement `ALTER TABLE Students ALTER COLUMN Name STRING (50)`. Cloud Spanner will leave the column in one of these states, but which one is not specified.

Data Loading

The best practices for bulk loading data into Spanner are as follows:

- Sort the data by primary key
- Divide it into 10 * number of nodes separate sections
- Create sets of worker tasks to upload the data in parallel

Since scaling the number of Cloud Spanner nodes up and down just requires a click, for quickly loading the data, you can consider boosting the instance to the maximum. Once the data is in the database, you can scale it back down to the number of nodes suitable for the usual load.

Limited Access Control

Google's IAM (Identity & Access Management) is used by Cloud Spanner for access control. It enables you to set permissions at a very high level,[1] which doesn't fit many of the production use cases, such as limiting user access to a specific table or to a subset of table columns, and so on. This limitation forces you to handle security measures through coding or configuration.

---

[1] https://cloud.google.com/spanner/docs/iam

In summary, Google Cloud Spanner offers scale-out right out of the box, which specifically means that Spanner is capable of the following:

- Scales out reads and writes without any change in the application

- Maintains transactional ACID guarantees across all nodes in the cluster

Cloud Spanner is best suited when you know the queries. However, it is not suitable for workload and business rules that require ongoing schema changes-type flexibility.

Summary

This chapter covered some of the best practices that you should be aware of for better and efficient use of Google database Cloud SQL and Spanner. With this, you come to a conclusion of GCP relational database services—Cloud SQL and Cloud Spanner.

Index

A

ACID property, 34
Add Column option, 249
Artists table schema, 200
Atomicity property, 34
Authorized network
    add new, 133
    communication, 133

B

Backup & restore
      mechanism, 150
    context menu, 154
    effect, 152
    list, 154
    maintenance
      activities, 156
      card, 159
      schedule, 157, 158
      timing options, 158
    manage, 151
    on-demand, 153
    tab, 151, 152
    target instance, 154
    top panel, 156
Binary logging option, 155
Blind writes, 222
Bounded staleness, 216

C

CIDR notations, 133
client-cert.pem files, 137
client-key.pem files, 137
Cloud console
    Create database, 242–244
    Create Schema
      (*see* Schema, Cloud console)
    Spanner Instance, connect, 242
Cloud providers
    benefits, 1
    core services, 2
Cloud proxy
    communication, 139
    features, 138
Cloud SDK configuration, 94
    command, 102, 103
    compute region, 98
    default credentials, 99, 100
    proxy client details, 101
    upload file, 101, 102
    verification code, 96, 97
Cloud shell
    activating, 10
    command prompt, 11, 12
    commands, 14
    connecting, 11
    gcloud command, 14
    google, 10, 11

325

D, E

Printed in the United States
By Bookmasters